Readings in
Sacramental Theology

PRENTICE-HALL INTERNATIONAL, INC., *London*
PRENTICE-HALL OF AUSTRALIA, PTY., LTD., *Sydney*
PRENTICE-HALL OF CANADA, LTD., *Toronto*
PRENTICE-HALL OF INDIA (PRIVATE) LTD., *New Delhi*
PRENTICE-HALL OF JAPAN, INC., *Tokyo*
PRENTICE-HALL DE MEXICO, S.A., *Mexico City*

C. STEPHEN SULLIVAN, F.S.C.

Academic Vice President, Manhattan College

Readings in
Sacramental Theology

Prentice-Hall, Inc.   *Englewood Cliffs, New Jersey*

© 1964 by Prentice-Hall, Inc.
Englewood Cliffs, N.J.

LIBRARY OF CONGRESS CATALOG CARD NO.: 64-18183
PRINTED IN THE UNITED STATES OF AMERICA: C-76100

Preface

The first session of the Second Vatican Council was something of a surprise to many people. A number of problems which captivated the modern mind by their scope (principally the problem of attaining unity with Orthodox and Protestants after centuries of separation) faced the Council, and while news media awaited word for a dramatic "breakthrough" on these problems, the Council fathers were discussing the sacred liturgy. The modern theologian was not surprised, however, because the history of the renewed interest in biblical studies, the catechetical revival, and the liturgical movements of recent years had prepared the theological world for this action of the bishops at Vatican II. Recent theological investigation and discussion had showed how intimately the liturgy is linked to the Church and to Christ. Hence, discussion of the liturgy was not merely a review of the ritual, but the first step in facing this great problem of the Church at any moment of her history, namely, the consideration of her nature.

During recent years, theologians and religious educators who have had their fingers on the pulse of our times have examined together the problems of the liturgy at various meetings. They have seen the liturgy as flowing from the nature of the Church, and they have come to focus on the Church as the foundation sacrament. While studying the Church, the primordial sacrament, they have considered the other sacraments of the liturgy within the incarnational structure. Thus, the whole liturgy has appeared as the exercise of the priesthood of Christ whereby sanctification is bestowed on man through symbolic activities, the sacraments. These studies have been incorporated in annual volumes of "Proceedings" published by various professional groups. Fear that these studies would not receive the attention they deserve prompted the compilation of this present volume.

Certain limitations were observed in the selection and editing of the articles, all but one of which were given at the annual meetings of the Society of Catholic College Teachers of Sacred Doctrine, the Catholic Theological Society of America, and the Liturgical Conference. It must not be surprising, therefore, that superb articles on sacraments which were published elsewhere have not been included. This limitation of selection also explains the apparent unevenness of the articles. Some of the articles are detailed, fully developed, and documented; others are short and provocative. All, however, reflect the lively discussions of the meetings of these learned societies and the stimulating restlessness of the contemporary theological world.

The audience for whom this anthology of theological essays is intended is, primarily, the college student. He is not usually a professional theologian but is the interested observer of theological development. In editing these articles, a number of footnotes which were found in the original papers have been omitted. Deletions were made where reference was made to works not usually available or useful to the nonprofessional. The texts of the papers are substantially unchanged, but remarks intended for a listening audience have, in general, been removed.

The editor acknowledges with gratitude the cooperation of the Boards of Directors of the Society of Catholic College Teachers of Sacred Doctrine (Regis College, Weston 93, Mass.), The Liturgical Conference (3428 Ninth Street, N.E., Washington 17, D. C.), and The Catholic Theological Society of America (St. John's University, Jamaica 32, N. Y.). They have been gracious in granting permission to reproduce the articles to which they own the copyright. Grateful acknowledgment is also made to the editor of *Worship* for his kindness in permitting the inclusion of Father Fransen's article. Finally, the editor profoundly appreciates the kindness of the authors of these articles; they have all shown an encouraging enthusiasm for the publication of this book.

C. Stephen Sullivan, F.S.C.
Manhattan College

Contents

Readings in
Sacramental Theology

GODFREY DIEKMANN, O.S.B.

Two Approaches to Understanding the Sacraments

It is the great limitation of the human intellect that it divides the objects it knows and thus exposes itself to the danger of over-emphasizing one aspect of truth at the expense of considering other truths. The history of theology makes clear the dangers involved in putting emphasis on one aspect while ignoring (but not denying) other essential aspects. In approaching sacramental theology, it is necessary to be aware of the limitations of human knowledge and the tricks which human history has played on the human mind. In this article the author indicates the mentality required to make a satisfactory synthesis of sacramental theology.

Father Diekmann is the editor of *Worship*. He is stationed at St. John's Abbey, Collegeville, Minnesota.

A revered confrere, Father Patrick Cummins of Conception Abbey, who is a distinguished Dante and St. Thomas scholar, likes to tell that his interest in the liturgical movement was aroused many years ago by his study of St. Thomas, especially his questions on the sacraments in the *Summa*.

This may come as a surprise to many of us. We are quite willing to make a reverential bow towards St. Thomas in every problem of theology. But we also know that there have been some notable developments of theological thought since his time. In our own day, besides the important field of Mariology, the doctrine of the

This article was first printed in *Education and The Liturgy*, proceedings of the Eighteenth North American Liturgical Week. It is reprinted here with permission of The Liturgical Conference.

Mystical Body and, as a consequence, the thinking about the sacraments, that is, the liturgy, have been in the forefront of theological concern. Especially since . . . [Pius XII's] encyclical on the Mystical Body and the *Mediator Dei*, they have led to vitally significant new insights into God's plan of redemption. Their impact on Christian life is, in fact, a primary feature of the spiritual quickening widely acknowledged to characterize our age.

This emphasis on the Mystical Body, on the Eucharist, and the other sacraments is something new. It may, indeed, be called a new discovery. For it is such so far as we are concerned. But I am convinced that Father Patrick is right, particularly in respect to the sacraments. Our spiritually stimulating discoveries about the sacraments are for the most part a rediscovery of what is contained in St. Thomas' *Summa Theologica* for all to see.

The trouble was that we failed to see it. The historical shift of emphasis to a more individualistic outlook occasioned by Ockham and the philosophy of nominalism and, even more, our preoccupation with Protestant attacks upon the sacramental system conditioned our thinking. We might say they proved a mental block which led us to look for, and to find, only those things which served our purposes—largely apologetic. In a word, we did not approach the *Summa* with an open mind.

It is really exhilarating, after reading modern liturgical-theological writings on the sacraments, to turn to questions 60-65 of the Third Part of the *Summa* (in which St. Thomas treats of the sacraments in general) and to realize that it is basically all there: not of course developed and explicit in every detail, but easily recognizable in his principles, and presented with that balance of component elements which is his chief merit in treating the sacraments.

It is quite as it should be, therefore, that most of the outstanding modern theological authors whose writings on the sacraments have stimulated and are stimulating the liturgical apostolate base their thinking squarely and frankly on St. Thomas: Vonier, Héris, Roguet, Journet, Congar, Philipon, and above all Schillebeekx in his important new volumes, and Vagaggini in his recently published *The Theological Dimensions of the Liturgy*. These men have rediscovered St. Thomas' key position in the development of sacramental theology, because they have recognized how St. Thomas insisted on, and maintained, the proper relation and balance between sign and causality in treating of the sacraments.

Sign and causality: these are the operative words in sacramental theology. The entire history of theology concerning the sacraments revolves around them. A sacrament is defined in our catechisms as "an external sign instituted by Christ, which confers grace." There we have the two terms: "sign" and "confers" (that is, causes) the grace which it signifies.

It is my purpose to sketch briefly how before St. Thomas the emphasis was on sign, and how after him it has been too one-sidedly on causality, and then to show how this imbalance since St. Thomas' day has led to an impoverished view of the sacraments and their role in the spiritual life—which is being rectified only in very recent times and which necessitated a liturgical movement or, as it is perhaps better named, a sacramental apostolate.

Historical Overview

The history of sacramental thinking can be found in such a standard work as Pourrat's *Theology of the Sacraments*, or in Michel's extensive study of "Sacraments" and "Sacramentals" in the French *Dictionary of Catholic Theology*. We cannot hope here to do more than sketch a briefest outline, at the obvious peril of oversimplification.

Quoting Pourrat, we can say that "in the first four centuries, the Church administered the sacraments without theorizing about them" (p. 396). For the next eight centuries, following St. Augustine who was the first to attempt a technical definition of a sacrament—"a sacrament is a sign of grace"—the sign or signification aspect of the sacrament dominated theological thought. The scholastics of the twelfth century, whose thinking was climaxed and balanced by St. Thomas, "completed the Augustinian formula by adding the specific idea: a sacrament is an *efficacious* sign of grace"—that is, the sacraments *cause* what they signify. And St. Thomas' personal great contribution lay in his exposition of how the sacraments are instrumental causes.

After Thomas, or roughly during the last seven centuries, theological interest has centered on the causality of the sacraments. To quote Vagaggini: Theology after Thomas, "and especially since the sixteenth century, in the treatment of the sacraments in general and in particular, has so relegated the concept of sign to second place that it has, practically speaking, forgotten it or, at least, has left it inoperative" (p. 464).

In brief—and necessarily omitting nuances—we can therefore speak of four introductory centuries, eight centuries of priority of sign, a brief period centering around Thomas which clarifies the concept of causality and relates it and balances it with that of sign, and then seven centuries of an unbalanced emphasis on causality. . . .

A Sacrament Is a Sign

A sacrament is a sign. St. Thomas did not think it a waste of time to devote his entire first question (60) with its eight articles to this statement; it runs, moreover, like a decisive motif through all his treatment of the sacraments.

A sign, he tells us, quoting St. Augustine's definition, is an object, the external perception of which suggests the idea of something else. The aim, the sole aim, of a sign is to suggest an idea, to call something to mind. In a word, to instruct. In the case of the sacraments it is Christ who instructs, insofar as He chose the sign; and it is the Church too that instructs, inasmuch as she expanded and further explained the essential sign, by surrounding it with additional rites and prayers. No one less than Christ and the Church themselves, therefore, are our teachers about sacraments and about their purpose and role in the divine dispensation. We couldn't wish for more competent teachers, and we can be confident that they teach us what is important for us to know as Christians.

Father Josef Jungmann, in fact, has shown that during the early centuries of the Church the liturgy was the *only* means by which Christians were normally instructed. The sacramental sign of the Eucharist, of the sacraments, and the other liturgical celebrations constituted the only school in which the Church taught her children the truths of faith.

To understand this rather startling statement we must recall, however, that the phrase sacramental "sign" is here interpreted in its traditional sense, embracing not only the essential matter and form, but all the supplementary rites, prayers, readings, and homilies that pertained to it. Thus, in the case of baptism and the other sacraments of initiation, it would include the richly instructive content of what we call the Lenten season, the entire catechumenate together with its sermon-instructions, the blessing of the water, and even the Masses and homilies after Easter. All these belonged to the sign of baptism through which the Church instructed the candidates.

It is particularly important to recall that the sign consisted not merely of the sacramental rites and prayers. The sermons or homilies were a normal part of the liturgy. And it is significant that it is precisely during these centuries, even though the prayers were in a language understood by the people, and the rites undoubtedly more easily intelligible to them than they are to us, that Sts. Cyril of Jerusalem, Ambrose, Augustine, and many others explained the rites and prayers of the sacraments of initiation in magnificent series of sermons that have come down to our day. As ministers of the mysteries of God, they knew it was their duty not only to explain the word of God contained in Scripture, but also the word, the teaching of Christ and the Church, contained in the sacramental sign. They had to help their people to read the sign.

For the same reason, the Council of Trent decreed: "That the faithful may approach the sacraments with greater reverence and devotion of mind, the holy council commands all bishops that not only when they are themselves about to administer them to the people, they shall first, in a manner adapted to the mental ability of those who receive them, explain their efficacy and use, but also they shall see to it that the same is done piously and prudently by every parish priest, and in the vernacular tongue . . ." (Sess. 24, Chap. 7).

The Ritual . . . reiterates this command of the Council (Tit. I, 10). "In the administration of the sacraments," it says, their power, use, and purpose and the meaning of the rites must be diligently explained.

It Causes What It Signifies

A second principle to recall, and one much stressed by St. Thomas, is that sacraments *significando causant,* by signifying they cause. Or, as it was formulated later, sacraments cause what they signify. The sign, therefore, comes first and must remain so. For the causality is coextensive with, and determined by, the sign. The sign is not just an interesting phenomenon which happens to be attached to sacraments (Hugh of St. Victor). Rather, only a correct and full reading of the sign can tell us what is being caused.

. . . Because the sign of the Eucharist, namely, food, daily strengthening spiritual food, was relegated to secondary promi- nence by other considerations, stemming originally from reaction to the Arian heresy in the fourth century, fifteen centuries of Christians were deprived of frequent Communion. There was no question of denial of truth: but the basic lesson of the sign was not generally heeded. Consequently, values were out of focus.

Perhaps we can now proceed to an analysis, however sketchy, of some of the historical consequences in spiritual life and outlook that resulted from neglecting St. Thomas' balance of sign and causal- ity, and from a too exclusive concern with the latter during ap- proximately the past seven centuries.

Faith and Sacraments

A first result can be seen in a certain obscuring in the minds of Catholics of the role and importance of faith in the process of salva- tion. . . . [There is] no need to enumerate the many Scripture texts which speak of the faith that saves. But also, only "he who believes and is baptized shall be saved." What is the relation, then, between faith and baptism, or faith and the sacraments? Are we saved by faith, or are we saved by baptism and the other sacra- ments?

For St. Thomas there was no problem. Faith and sacraments are not two separate compartments, as it were vying with each other for priority. Repeatedly and as a matter of course he speaks of the sacraments as "signs of faith," "signs proclaiming or expressing faith." The sacraments themselves are the great acts of faith. (Both Vonier in his *Key to the Doctrine of the Eucharist* and Roguet in his *Christ Acts through the Sacraments* treat this subject well.) Sacraments, as signs, are acts of faith of the Church, first of all. But they are also the great acts of faith of the individual Christian. Moreover, active and understanding participation in the sacraments, besides manifesting the faith of the individual Christian, also deep- ens and develops it. There is no opposition, or a question of either-or. The faith which is the root of all justification must be manifested in the manner prescribed by Christ Himself, that is, by the sacraments. The sacraments (especially baptism and the Eucharist) are the acts of faith demanded by Christ. Thus St. Thomas in treating of baptism, for instance, no less than fifteen times simply calls it *sacramentum fidei*, the sacrament or sign of faith.

Subsequent neglect of the sign, and relative overemphasis on the causality of the sacraments as producing grace, was bound to result in an overshadowing of the role of faith in the popular mind, and in a corresponding naïve isolation of the sacraments as channels of grace. With what explosive results—we witness in the Protestant rebellion. In fact, Lortz in his volumes on the *Reformation in Germany* echoes other authors in wondering whether the Protestant Reformation could have had such spectacular success if Trent's clarifying statement on faith and justification had been promulgated —and preached and understood—before the revolt.

Mechanistic View of Sacraments

A second result of an unthomistically one-sided stress on causality was a more or less mechanistic view of the sacraments. This, perhaps, the most baneful result, is still doing its damage today. I believe the average view of the sacraments is something like the following. The sacraments produce grace *ex opere operato*, by their very conferring. Christ instituted them, yes; but entrusted them to the Church. And the Church guarantees the results, relying on the word of Christ. The sacrament is a holy *thing* which contains and confers grace. If matter and form are there, the result is infallible.

Despite all our protestations to the contrary, it sounds like magic. And there can be no doubt that, in practice, sacraments were regarded in this mechanistic fashion by vast sections of the faithful before the Reformation. Superstitious uses of sacraments abounded. To all intents and purposes, they *were* medicine chests. The Protestant accusation that sacraments are a man-made machinery interposed between Christ and the soul, the Protestant revolt against sacramentalism, and their appeal for a personal religion, a religion of personal union with Christ, could not have found a willing audience otherwise. Luther's denunciations of the *ex opere operato* were justified if we recognize how that term was then widely understood, and, I'm afraid, how not a few of our people understand it today.

Reflection on the sign, on the essential forms—This is *My* Body, *I* baptize you, *I* absolve you—which can only refer to Christ—makes such a mechanistic view impossible. Christ is not merely the distant historical Christ who founded the sacraments two thousand years ago. To say He instituted the sacraments means that He chose these signs through which He has willed Himself, here in the present, to effect salvation. The sacraments are not things: they are actions, the saving actions of Christ. This is what St. Thomas clarifies by the philosophical concept of sacraments being instrumental causes. *Ex opere operato* means really, *ex opere operantis Christi*—sacraments effect grace because they are the actions of Christ.

We must be grateful to . . . [Pius XII] that in *Mediator Dei* he has again put primary emphasis on this fact. The sacraments, he says repeatedly, are the continuation in the present of the priestly activity of Christ. Or again: "Christ is present in the sacraments, infusing into them the power which makes them ready instruments of sanctification" (20). Pius XII has again *personalized* the sacraments in a way that makes impossible any mechanistic misconception. If that emphasis had been present in the sixteenth century, one wonders whether the Protestant revolt would ever have amounted to more than a local theological dispute in a provincial university.

Reducing the Sign to Essentials

A third historical result of overstressing causality to the detriment of sign was that the sign was narrowed down more by theologians to what was essential *ad validitatem*, for validity. "What is necessary for validity" became the decisive question in theology textbooks, rather than: "What does the *full* sign teach about the effects of this sacrament?" In other words, what is the legitimate concern of the moral theologian and the canonist has been substituted for the broader considerations of dogmatic theology in our textbooks. Vagaggini in his recent study has documented this fact in the case of every well-known dogmatic theology manual since Trent. Not one of them bases its treatment on an inquiry into the full sign—a sign given to us for our instruction by Christ and the Church in the wealth of sacramental rites and prayers. . . .

How this whittling down to what is essential *ad validitatem* has effected practice needs no elaboration. I am not advocating pontifical Masses every day. The time is past, thank God, when a liturgist was expected to profess enthusiasm for Byzantine court ceremonial baptized into the Mass rite. But I do think, to give a minor example, that streamlining is not necessarily a virtue in such instances as holy-water fountain pens. (And you all know the story of the priest at a sick call who got his holy water and ink fountain pens mixed up.) *Sancta sancte!*

Again it is . . . [Pius XII] who has called a halt to viewing the sacramental sign solely in terms of what is essential *ad validitatem*. In his constitution on holy orders (1947), he points out the essential words in the ordination rites of deacons, priests, and bishops, but he calls the entire respective preface the "form" of the sacrament.

Valid or Worthy

The spiritual disadvantage resulting from the utilitarian emphasis on causality at the expense of sign is illustrated fourthly by the interpretation commonly given to a phrase used by the Council of Trent: *non ponentibus obicem.* "If anyone says that the sacraments of the New Law do not contain the grace which they signify, or that they do not confer that grace on those who place no obstacles in the way . . . let him be anathema" (Sess. VII, Can. 6, Denz. 849).

What the Council obviously intended with this Canon was to safeguard the basic truth that the grace of the sacraments is caused, not in any way by man, but by the sacraments themselves, that is to say, by Christ acting through the sacraments. Man cannot merit saving grace, which is a gift of God's sheer mercy. The phrase itself, "not placing a hindrance," the Council took over from St. Augustine (Eph. 98:10), who used it in regard to infants, who, he points out, cannot personally place a hindrance to the effects of the sacrament of baptism and therefore receive it fruitfully. The Council applies parallel thinking to all of the sacraments: it is not the personal merit of the recipient that causes the grace received. On the other hand, God does not force the human will.

And so the Council's declaration has passed over into our common definition of a sacrament, "An external sign, instituted by Christ, which confers grace on those who do not place an obstacle."

What does such a definition convey to the average Catholic? My own experience in teaching on several levels is that ten out of ten will understand it to mean: "All that I have to do in order to receive the graces of the sacraments is *not* to place an obstacle: that is, not to be in mortal sin." The impression given by the definition is that of passivity on the part of the recipient.

Certainly such an impression was furthest from the Council's mind. The Council was defining essential truths, defining also what was necessary for the validity of the sacrament. It was not intending to give a full description of how the sacraments are to be received. It did this eloquently, and at length, elsewhere, especially in speaking of baptism and penance. Man cannot contribute to causing the grace of the sacraments; but, to cite an example, the closer a man approaches to fire, the more he will be warmed; so also, the better a man is disposed for the reception of a sacrament (which disposition itself of course is possible only through grace), the more fruitfully he will receive the sacrament.

The Council was stating a minimum. By our one-sided stress on causality, we have made its declaration into a norm about receiving the sacraments. "Valid" and "worthy" reception have become synonymous. The Council itself, following St. Thomas, elsewhere insisted on the sign, on the faith which the Church wishes to arouse and quicken in the recipient by the sign, by the prayers and rites of the sacrament. St. Thomas, for his part, does not use the phrase "not placing an obstacle." He knows the doctrine, of course. But in speaking of the recipient, he consistently refers to the sign of the sacrament, and how it is meant to dispose one more perfectly for receiving the sacramental graces. He calls for an interior conversion to God, for a personal encounter between the soul and its Savior. Receiving the sacrament must be a personal act of faith and submission to God's redeeming love.

Rarely does St. Thomas speak of "valid reception": he is more concerned with emphasizing the positive *recta dispositio*—the right disposition, worthy of a Christian. We often seem to be more interested in teaching the minimum, than in urging the optimum. This is not how saints are made, and sacraments are supposed to make saints.

Fides et devotio: faith and devotion (self-surrender), St. Thomas calls for—incidentally, the very words used in the Canon of the Mass concerning God's holy people. Not only in regard to the Eucharist; of the recipients of every sacrament, St. Thomas expects that their faith be known to God, and their self-surrender manifest. And, to repeat, it is chiefly by the sign of the sacrament that he presupposes such faith and devotion to be stirred up. To cite but one instance: since the sacrament is a sign of Christ's passion, we too must be ready and willing to enter into, to be conformed to, Christ's passion in our innermost wills and daily life.

This is clearly an entirely different spiritual climate from the largely passive, if not outrightly mechanistic, view of the sacraments that concentrates on their causing grace in those not placing an obstacle. The Church *must* be concerned with encouraging the right disposition of faith and self-surrender; for she cannot forget that Christ too on earth was eager to work His most generous signs and wonders in favor of those whose faith was great.

Sacraments and Sacramentals

Another area in which the neglect of the sign aspect of the sacraments has had repercussions is in our view of the sacramentals. It is generally known that until the twelfth century all outward signs of grace were simply called sacraments. Distinction of course was made between the major sacraments, the more important signs according to Holy Scripture and traditional theology, and the minor sacraments, the signs which are of obviously less significance in the life of the Church. It was Peter Lombard who in his famous *Summa Sententiarum* laid down the principles which, for all posterity, clearly distinguished between the seven major signs, called sacraments, and the multiple minor signs which henceforth were known as sacramentals.

Now, if we approach the question of sacraments and sacramentals primarily from the standpoint of their causality, their distinction looms large, and rightly so. For only the sacraments confer grace *ex opere operato*—by their very conferring. And because the stress since St. Thomas has been one-sidedly on causality, the valid and necessary distinction between sacraments and sacramentals has resulted in what amounts to an undue separation of these two kinds of sacred signs. Sacraments confer grace, and therefore they are all-important, in a category all by themselves. Whereas sacramentals, which do not of themselves confer grace—what of them? In contrast to sacraments, they don't seem to amount to much.

Theologically they have become therefore seriously neglected. . . . And yet sacramentals constitute the greater bulk of one of the basic liturgical books of the Church, the Ritual. This theological neglect has led to a corresponding neglect in practice. And so far as explaining them is concerned, our principal aim would almost seem to be to avoid any danger of superstition by insisting that their effectiveness is *ex opere operantis*, that is, depending on the effort of the user.

In a word, we have quite thoroughly isolated the sacramentals. They are a world apart, a world we don't exactly know what to do with. There is even a modern trend in theology of denying the name sacramental to the rites and prayers surrounding the essential matter and form of each sacrament.

We forget that there is another way of viewing sacramentals, the way of St. Thomas, the way of the sign. St. Thomas has no special treatment on the sacramentals, but he brings them in constantly in connection with his treatment of the sacraments. He views the entire sacramental system, including the sacramentals, as a unified whole, with the Eucharist as the source and center, the other sacraments surrounding it, and the sacramentals, all of them, relating to the sacraments, and ultimately to the Eucharist, as disposing man for the sacraments. Thus the catechumenate, or the exorcisms before baptism, are signs of faith, or of rejection of Satan and sin, effectively preparing man to receive the grace of baptism itself. All sacramentals, moreover, not merely the rites and prayers of Mass or the other sacraments, are expressions, signs, of our faith in the saving action of Christ, and therefore to some degree share in bringing it to man. They assist the sacraments in doing their uniquely essential work. They belong, as minor ministers, to the hierarchy of the sacramental world.

I am not . . . trying to erase the essential difference between sacraments and sacramentals. But I am saying that if we regard sacramentals as sacred signs, chosen for the most part by the Church in order to stir faith and devotion in the faithful with a view to their reception of the sacraments, we will rescue the sacramentals from their isolation, and fit them again into the total pattern of Christ *and* the Church acting to save us through signs.

Greater emphasis on sacramentals as signs, signs of the faith of the Church, and not only of the faith of the Christian who uses them, will consequently result even in crediting them with greater effectiveness than we have hitherto been inclined to attribute to them. No longer will we be tempted to regard them as working solely *ex opere operantis* of the faithful—that is, the personal effort of the recipient or user. . . . [Pius XII] in *Mediator Dei* says: "their effectiveness is due rather to the action of the Church (*ex opere operantis Ecclesiae*), inasmuch as she is holy and acts always in closest union with her Head" (27). It is of considerable significance for the theology of sacramentals that this phrase, *ex opere operantis Ecclesiae* (by the action of the Church), a phrase much used and urged by liturgists, is here used, it would seem, for the first time in an official document of the teaching Church (cf. Vagaggini, p. 97).

In fact, this encyclical should be a major impetus to a theological rediscovery of the importance of the sacramentals. As a consequence of viewing sacraments and sacramentals too exclusively from the pragmatic standpoint of efficacy, we have associated sacraments with Christ (external signs, instituted by Christ, and so forth) and sacramentals with the Church (external signs, instituted by the Church, and so forth)—thus, as it were, divorcing Christ from His Bride, at least in the minds of our faithful. Pope Pius XII however states: "Along with the Church, her divine Founder is present at every liturgical function" (20). And then he explicitly applies the principle to the sacramentals of the divine office and the liturgical year: "Christ is present in the prayer of praise and petition we direct to God" (20). And: "The liturgical year . . . is not a cold and lifeless representation of the events of the past. . . . It is rather Christ Himself who is ever living in His Church. Here He continues that journey of immense mercy which He lovingly began in His mortal life, going about doing good" (165).

That is to say, not only sacraments, but sacramentals too, are in their own minor but supplementary way a continuation of the priestly activity of Christ Himself. To use the simile of the late Dr. Pinsk: sacramentals cannot be less than the hem of Christ's garment, from which too, as the Evangelist records, power went forth.

Other areas in which a return to St. Thomas' balance between the sign and causality of sacraments would enrich our spiritual vision . . . [will] only be briefly alluded to. . . . Yet each of them is of such importance that it would deserve full treatment in a separate . . . [article].

The Social Nature of the Sacraments

There is, first of all, the social character and role of the sacraments. Viewing the sacraments primarily in terms of causality has inevitably led to the rather individualistic outlook of: "What does this sacrament give me? What graces do I get out of baptism, penance, holy Communion?" Yet the whole of tradition, embodied and proclaimed in the sign, that is, the prayers and rites of the sacraments, urges that every sacrament involves the whole Church: that every sacrament, and especially the Eucharist, is a bond that unites the whole Church and member to member; that the Mystical Body is a *communio sanctorum*, an organism of sacraments; that she is constituted by sacraments, lives and grows and flourishes through the sacraments; that baptism is not only membership in Christ, but is such because first of all it is membership in Christ's Body; that the purpose of the Eucharist is, to use St. Thomas' favorite phrase, "the unity of the Mystical Body," and so on.

This social character of the sacraments is moreover eloquently borne out by the sign of the sacraments insofar as it tells of the relation established through the sacraments between the individual Christians and their common father in God, the bishop of the diocese. This relationship with the bishop through sacraments has, we know, been highlighted again by . . . [Pius XII] through his reform of Holy Week, especially by the prominence restored to the Mass of Holy Chrism on Maundy Thursday.

Sacraments are signs of salvation, yes; but salvation is in and through the Church.

A modern English theologian, Father Bernard Leeming, S.J. (*Principles of Sacramental Theology*) has therefore even ventured to attempt what he considers a better definition of sacraments: "Might not a sacrament be better defined as 'an effective sign of a particular form of union with the Mystical Body, the Church, instituted by Jesus Christ, which gives grace to those who receive it rightly'?"

At all events it is not just a coincidence that underestimation of the social character of the sacraments as embodied in their sign runs parallel, historically, with the gradual loss of awareness or obscuring of the doctrine of the Mystical Body. Conversely, what might be called the rediscovery of the Mystical Body in our own time has meant a corresponding discovery of the role of the sacraments in Christian life. The encyclical on the Mystical Body was continued logically, as Pope Pius XII himself says, by the encyclical on the liturgy.

Sacraments Are Worship

Another new (or restored) insight of our day, consequent upon studying the sign of the sacraments, has been a better realization that all the sacraments—and sacramentals—are not merely means of sanctification (that is, important because of their effect on man), but are basically and intrinsically worship. Emphasis on causality, on effect, has given rise to the axiom *Sacramenta propter homines*. Sacraments are for man. True. But this is only half the truth. As Cardinal Suhard reminded us in his *The Meaning of God*:

> The expansive phrase is often repeated, and rightly, sacraments are for men. But it is not sufficiently realized that if the reception of the sacraments must always be made possible to the faithful, the reason is that they can thus the better appropriate them and be carried along in the great movement of praise and thanksgiving rising from this earth to God through His Son. If the sacraments are emptied of this essential content they will soon become lifeless rites.

Sacraments are for man: but man is for God. Or, as Pius XII said succinctly in *Mediator Dei*: "Let everything, therefore, have its proper place and arrangement; let everything be 'theocentric' so to speak" (33). To how many of our faithful would it nowadays occur that receiving the sacrament of penance is worship? Yet the sign of the sacrament is intended to arouse "faith and devotion" (self-surrender), the root and primary act respectively of the virtue of religion, which is worship. The indelible characters or signs of baptism, confirmation, and holy orders are deputations to worship. St. Thomas therefore, in summarizing the purpose of the sacraments, says quite indiscriminately: "They are for the sanctification of man" or "they perfect man in those things which pertain to the worship of God"—as if these two ideas were interchangeable. And they are. For by active and intelligent participation in the sacraments, man is lifted out of his own narrow self-centeredness, to become one with Christ. And Christ gave His life for the salvation of man—but in order that, together with His new brethren, He may now give glory to the Father.

This view of sacraments certainly widens our horizons, frees us from a suffocating spiritual selfishness. Peace, grace, to men of good will, yes—but for the purpose of giving glory to God.

Sacramental and Biblical Thinking

Two final ways in which St. Thomas' balance between sign and cause would profit our spiritual maturity I can no more than mention. The Church in her sacramental signs steeps us in biblical thought. She loves to recall the signs and sacraments of the Old Testament, and the signs and wonders of Christ in the New. Liturgy and Scripture are blood brothers. And a true understanding of the liturgy would again make us Bible Christians—a consummation devoutly to be wished. . . .

Citizens of Heaven

Finally, reflection on the sacramental sign would bring back more vividly to our consciousness the eschatological nature of our Christian existence; that is, it would bring heaven and our eternal goal into the present. Concentration on the graces received here and now has made us forget more or less that, as St. Thomas insists, every sacrament as a sign signifies, not only present graces, but the past, the passion and death of Christ, and the future, eternal glory. It is well to remind our faithful: "Remember thy last end, and thou shalt not sin." But it is by means of the sacraments that the Church herself gives that reminder to the active and understanding participant. Every sacrament should make us less earthbound, should, may I say, give us wings. Every sacrament, since it actually confers the seed of eternal glory, should make us homesick for our eternal home, should lift up our hearts, for we are in fact, and not only in hope, citizens of heaven. Every sacrament is a joyful *sursum corda*.

Conclusion

. . . What conclusion would I draw? . . . The sacramental apostolate, if properly understood and realized in practice, does have major contributions to make to a fuller and more mature Christian life and outlook. Sacraments are formative of the will, and also of the mind. They are not sufficient by themselves, however, in their teaching. It would be foolish—and very likely fatal—to depend solely on the sacramental sign, no matter how broadly interpreted. But Pius XI did say: "The liturgy is the most important organ of

the ordinary magisterium (that is, teaching power) of the Church."
Not the only, but the most important. Far from being exclusivists,
. . . [the] liturgists want to be inclusivists: . . . [they] want (we
honestly believe) what the Church wants: that the liturgy, after
seven centuries of relative neglect as a teaching organ, be again
more fully included in the normal teaching activity of parish school
and church. That is instructional and spiritually formative wealth,
put there by Christ Himself and the Church, be exploited to a
greater degree than it has been. That in all things, including the
sacraments, and especially through the sacraments, God may be
glorified.

TERRENCE TOLAND, S.J.

Christian Sacrament:
Sign and Experience

The Catechism definition of a sacrament as an "outward sign" leaves something to be desired. In contrast to sign is the motion of symbol. The latter suggests a dimension of experience, and it involves the imagination, sensitivity, emotions, and history of man. In this article sacraments are considered as symbols and sacramental experience is seen as a response to personal salvation history. The author examines the sacraments in the light of the Word's Incarnation and enables us to see that a basic principle of sacramental theology (that matter can channel spirit) rests upon the fact of the Incarnation. Instead of a conclusion, Father Toland raises a series of questions at the end of this essay. These questions show the direction in which the theology of the sacraments is moving.

Father Toland is professor of theology at Woodstock College, Woodstock, Maryland.

With an understanding of faith, we know that the Christian sacraments are signs. They are, first of all, signs of grace, of the grace they ultimately produce. And we are aware that a sign which produces anything—let alone grace—is a very extraordinary sort of sign, for normally a sign will represent, point to, but hardly produce the reality in question. A tear is not the sorrow, a falling leaf not the autumn, a footprint not the walking man. The sacraments both point to and produce. This sacramental sign-function is itself rich in its

This article was first printed in *Participation in the Mass,* Proceedings of the Twentieth North American Liturgical Week. It is reprinted here with permission of The Liturgical Conference.

complexity since it points to grace in a three-fold dimension of present, past, and future: it looks to the present possibility of receiving grace; it looks to the past, to the source of grace which is the redemptive Christ-act; it also looks to the future, to the eschatological fulfillment of grace, eternal life itself of which grace is here and now the pledge. All of this—at least all of this, I would say— the Christian sacraments represent, and in point of fact likewise produce the grace represented; they put us in contact with the redemptive power signified by the rite.

We know the Christian sacraments are also signs of faith. To receive a Christian sacrament is to engage oneself in an act of worship, a creaturely self-reference to the Creator. And so we are wisely cautioned not to overplay the common distinction between the upward thrust of sacrifice and the downward movement of sacrament, as though the former were exclusively for God's sake and the latter for the sake of man. A true reciprocity is necessarily involved in both. The sacraments demand a conscious adherence to the truth which makes them what they are. The intelligibility of the Eucharist is scarcely exhausted by calling it a gift of divine food. No more than magic, sacramental reception is not mere passivity. To receive a sacrament is to say prophetically, cultically, humanly: "I believe."

Further, the sacraments are signs of the Church. By the sacraments the Church expresses herself; by them she makes visible her role as sanctifier. It makes little difference which of her ministers sits in the confessional, but it is wholly essential that he be her minister. The sacraments sketch the face and structure of the Church; they give her members. And they give her members life and food and union and office.

Although this sign-aspect is an ancient and basic tenet of sacramental theology (this is Augustine; Thomas begins what he has to say about the sacraments by first establishing the fact that they are signs), post-Tridentine history records a far greater theological preoccupation with sacramental efficacy. The Council of Trent, it would seem, is more properly an occasion than cause of this subsequent concern with an effect produced and the requirements for this objective efficacy on the part of the minister, recipient, and the rite itself. The Protestant assault had to be met; and if sacramental efficacy was being reduced to merely subjective, psychological goodliness, the Spouse of Christ necessarily anathematized this distortion of God's revealed truth. And it should be noted that the Council itself encouraged no imbalance, either speculative or practical, for bishops, as we read in the informative Catechism of the Council of Trent, were to see to it that proper instruction on the meaning of the sacraments should precede their reception by the faithful.

Whatever the provocation, theologians, who long busied themselves more with what happens than with what is meant, have recently directed our attention back to the classic Augustinian-Thomistic insight: whatever else we might say, the sacraments are signs; and more, the sign-function of the sacraments is the key to understanding their purpose and effect. For it is not enough to say that the sacraments cause grace and also happen to signify grace, as though grace and meaning emerge concomitantly from the rite like parallel railroad tracks. It is not that while the sacraments give grace they also illustrate Christian doctrine; nor that while man receives divine life he can also receive a communication of the *Logos*, if, that is, he adverts to it through proper instruction. Rather we are today emphatically reaffirming the principle set by Thomas: "God's word operates effectively and sacramentally, that is, in virtue of its meaning" (III, q. 78, a. 2, ad 3). And also: "The words operate in the sacrament with respect to the sense which they make" (III, q. 60, a. 8). The point is that everyone sees in the words of the sacramental form a participation in the sacramental causality. The relationship of efficient and exemplary causality, then, again enjoys its proper balance. There is no rivalry, nor even concomitance; there is a mutual dependence, a congenial fusion. The effect of grace is produced through the medium of significance. . . . The effect is not arbitrary but precisely what is signified by the liturgical rite; the supernatural life produced directly corresponds to what is dramatized in words and actions (one obvious reason for seven different rites with distinct meaning and distinct effects). It is not that you merely miss the richness of sacramental intelligibility by ignoring the sign. You simply would not even begin to understand what happens.

Further encouraging indications of balance are found in the current trend to clarify, if not eliminate, the false and unfortunate dichotomy between the notions of *ex opere operato* and *ex opere operantis*. Every grace in this present order is the grace of Christ through His Church. Every grace, then, can be said to have an internal inclination toward social visibility in the Church. This incarnational and ecclesiological tendency of grace reaches its summit in the sacraments. But it is never just a rite; it is always a rite of the

Church having to do with a man who will function as the social, visible, knowing-willing creature that he is. We have come a long way from our siege complex occasioned by charges of magic-cult. For both ecclesial and personal reasons, the *opus operantis* is not opposed to the *opus operatum* but is its continuation and fulfilment.

To suggest that the Christian sacrament is something to be experienced is to move beyond the function of sign to the dimension of symbol. This will have about it more of living than of something produced. In this light the sacraments, like Scripture itself, are seen as sacred history; they become themselves salvation events in the history of an individual soul. And an event, even a symbolic event, is to be experienced personally, humanly. My thesis would come to this: the sacramental experience is the fully human response to the symbolic events of personal salvation history.

However briefly and inadequately, a few words must be said about symbolism since it is essential to our present discussion. True, this is not a fashionable conversation piece during coffee-break. Many in fact will berate the modern man of the market place for his disregard, if not contempt, of the world of the symbol. We are, it is said, much too immersed in the comfortable, the here-and-now, the scientifically efficient; too preoccupied with the gadget, the immediate payoff, the functional, the lucrative. Encouragement comes from a pseudo-philosophizing which would oppose the symbol to reality. A symbol is taken only to stand for something else (the something else of course is always the reality—the "really" real), and once you grasp the something else the symbol has served its turn, is no longer of use, can and should be scrapped. Continued concern and success with the control of nature's forces further reassure this attitude, since man is led to believe he is now in more direct contact with "reality," and any symbolic expression is proportionately superfluous. In brief, those who worry about this sort of thing will contend we have disastrously condemned to so-called "unreality" just about everything that cannot be measured, mechanized or, we might add, syllogistically packaged.

Less dramatically, others will summarily dismiss the whole business by making symbolism the concern of the esthete, the poet—and perhaps they are closer to the truth than they realize, since symbolism is for the poet, in the sense in which every man is and ought to be a poet if he wants to be human. Still others with a more academic flair will question the validity of any truth derived from symbols. They make of this an epistemological problem. Accustomed to the methods and accomplishments of efficient causality, they have little taste for research into exemplary causality and tend to regard as an inferior order of knowing whatever has its origin more in poetry than in science, and is thereby incapable of that rigorous methodology which is for them the sole foundation of real certitude. Symbolic thought is seen to proceed from some vague, prelogical mentality which is not a permanent form of thought, even of religious thought, but at best something of possible archeological interest.

Though these observations of our modern thought and ideal patterns might smack of the jeremiad, we have genuine cause to be concerned. And positively, not just polemically. The world of symbolism is real, and it is here to stay. And it is thoroughly Christian. And it is, I propose, wholly relevant to sacramental theology.

The theoretical explanation of the symbol is admittedly still much in dispute, but most will readily assert its reality and there is a certain general consensus about the elements of its makeup. A kind of phenomenological description perhaps will help us recognize this something which points to a deeper or higher reality—to something either too big to be thought of comfortably or too mysterious to grapple with directly. A good way to describe a symbol is to contrast it with a sign.

The sign is a representation of a concept or a judgment. It is rational and discursive. There is nothing mysterious about it. Its signing function is one for one; once it points, leads to the other, the sign—if indeed it is only a sign—has finished its work. It has lost its value, in fact, except to point out again. The purpose and content of the sign are clear: stop, go, curve ahead, sixty-nine cents a pair.

But the symbol is essentially mysterious; it carries with it all the mystery of the personal encounter. The lock of hair is just a sign to the lover if it merely indicates the fact of his love. But if the lock of hair carries with it all the intimacy and mystery and involvement of his relationship with the person of his love when they encounter one another, then it is a symbol. Rather than being just a concept-bearer, the symbol is an experience-bearer. It has in itself all the elements of an intimate I-thou relationship. To use a standard division, the symbol contains not only rational elements, but imaginative, sensitive, and emotional as well, and all of these on both the conscious and unconscious levels. This descriptive division is inadequate, of course, because the total experience is more than just the sum of these elements. It is a reality in its own right.

For the symbol has a life and growth of its own besides its function of reference. It opens up a level of reality, of being and corresponding meaning, which otherwise we could not reach, and in doing so the symbol participates in that which it opens to new awareness. Symbols result from a creative encounter with reality. They are not invented and they cannot be abolished, but they will die if this encounter with reality should ever cease. Originally, prehistorically, the important elemental symbols of fire, water, bread, and so forth, may have been just single meaning-bearers, but each picks up in its long use in history the subtleties and elements which express newer and newer relationships to the men who use it—the fire of Prometheus, Pentecost, Hiroshima. Unlike the sign, when we see beyond the symbol to something else, the symbol retains its value—there is always more to see, and experience. Each symbol contains within itself all of history, and not history as recorded in writing but history as lived. And if it is a religious symbol, the more to see and experience is infinitely meaningful and unconditionally valid. The symbol itself will take its material from the natural, personal, historical realms of life; it will itself remain limited and conditioned, but it will point to what is of ultimate concern to us; it will point to what is unlimited.

The symbol will evoke different reactions in different individuals depending on the personal conscious and unconscious equipment of each. If the symbol itself has its own organic growth, so too does my experience with it—if, that is, I condition myself to approach the symbol with openness. My reaction to bread will be slightly different from yours, but our experience of it will in both cases contain all the relations of all men to bread.

Really I have not been defining the symbol, but only trying to point to its reality. I am not sure it can be defined, as you cannot define so many elemental things. The best one can do is set up a circumstance in which an insight might be shared. I cannot tell anyone why the *Verbum caro factum est* is meaningful and beautiful to me; I can just point to it.

With this said about the symbol, we might return to the proposal that the sacramental experience is the fully human response to the symbolic events of personal salvation history. Let me now sketch the theological principles which I believe support the validity of this interpretation. What I intend is a value more than didactic, or esthetic; it is more than a recovery of our sense of Christian tradition, and more certainly than a pastoral come-on to get as many to the church on time as to the parish festival. Theologically, I would say, the sacraments are presented to us as events to be experienced.

The first is a well-known, but hardly overoperative, principle usually proposed by the rubric: grace builds on nature. The danger is to see this as a building-block design rather than an organic structure. Better: grace supposes nature, for man will not be saved without man. Grace is not a precious veneer coated over nature as on an ugly and embarrassing piece of family furniture. Better still: grace perfects nature, and this means body and soul (isn't it curious how we speak of saving our souls though Christ our Lord died to save men; and we note the Communion formula: *"custodiat animam tuam . . ."*). The whole man, then, is involved in this process of new life through death, of strength and gain and growth and union. To dispose oneself for grace is not a departmentalized enterprise. It involves me, the fully human graced me in whom the Spirit operates. (And we wonder in this regard if the "Sunday-weekday Catholic" bit is not overdone in our pulpits. Is what I do outside of Church and formal prayer, the ordinary task of life-providing, so alien to the workings of grace that God looks for a constant, explicit baptism by pure intention?) There is a graciousness of nature and, in this qualified but valid sense, a naturalness of grace.

The second theological principle is a pertinent elaboration of the first: it is what we label the sacramental principle itself. Just as God will not save man apart from man's human nature, so did God freely choose to make of human nature the very channel of redemption. In the Epiphany of God in created flesh we have also the manifestation of the prime analogate of Christian sacramentality: matter can channel spirit. When the first man had sinned, the bond between body and soul was loosened, as well as the bond between man and the universe which is a kind of prolongation of his body. The message of nature became ambiguous (cf. Rom. 1). Like man's body, nature was more easily abused than used, more easily misread than read aright. But in the Incarnation, by assuming the composite nature of man, the Son of God likewise took up to Himself all the elements of the universe. In root, all of creation is restored, men and things. And the world is not only to be transformed and returned to the Father; the material world itself will be used to facilitate that return. All of creation is capable of supernatural instrumentality, and certain privileged parts of creation will in fact be so commissioned. The sacramental principle confronts us with a divine *fait accompli:* matter does channel spirit.

There is a relevant analogy between God's contact with men through His word and through His life, the life we can call grace. Scripture scholars today invoke a more dynamic dimension to the notion of revelation. Revelation is not so much an utterance spoken forth by God, corroborated by divine testimony (*locutio Dei attestantis*), as though spoken merely for the objective record. Rather, it is an utterance of God to someone from whom God seeks the response of faith. It involves encounter. And man must accept or deny this revelation, for unlike the case of your words or mine, God's word cannot even be ignored. To ignore the revelation of God is itself a denial. Not just the fiats of Genesis, but every word of God is efficient; it produces an effect; in the word is a power that can save, but it is a power that demands a human response. The analogy with the sacramental word was an immediate insight of the Fathers. Here, too, is a power, a power to communicate both the knowledge of God and—by divine design and institution—the very life of God. We do no service to the Incarnation to separate the divine from the human by isolating the divine. The Incarnation has established the sacramental principle: nature communicates the supernatural, matter channels spirit.

The third and final theological foundation of our proposition deals with the content of God's communication to man; it is called "salvation history." Accordingly, revelation is seen as composed not of bits of information imparted to man from time to time in the course of history. Rather, history itself, the recorded saving events, are the revelation. It is the record of God saving his people. In word and deed, God unfolds to man a plan whose central fact was the redemption of the race which had been lost in the sin of Adam. We read in 1 Corinthians 10:11: "The record of it was written as a warning to us, in whom history has reached its fulfillment." Taken in this light, the whole of sacred history assumes the character of a continuous revelation in which each event, each communication, resumes and continues what has gone before.

Prefigured and begun in the chosen people of Israel, the central fact of this revelation is of course Christ our Lord—the incorporation of the Godhead into mankind and mankind into God in the

Incarnation and Redemption. The prophets speaking of this as "the last days" described this new era as a new level in sacred history; but it is described as taking place in terms of former events. The "last days" are a new creation, a new deluge, a new exodus; God's people are called forth in a new Adam, a new Noe; the judgment of God descends once more on the Leviathan of the deep, and the waters of death bring forth a new life. Over and again the pattern repeats itself: election, sin, judgment, redemption—the return, that is, to former election. Thus the Redemption is seen not merely as a total climax of sacred history, but as the initial point of a whole new plane of sacred history: the beginning of a new dispensation of Providence to be accomplished in the Church which is the extension of Christ. When Christ took to Himself a human body, He made it possible to prolong Himself, through human beings, in a mystical body. It is not that the Church is the instrument of a new revelation but she dispenses, at each moment of her visible evolution, the content of this economy of salvation and she renders present at each moment of time, these "last days" of the Christ.

The gesture, the dramatic use of material things, are highly significant in the Johannine Gospel account written for an audience already accustomed to the Christian liturgy. This Christological typology—and, in its turn, sacramental typology—is a viewpoint of sacred history in which an analogy is noted between the great moments of salvation. Not just concepts but events, of themselves multiple and distinct, are drawn into an objective unity by their participation in something which is one. Creation, flood, exodus, covenant are distinct in time and space, distinct moments of sacred history. But the Providence decreeing these events draws them into an objective unity and uses them for the continuous unfolding of the one revelation. And in Christ, all is summed up, the same material things and human things of oil and bread and fire, of meal and contract. These Old Testament events and event-symbols all point to Christ and take their unity from reference to Christ. Instituting the sacraments, Christ has charged them with this complex content of sacred history. The sacraments are themselves events, salvation events in the history of the life of the Church as well as salvation events in the history of each individual soul in these "last days." (And might we have here a basis for the psychological acceptance of the liturgical cycle? Christ comes and dies no more, but the Church does, and so do I. I who live in time am schooled in the sanctification of time. This is the law of growth, and the rhythmic wheeling of the liturgy is not a one-dimension circular recall of what he did but a spiralling repetition of saving events which, if experienced, effects the maturity of the Church and individual in Christ.)

Here, then, is the mystery: the possibility by means of the sacramental economy—by the liturgy, that is—of our insertion into the history of salvation. For the liturgy is the mode this history assumes in the period from Pentecost to Parousia; necessarily ritualistic, it is the means by which the saving events of God are sacramentally communicated to man, and man's personal, fully human response is carried to God. Whether we are conscious of it or not, this mystery is present in the sacraments, for Christ is living in His Church; what Christ did comes in contact with what we are and becomes for us a reality of the moment. *Hodie Salvator apparuit.* This is not to enable us to do something similar to what He did (a too-literal appeal to the *alter Christus* is as psychologically discouraging as it is ontologically impossible), nor even to supply us with the supernatural power to repeat what He did (even in the Mass this is not done), but rather to make it possible in all the things we must do (the simple, undramatic business of living) to participate in what He did once and for all.

This, I submit, is what the Christian sacrament is ontologically: not a static this-for-that sign, but a mysterious, "presenced" symbol which can introduce my soul to the new, richer level of both conscious and unconscious participation in salvation history. If by prayerful reflection I become more and more aware of the personal salvation history being lived out in my own soul, if I approach the sacraments as more than a single truth to be acknowledged and a gift to be had, if I realize that to receive another is to give myself openly—almost incautiously—then I will go beyond the sacrament sign to the sacrament symbol. Then, even though much of the Spirit's breathing will still take place on the subconscious level, nevertheless I will more genially blend the fully human psychological me with the ontological reality I confront. Then the Christian sacrament will be an experience.

Let me conclude with some questions:

1. Are we too hesitant to admit, to explore, to value, to encourage the symbolic experience? Do the polemics of magic and fideism make us shrink from the acknowledgement of mystery? (I don't say the mystifying!) Do we tend to reserve religious intuition to the

rare mystic, and that suspiciously? Because the grasp of symbolic meaning is ever elusive, do we condemn the pursuit of the unfamiliar as a sort of religious but capricious moon-chasing? Are we reluctant to admit that once I say I know just what happens in the sacramental experience I don't really know?

2. Does not our response to a religious symbol depend more than we might suspect on our response to all symbols, especially the elements of nature? In the past few years commendable and intelligent efforts have been made to explain the salvation-history content of the liturgy. This is the water of creation, the flood, the Red Sea, the rock of Horeb, the Jordan; the water of Christ's baptism, the pool of Probatica, the flow from the pierced Heart of Christ; the water of baptismal immersion when the soul is plunged into death with Christ to rise with the new life of the risen Christ. But has it not been observed that despite the best of translations, the best of commentaries and commentators, there is still an inadequate response. The life-through-death water of baptism; but what does water itself on the natural level mean to me? And am I conditioned to respond to the mysterious ambivalence of water if in its purely natural context I normally experience it only by the turn of a faucet? *Lumen Christi*, the light of Christ; the light is Christ. But what is light itself but neon and the click of a switch? What I am suggesting is that we are remedying the symbolic content of the upper religious level but cannot depend on the wealth of human response to these elements on their lower-story plane. And is there perhaps a connection with the development of the imaginative faculty within the broader context of general Christian education? From earliest years should not the accumulated memory of God's truths be organically fused—not paralleled only, but fused—with growth in the awareness that all of creation belongs to God and speaks of God, and in the realization that all the mysteries of our faith are connected one with the other and with all pertinent facts of day-to-day living, though many of the latter remain naturally mysterious? And could it be that this lack in depth of response, conscious and unconscious, to natural as well as religious symbolism can tend to force liturgical functions into the class of a theatrical production (and TV is far less demanding and, probably more, spectacularly exciting)?

3. Do we need new symbols? There is the obvious problem of anachronism which no interest in liturgical participation will long

tolerate. Since water is in pipes and the family meal hardly an *agape*, should we look elsewhere? In baptism, for example, might we better stress the symbolism of receiving a new name (the initiation idea) than washing (our pouring is not even a weak substitute for immersion)? Furthermore, when symbols are objectified, a given individual might tend to see the canonized pattern as an imposition on his personal aspiration and needs, especially when offered in unfamiliar language which makes the ceremony more mystifying than mysterious. This conscious or unconscious resentment can reduce worship to mere routine, superficiality of participation, and even a consequent ignorance of, or unconcern about, what is actually going on. But this is not just the problem of the vernacular; any theme can become a cliché, any symbol a counter. There is a problem here for the Church as she prolongs in her being the Incarnate Christ. Her charismatic moments must be continually meaningful to every historical moment in which she flourishes, to every cultural milieu. Her teaching and her symbols must confront the man of the now with his reciprocal expectations and allegiances, his obligations and loyalties. But her symbols and teaching must likewise be stable and transhistorical and will therefore be locked in a necessarily institutionalized context so that every culture, every human longing, every crisis, every mixed motivation can be purified and dynamized by a return to the source of power and truth. Is the answer education—in awareness, in response especially to the nature obscured by industrialization? And in flexibility in attaching different dimensions, if not new meanings, to any given symbol? This would not so much reject the emphases of previous ages but gather up the significant riches of the past and offer them in a new guise with new meaning for the present, for if truth is to be expressed symbolically on the world stage, it will take into account that all the psychological differences of the centuries are somehow present in today's cross-section of humanity. Most of all, there seems to be a need for education in personality growth, a realization that my very submission to communal, patterned activity achieves more than social values unattainable by individual effort alone. The self-giving process is itself a humility that enlarges and matures the individual soul, though not in an individualistic way since personality maturity, if genuine, necessarily involves a social dimension in both natural and supernatural life.

Whatever the value and validity of the thesis I propose, we are agreed in this: the Christian is formed, nourished, and continually re-created through the sacramental encounter by the God who gives joy to His youth.

BERNARD COOKE, S.J.

The Sacraments as the Continuing
Acts of Christ

The most important aspect of the efficacy of the sacraments is the fact that Christ acts through sacraments. Yet it is more important to go beyond this doctrine and examine more fully what it is that Christ is doing when He acts through the sacraments. In the following article, Father Bernard Cooke shows that in the sacramental economy the redemptive intent of Christ unfolds throughout history and moves toward the final stage of eschatological fulfillment.

Father Cooke is Head of the Department of Theology at Marquette University, Milwaukee, Wisconsin.

One of the ideas that has been working most fruitfully in recent Catholic philosophy and theology—one that brings us into profound and important contact with the evolutionist character of contemporary thinking—is the idea of finality. Discussion of the eschatological aspect of biblical thought, investigation of the theology of history, study of the development of dogma—all of these are facets of this common thought trend. . . . [This article] on the continuing action of Christ in the sacraments hopes to draw from this current of theologizing, to study the final causality of the sacraments, to examine a little more closely the link between biblical eschatology and the understanding of the Christian mysteries. Our purpose is not to show that Christ continues to act in the sacraments;

This article was first printed in the *Proceedings of the Sixteenth Annual Convention of the Catholic Theological Society of America*. It is reprinted here with permission of the Society.

this is obvious. Rather, we wish to attempt some answer to the question: what is it that Christ continues to do in the sacraments?

To speak of finality is to bring under discussion the divine intent in creation. That there is a divine purpose guiding in orderly and purposeful manner the development of the world and the course of human history is at the very basis of revealed thought. To the faith vision of the people of Israel, this intent of Yahweh was manifested in the historical events in which they were involved. Their very notion of God was of one who had brought them out of Egypt in the Exodus experience, saved them from the evil of the Pharaoh so that he might bring them to a promised land.[1] And this primitive experience of their God in act is repeated in varying fashion throughout their centuries-long existence.

That the action of Yahweh in history is highly personal and intelligent is reflected in the Israelitic notion of the power of Yahweh's word.[2] It was by His word that the world came into being; it is His word channeled through the human speech of Moses or the prophets that roots up and destroys, builds and plants (Jer 1:10); His word is an irresistible power that comes down like the rains and will not return unfruitful (Is 55:10-11). This word of God is not a dumb force shaping the events of man's life; it is revelation (Am 3:1-7; 4:13). The very events themselves speak of the God who has chosen Israel and who guides her history (Dt 32). For the Israelite of faith, and therefore in the faith record of Israel's history which is enshrined in the Old Testament books, what is important about the things that happened to them is not just the brute fact, but the significance of the fact; and it is this significance which is seen as the deepest causal influence.

What it was that the events of their early history signified was seen by the first centuries of Israel in very superficial fashion. Only with the passage of generations and the maturing experience of suffering and defeat does the deeper significance of exodus and covenant, of kingship and prophecy, of sin and salvation begin to dawn on them. As later events bring a greater insight into God's dealings with them, the Israelites see these more recent happenings as a fuller revelation of what God was already trying to tell them in his earlier interventions in their history. The history of Israel is a progressing revelation, a deepening word of Yahweh, in which earlier stages are types of later happenings, and these in turn are types of actions still to come.[3]

than empty occasions of grace, with no effectiveness of their own.[9]

If the events and institutions of the Old Testament are the "sacraments" of the divine intent to save mankind and bring it to a supernatural destiny, the redemptive Incarnation fulfills in transcendent fashion this process of revealing Yahweh's redeeming love. Careful reading of the New Testament literature makes it abundantly clear that the primitive Christian community saw that a new epoch had begun: the Father had spoken to men His own Word, had sent His own Spirit to work through the humanity of Christ and the mystery of the Church.

To this unparalleled fact the actions of Christ's own public life bear witness in the purest and fullest sense of Israelitic prophetism. Like the great prophets before Him, it is not just by His words that Jesus gives testimony to the will of His Father to give life to men, it is above all by what He is and what He does. His very presence among the Jews of His day was—as Matthew points out in relating Christ to the Emmanuel prophecy, and as Luke does by narrating the presentation of the infant Christ—a sign of a new and active dwelling of God-among-men. It is a coming that restores the true eschatology of the prophetic view; because Christ claims for Himself as Son of Man the power and kingdom given the apocalyptic figure in Daniel 7, but claims them as something that is to operate within human history, not just beyond. Eternal Wisdom comes actually to live out the wise way of human life, to let men actually see in Him the destiny which lies at the end of that way: he who sees me sees the Father (Jn 13:9).

It is in this context that the Gospel writers describe the miracles of Christ, and our contemporary re-evaluation of the role of miracle is fortunately recovering some of this mentality. Christ's extraordinary actions are *signs*, signs that are consciously related (by Jesus and by the faith of the primitive Christian community) to Yahweh's Old Testament actions—whether these were worked directly or through some human mediator. Jesus' deeds go beyond those of Moses, or Elias, or David, even beyond the promised deeds of the Messiah; for Jesus is Yahweh fulfilling the process of giving the word of life to men. These signs of Jesus not only speak the *fact* that He is Messiah and God, they speak of the *way* in which the Word become flesh is carrying out the mission given Him by the Father. Through Christ, the Spirit is working to overthrow the powers of evil, but it is the humanity of Christ that translates into finite expression the undefined immensity of divine love and power.

What precisely is the role played by the human nature of Jesus in transmitting the divine causal intent? Obviously, whatever it is that Christ as man does in contributing to salvific causality involves His human consciousness and free choice; so we can immediately proceed to a more specific question: what in the area of salvific action is the causality exerted by Christ's human intent?

First of all, it is good to remember that all the human acts of thought and love performed by Christ flow from and are the expression of His sanctifying grace which is the *gratia capitis*. Thus there lies behind His human acts, not just the infinite causal principle of His divine Person, but that grace which, being unlimited in its own species, is completely co-extensive with the whole mystery of man's transformation in grace.[10] In all giving of grace to men, this unique grace of Christ functions in an instrumental fashion; for this reason all grace is a participation in the grace of Christ and bears as a result a resemblance to Christ.[11]

However, it would be unbecoming the dignity of Jesus' humanity to think of His grace being utilized by the Trinity as an impersonal force. Christ's nature and the transformation of that nature which was His grace found expression—as it does in all us humans— through the actions of His human powers of activity, themselves supernaturally transformed so that they could be the bearer of this new causal stream. It was, then, the human intent of Jesus to accept His Messianic role, to give up His life so that He could then give new life to men, it was this basic choice (which governed all Christ's acts) that was and is the medium for the divine causality of grace.

Christ's own conscious finalistic orientation of Himself to man's redemption is the instrument that enters into each man's sanctification; and because His human intent does occupy this instrumental role, we can speak of a certain "addition" that it gives to the divine creative activity that flows through it. Clearly, we are using the word "addition" loosely in this context, because we know that the precise proper effectiveness of such an instrument lies in the area of specification, that is to say, of limitation. What actually happens is that all grace given to men bears not just the specification coming from Christ's grace, but the specification coming from that sacrificial acceptance of death which is the cause of our redemption. We can see that Jesus' acceptance of Calvary is not just a meritorious cause of our grace, but an instrumental specifying cause as well.[12] Our grace is very profoundly an assimilation to the redemptive mysteries of Christ.

When we return now to a consideration of the "signs" that Christ worked, we can see that they are much more than pedagogical devices, more than a claim to be recognized as Messiah and God. They are, as conscious expressions of Christ's redeeming intent, and culminating in the actions of Holy Week, actually part of the Christian specification of grace.[13] As we shall see in just a moment, Christ purposely introduced into those acts all the religious significances of the Old Testament dispensation, so that the specification given grace by the signs of Christ is a recapitulation of all the "words" of God in the centuries prior to the Incarnation. Possessed as He was of beatific vision, Jesus was completely aware of this role and able to catch up into His intent the entire history of the human race.

Intent says more than just knowledge; so we might briefly recall the instrumental function of Christ's human love in the causing of redemption. This love, natural and supernatural, was the intrinsic motive force directing all Christ's activity towards the fulfillment of that cosmic finality described in the beginning of Ephesians. Everything in Christ as man was eschatologically oriented by this act of love of His Father and of men. This human love provided a deep and complete dedication of Himself to His Father, a dedication that finds expression in the action of sacrifice; and this act flows into our grace and charity which gives us a share in this Christian dedication of our selves and our activity.[14] Again, as with Christ's grace and His consciousness, it is not the charity of Christ as an unspecified power that works in our sanctification; it is the charity of Christ expressing itself in His actions of Cenacle, Calvary, and Resurrection that flows into the causation of our grace and our charity.

As a moment's reflection suffices to indicate, this specification of our Christian sanctification by Christ's own sacrificial love points to the profound link between sanctity and sacrifice. As preparation for considering this in terms of the Christian sacraments, let us discuss one last area of Christ's own fulfillment of the Old Testament eschatology: the *ritual expression* by Jesus of His divine-human intent to save men.

No matter what particular theories one may hold as to the sacrificial nature of the Last Supper and of Christ's death on the cross, it seems beyond question that that which was most important in this redemptive act, that which was most properly redemptive, was Christ's internal attitude of self-giving to His Father and to mankind.[15] Not that one would wish to discount the true causal efficacy of the externals of His action; but it was the humanly conscious choice that gave the action its moral specification and therefore made it a meritorious cause; and it was this same conscious choice of Jesus that can and does act as the instrumental exemplary cause of that Christian orientation in us that constitutes our intrinsic redemption.[16] This attitude of Jesus, which upon examination is seen to be the internal element of an act of sacrificial worship, links together Cenacle and Calvary in an inseparable unity. Moreover, this sacrificial choice flows on unbroken in the mystery of the risen and ascended Christ, and as long as it exists it possesses a finality directed to the redemption of man and an intrinsic specification coming from the death on Calvary that is the object of the choice.

Ritually expressed in actions whose symbolic richness is so great that centuries of theological investigation will never comprehend it, the redemptive sacrifice of Christ was the goal towards which tended everything else Christ said and did. The Gospels witness to the fact that Jesus and the primitive Christian community saw these events of Holy Week as the *eschata*, as the day of the Lord; everything that is narrated of Christ earlier in the Gospels is preserved by the Evangelists as a means to better understanding the final redemptive act—and its continuation in the Christian sacramental life.[17] Careful examination of the Gospels, Synoptics as well as John, shows that earlier scenes in the public life of Christ are seen as the inchoative stage of that ritual which finds full expression from the Last Supper onwards. All the significance of these earlier events is contained eminently in that which was seen clearly by Christ as their fulfillment; in a sense, we can say that the Supper, death, and resurrection of Jesus had a kind of pre-existence in the intrinsic finality contained in these earlier actions—and extending this principle to the realm of Christ's divine causative intention, we can see a pre-existence by way of finality even in the events of the Old Testament. Already in the Baptism of Christ, in His Transfiguration, in the multiplication of loaves, in the miracle of Cana, there is evidenced Christ's identity as the Servant of Yahweh who is going on to establish the Eucharistic covenant and seal it with His blood, and the externals used by Jesus to express this sacrificial intent are themselves highly symbolic and ritualistic. In Luke, particularly, the atmosphere of priesthood pervades the narrative, from its first scene of Zachary in the act of sacrifice until the final lines which tell of the Apostles expressing in the Temple their gratitude for the glorification of Jesus.

If the earlier "signs" of Jesus functioned, as we have seen, to reveal the manner in which God is redeeming mankind, this is eminently true of the final stage of Christ's ministry. Not as some detached and neutral meritorious cause does the action of Supper and Calvary and Resurrection bring about our salvation; in all the significances of this three-stage action Christ speaks to us of the kind of salvation that is ours (one of being fed with His life-giving body and consecrated by His sacrificial blood), speaks with a sacramental word that is efficiently operative according to its significances. To know what Christian redemption truly is, one must probe in faith and charity the meaning of that act of sacrifice begun by Jesus in the upper room; the great orthodox traditions of spirituality in the Church have always seen this and have made the redemptive act of Christ a privileged object of contemplation.

Nowhere does Christian eschatology come to richer focus than in this redemptive sacrifice of Christ. This is the long-awaited "day of the Lord" and the fulfillment of Messianic expectation; this is the end of the Old Testament in the triple sense of termination, goal, and fulfillment. From one point of view, this is the *eschaton* beyond which nothing else can lie; yet it itself, as a fullness that must flow out to share itself, is ordered finalistically to Christian history and to the life of man with God beyond history. Two aspects of this eschatological orientation might be mentioned. First of all, and quite obviously, the redemptive intent of Jesus that is the abiding internal core of the events from Cenacle to Ascension is a causal orientation to our salvation through grace (Hb 7:25). Secondly, and less obviously, the externals of Christ's action point in their significances to a fulfillment beyond themselves, a fulfillment which they already contain *in causa;* for example, to give food which is source of life points to an expected increase of vitality, an increased vitality already somehow contained in the food. Because it contains in its causal fullness all the future development of the Christian mystery, the redemptive sacrifice of Jesus is truly "realized eschatology."

Even among those Scripture scholars whose view of Christ's human consciousness is limited by their rejection of His divine personality, one finds today a more moderate view of the so-called "eschatological" mentality of Christ. Whereas before some tended to see in Him a disappointed visionary, now there is increasing recognition that Jesus was aware that a long interval would separate His death and resurrection from the definitive realization of His kingdom, and that He purposely established a religious society to provide for this interval.[18] Along with this has come an increased understanding of the extent to which the primitive Christian community was aware of the abiding presence of Christ in its midst; in the mystery we denominate the Mystical Body, a mystery accomplished by the continuing gift of the Spirit. Thus, the mystery of Resurrection and Ascension does not involve a separation of Christ from His followers, but rather a new and all-pervading, though invisible, presence.[19] Christ continues to work redemptively, the driving intent to bring true life to men still continues to move Christ in His human activity, and the sign of this salvific intent and its effective presence in our midst is the mystery of the Church. Just as Christ's deeds, His signs, bespoke His saving love during the days of Palestinian ministry, so now the redeeming word He continues to speak is His Church.

This Church, implementing as it does the redeeming love of Christ who is the source of its life, pertains essentially to the risen glory of Christ. Semantic studies have pointed out for us that the revealed notion of "God's glory" is inseparably linked with that of salvation. It is at the great turning points of Old Testament salvation history that the *Kebod Yahweh* is manifested, and the later centuries of Jewish thought looked on the abiding of the "glory" in the Temple as the guarantee of God's saving action in Israel (Ez 10:18, 43:1). From the scene of the Presentation onwards, the Gospels point to Christ as the replacement of the Temple and its *Kebod;* and the Church in turn becomes the glory, the salvific manifestation, of the risen Lord who like His Father "works until now" (Jn 5:17). Throughout her history, Christ purifies and sanctifies the Church, so that without wrinkle or blemish, she can be His glory in the hereafter (Eph 5:27)—as a wife is the glory of her husband (Prv 12:4; 1 Cor 11:7).

But the salvific intent dynamizing the activity of the Church is not just the human redeeming love of Christ; behind that lies the divine creative will of the eternal Word. He who abides with His own is the Son of God, and as such there is only one adequate way of expressing the love which is His: by the gift of the Holy Spirit. Christ's own public life had been a sacrament of the Spirit's redeeming work among men; yet the fuller messianic manifestation of the Spirit comes with Pentecost when, through the accomplished mysteries of redemption, the Spirit is able to work towards the *aedificatio corporis Christi*. It is clear that Pentecost is an eschatological event par excellence: the Spirit is sent to build, to form, to develop life. A new creation, a new man, is in process of being achieved; Pentecost is but a beginning, a beginning of something in a sense already accomplished: the rule of human history by the Incarnate Word. It is not accidental that to establish His rule, Christ sends the Spirit who proceeds from His love, for Christ has made it abundantly clear that the very principle of His own redeeming effectiveness is His love—and the same is to be true of His Church. Those who follow Christ are by their love to be signs of His own abiding love, of the abiding among men of the Spirit of His love (1 Jn 3:23-24). The Church is the word of love that Christ speaks to mankind throughout its history, a word of invitation and promise; it is the Church's role to be the sacrament of this love.

That work of redemptive love which Christ continues to carry on in His Church is a priestly one of mediating His own divine life to men. At the very heart of this work, as we will see shortly, is the act of sacrifice; and at the heart of the act of sacrifice is found that which we have made the object of this [article], the redemptive intent of Christ. To enable His Church to participate this redemptive sacrificial intent, Christ has communicated to His followers that share in His own priestly power that we call the sacramental character. Situated by rather common agreement in the area of operative power, the sacramental character is a germinal assimilation to Christ in His redeeming sacrificial attitude that is meant to come to actuation in the Christian's conscious participation in sacramental life. It is obvious how prominent finality is in the notion of the character: as an operative power it is an orientation to action, and the very action in question is the entry into communion with Christ's salvific intent. Since it is the character that incorporates us into the Mystical Body,[20] it is clear that Christ's causing of this character in His members gives to His Church an essentially apostolic—or if you will, eschatological—orientation.

The causal finalization of the character is directed towards man's two final goals: towards his internal final goal of unending possession of supernatural life in glory, towards his external final goal, the Father, through an act of sacrificial worship in this life and through beatific vision in the next. By virtue of this character, the members of the Church are able to speak the effective words of Christ, to impart His transforming influence to the world in which they are situated, to mediate the finality of the created universe in an act of worship of the Father.[21] Or, to put it another way, by virtue of the character members of the Church are rendered apt instruments in and through whom Christ can continue those salvific actions He began two thousand years ago, and the precise acts of the Church in which Christ's continuing activity finds highest expression are the sacraments.[22]

It is in the sacraments above all that Christ continues to give witness to the eschatological action of the Trinity in human history. In the Mass is to be found an unparalleled fulfillment of Old Testament and New Testament prophetism, for the Eucharistic action is the continuation of Cenacle and Calvary.[23] Through the self-offering of the Last Supper and Calvary, when with full consciousness He fulfilled the prophetic vocation as idealized in the Servant of Yahweh, Christ bore unique witness to God's covenant dispensation by establishing a new covenant in His own blood.[24] St. John's account of the last discourse emphasizes the new finality of this Christian covenant: the peace towards which it was directed, the inheritance promised to those who accepted it, the promised land in which Christ would join His disciples to Himself, the force of fraternal charity which would lead them to this goal. Each celebration of the Eucharist, showing forth as it does the death of Christ until He come in final judgment (1 Cor 11:26) bears witness to the triumphant and redeeming power of that death by which we gain life. Each celebration of the Eucharist is a step towards that final manifestation of Christ's risen glory that will come at the end of human history.

Being the continuation of Christ's action of the Cenacle, which in its significances carries us back to the entire history of Irsael, the Mass is a recapitulation of all sacred history; and the same is true in somewhat less complete fashion of the other Christian sacraments. The very fact that the sacraments cannot be understood adequately without a wide and deep knowledge of both Old Testament and New Testament happenings indicates the extent to which the meaning of Israelitic and Christian history is involved in the sacramental system. However, we must be careful not to miss the depth of this recollection; the sacraments are not simply a reminder of what happened; they catch up into themselves—and this precisely because they are the personal conscious acts of Christ—all the religious reality of those previous stages of salvation history. Just as in our human knowing, each experience is conditioned by everything we have known previously and, in a sense, our latest experience is the fullest because drawing on everything before it; so the celebration of the Eucharistic sacrifice is, day by day, the fullest expression up to that point of the redemptive mystery of Christ.[25]

In the sacraments Christ still speaks to us of the *Magnalia Dei* which found their fulfillment in Him and of the "signs" He worked to prepare for the understanding of the sacraments; but the word He speaks is not just an explaining word, it is an effecting word. The sacramental word that Christ speaks through the voice of His Church bears witness to the presence of His redeeming act in human history, not only bears witness, it forms part of that redeeming act, for this sacramental word (and we use this to signify the entire sacramental action which finds its supernatural specification in those words that are the "form of the sacrament") is the bearer of Christ's divine and human intent. Thus, the sacraments are the key actions —conjoined actions of God and man—in what is the last period of salvation history, in the march of the new man in Christ towards unending glory.

That mankind will reach this glory is absolutely assured by the presence in the sacramental acts of Christ's redeeming love. This human love, revealed as present by the sacramental actions, is itself the sacrament of the creative divine love that is operating to transform man supernaturally. The very nature of God demands that this divine love work to draw men to God as their final end; reason can tell us this. Christ's redeeming love in the Church is a sign of something sublimely greater: man has been offered the gift of the divine Persons in friendship; it is Their fidelity as lovers that is in question and that is attested to in the Christian sacraments. Since it is this divine love that is the dynamic power at the source of all creation, natural and supernatural, its operative presence in the sacraments is the unshakable foundation of Christian hope. Only man's free acceptance is needed to complement this love, so that it can work out man's divinization; and in the sacramental context this condition is fulfilled, for the human part of the sacramental action is free response in an act of love. The loving union of man with God in the sacraments is actually the beginning, and therefore the promise, of the unending life of union, which is man's destiny.

Not only Christ's word and love in the sacraments make of them a witness to the divine action directing mankind towards supernatural fulfillment; the very presence of Christ in His risen state in the sacraments means that these actions, at least partially, are already *eschata*. Christian sacraments are actions both of Christ and of His Church: as actions of the Church they are limited by all the restriction of the temporal process, and their enactment can be a progressively more intelligent and meaningful process as the Church matures in faith and charity and moves towards its fulfillment beyond history; as actions of the risen Christ the sacraments are already beyond the limiting influences of time, for in Christ Himself there is nothing to be achieved; He is already present to the goal of human history because He is Himself that goal both as God and as man. In the sacraments we find a rich exemplification of that "realized eschatology" of which we have already spoken. More importantly, we find the key to understanding somewhat the relation of time to eternity, a problem that has vexed human thought throughout the centuries.[26]

Earlier in the paper we spoke of the interesting process by which Old Testament thought incorporated into itself the religious significances of natural religions and transformed them in doing so; and we then saw later that a similar process takes place in Christ's transformation of Old Testament significances. This progressive transformation of the meaning of the world and man's existence is one of the key elements in a Christian understanding of evolution or in the development of a theology of history. It is intrinsically bound up with the institution of the sacraments, which in turn play their role as the focus of the gradually unfolding significance of history.

What interests us here is that it is Christ Himself who, working in the sacraments, directs this process of transformation towards the last day when all mankind will see in final judgment the true meaning of man. There are two levels to this transforming influence of Christ. Insofar as He, the Incarnate Word, reveals Himself ever more fully and as He gathers the significances of all creation into Himself and speaks of them to the Father, He communicates to creation a constantly deepening *Christological* meaning. Insofar as He accomplishes this in and through His Mystical Body, which has its own proper though derivative causation, Christ adds the *ecclesiastical* dimension to the significance of human history. It is not just Christ that is the principle of interpreting God's action in history; it is Christ in the continuing mystery of the Church.[27]

This double transformation takes place supremely in the sacraments which as actions of Christ and actions of the Church are signs of the nature of Christ and of the Church, signs of the role each is playing in the redemption of mankind. Nor is this transformation a static reality, accomplished once and for all when Christ instituted His Church; as the Church moves through history, each succeeding step in the advance of man is given its ultimate significance because the Church of men absorbs into its transforming sacramental life all the deeper consciousness of himself that man has gained, and because the Church then goes out again to men with this transformed understanding so that it can be the root of still further advance.

However, we must not think of this sacramental transformation as a mere natural advance in understanding human life, as something that is quite clear and comprehensible. Such a transformed meaning of life pertains to the vision of faith; for the action of Christ in the sacraments is not mere instruction about the deeper meaning of life. The sacraments cause what they signify; Christ in His Church actually is engaged in a progressive supernatural transformation not just of individuals but of man's social existence; and the sacraments are the Christ-Church actions that cause this transformation significantly.

We can make a mistake in excluding from the significance of the sacraments the interior consciousness of the Church and treating the sacraments as things rather than as personal actions. Schillebeeckx has drawn attention to the *signifying* as the heart of sacramental act;[28] and in this perspective, whose truth can scarcely be disputed, the deeper the understanding possessed by the Church of the significance of the sacraments (indeed, of the entire Christian mystery) the deeper will be the signifying action performed by Christ through the mediation of His Church. Our task in the Church is to be leaven, imparting a transforming and life-giving

influence to human life; the new meaning we communicate in the
sacraments is not just the meaning of ourselves as the Church but
the meaning of Christ Himself, and the extent to which we communicate the meaning of the one and the other is necessarily dependent upon the level of our understanding. The sacraments are
the word that Christ speaks and they are simultaneously the word
of the Church. This is a word of life, and the life caused by this
word will be richer as the word of the Church itself is more meaningful.

If growth in understanding of the Christian mystery is required
so that sacraments cause more deeply, the sacraments themselves
exist to provide this growth; for they are not only the expression
of the Church's faith knowledge, they are the object of that faith.
In the experience of the sacramental acts, the Church comes into
concrete contact with all the mysteries of revelation; it is here that
the Church is meant to gain existential knowledge of the divine
persons whose acts the sacraments are, existential understanding of
the Incarnation's redemptive fulfillment that is being accomplished
in the sacraments, existential insight into itself as it becomes aware
of what it is doing in the sacramental acts of redemptive worship.[29]
As a man comes to know his own personal being by observing
those acts of cognition and appetition that are proper to him as
man, so the Church comes to deeper understanding of that mystery
which she is by faith experience of her own proper actions, the
sacraments. In the consciousness of being redemptively loved by
Christ, the Church becomes aware of her own proper role as the
"redeemed." In the experience of offering the supreme sacrifice in
union with Christ, the Church comes to know her own priestly
dignity and vocation, comes to discover the profound role she is
meant to play in mediating divine truth and divine love to men.[30]
It is in the Mass alone that man can discover the true nature of
religion and therefore the true meaning of man.

It would be interesting to pursue this line of thought, to show
the central role that religious tenets and practices play in human
cultures, and to point to the reciprocal influence of sacraments and
culture. This would be a study all by itself, one that would involve
a theology of man's imagination.

We have seen, then, how Judaeo-Christian revelation tells us of
the divine intent at work in human history, specified and described

by the whole course of Old Testament events and religious expression, incarnated in the mystery of the Word become flesh, expressed and implemented by His redeeming actions, finally carrying on through Christ's continuing actions in the Christian sacraments. In this process the human intent of the Church is the instrument of the human intent of Christ which is in turn the instrument of the divine creative intent; the sacramental words that the Church uses to express this intent are the words that Christ is speaking through His Church, and are also the words that the Father is speaking to men in His Son. It is above all in the Eucharistic sacrifice that the Christian community encounters the Word that the Father is speaking to it and through it; but it is also in the Mass that the Christian community speaks the Word back to the Father in worship. This is the concluding point . . . [of discussion], for it is this response of worship that is the last link in the eschatological orientation of the Christian sacraments.

With a depth of meaning to which we (who speak of "*receiving* the sacraments*") are unaccustomed, the early centuries of the Church looked upon the sacramental actions as professions of faith in the God of revelation. Today, with the added interest in the sacramental character and in the sacrificial nature of the Eucharist, we are again awakening to the sacraments as acts of acknowledging the Fatherhood of God. In this protestation of Christian faith, the sacramental actions serve as the word of worship for the individual Christian and for the Church as a whole; in the sacramental word the human personality finds fullest expression, and the Church fulfills its principal purpose for existing. But the richness of the Church's sacramental worship is increased immeasurably by the fact that it is Christ Himself, standing in the midst of His brethren and joining them to Himself, who is the chief agent of the sacramental praise of the Father. If His human intent was directed to the redemption of men, it was directed still more ultimately to praise of the Father; and Christ's intent operative in the Church still bears that finality.

In the task of assimilating his own worshipful attitude to that of Christ in the sacramental actions lies the Christian's most profound application of the Apostle's exhortation, "Put on Christ Jesus" (Rom 13:14). That human mentality of Jesus which the Gospels portray, a mentality that in deep mystery participates in the filial orientation proper to Christ as second Person of the Trinity, is the exemplar and goal of Christian virtue. But more than that, as we already saw, this human attitude of Christ that expresses both His priesthood and His grace, is itself an instrumental cause effecting the Church's sacramental act of worship.[31] Through the attitude of sacrificial worship which animates the Christian in his sacramental actions flows Christ's own attitude; and it is this latter that communicates to our Christian sacramental activity its priestly efficacy. Conversely, there is a certain dependence of Christ upon His Church in that the historical manifestation of Christ's worship of the Father is conditioned by the extent to which awareness and sincere worship characterize the Christian community's sacramental action. Just as the Church's signifying action does have a genuine effect in the causation of grace, so also does it have a true efficacy proper to itself in the unique Christian act of worship. Christian contemplative effort to probe into and to conform to the mind of Christ should be oriented to the sacramental actions in which the Christian identifies his attitude towards man and God with that of Christ.

If the Christian community in each succeeding stage of human history thus joins its acknowledgment of the Father with Christ's sacrificial acknowledgment, there results a profound consecration of the entire historical process. Caught up into the lives and experiences of Christians, the otherwise disordered and unintelligible events of human living fall under the influence of an ultimate finality. As the objects of man's knowing and as the goods that man employs to develop himself humanly and supernaturally, even the subpersonal creatures become part of the Christian reference of human life to God the Father. In the sacraments, then, occurs that fulfillment of creation's finality to which the "*Per ipsum*" of the Eucharistic action refers. In the sacraments Christ is working to reorder, to redeem, man and all creation through man. As the Church moves through history, this process of Christ revealing and effecting His redemptive intent gradually unfolds until it attains to its realization in the final stage of eschatological fulfillment. Until that happens, our Christian sacramental life will remain not only anamnesis and presence but also promise: *Recolitur memoriam passionis eius, mens impletur gratia, "et futurae gloriae pignus nobis datur."*

References

[1] Nehemia 9:6ff.; Deuteronomy 5:2ff.; Jeramia 2:6.

[2] As an indication of the attention paid recently to the Old Testament "theology of the word," cf. J. L. McKenzie, "The Word of God in the Old Testament," *Theological Studies*, 21 (1960), 183-206.

[3] On the deepening understanding of Old Testament happenings, see the valuable study of J. Guillet, *Biblical Themes*, trans. 1961.

[4] See the polemic in Isaia 43 against the false gods; in this passage emphasis is laid on the fact that Yahweh alone knows and communicates knowledge of the future.

[5] Cf. J. McKenzie, *The Two-edged Sword* (Milwaukee, 1956), pp. 60-71.

[6] In view of the widespread dispute on the notion of eschatology (and consequent ambiguity in use of the word), it would be well to state the sense in which . . . [we] will use the word. By *eschatology* we will mean that aspect of historical events (or manner of viewing these events) that points towards a future fulfillment which, being itself a new beginning, will mark the end of the present historical sequence.

[7] See especially Isaia 52-55, where one finds the famous passage on Yahweh's word (Is 55:7ff.) almost immediately after the final Servant Song which concretizes the ideal of prophetism in the Messianic figure.

[8] On Messianism, cf. J. McKenzie, "Messianism and the College Teacher of Sacred Doctrine," *Proceedings of the Society of Catholic College Teachers of Sacred Doctrine*, 6 (1960), 34-53.

[9] *S.T.*, III, 62, 6, ad 3.

[10] *S.T.*, III, 8, 5; *Mystici corporis* (America Press), pp. 63-64.

[11] *S.T.*, III, 7, 11; 8, 5; 56, 2, ad 4.

[12] *S.T.*, III, 48, 6.

[13] It is interesting, too, to recall that all the actions and experiences of Christ "left their mark on Him," so that they all flowed into His final act of knowing and loving.

[14] Cf. *Mediator Dei* (NCWC), 93-99.

[15] *S.T.*, III, 48, 1, ad 1.

[16] *S.T.*, III, 48, 6; *DB*, 799-800.

[17] Cf. B. Vawter, "The Johannine Sacramentary," *Theological Studies* 17 (1956), 151-66.

[18] Cf. O. Cullmann, *The Christology of the New Testament* (Philadelphia, 1959), pp. 43-50.

[19] Cf. E. Schillebeeckx, "Ascension and Pentecost," *Worship*, 35 (1961), 336-63.

[20] *Mediator Dei*, 88.

[21] *Mediator Dei*, 99-104. Cf. J. Van Camp, "The Sacramental Character," *Theology Digest*, 1 (1953), 28-31.

[22] Cf. C. Vagaggini, *Theological Dimensions of the Liturgy*, I (Collegeville, 1959), 74-83.

[23] Most authors—like Durrwell, *The Resurrection*, 144, and C. Spicq, *L'Epître aux Hébreux*, 1, 312—regard passages in Hebrews, such as 9:12, as indicating the perduring nature of Christ's redeeming action. However, A. Vanhoye, "De 'aspectu' oblationis Christ secundum Epistolam ad Hebraeos," *Verbum Domini*, 37 (1959), 32-38, insists that such passages point, not to the

continuing sacrifice of Christ, but to the uniqueness of this sacrifice as a past and unrepeated historical event.

[24] See page 22 in my article "Synoptic Presentation of the Eucharist as Covenant Sacrifice," *Theological Studies*, 21 (1960).

[25] See E. Mersch's stimulating discussion of this aspect of Christ's death: *The Theology of the Mystical Body* (St. Louis, 1952), pp. 264-70, 278-96.

[26] See the provocative remarks of Karl Rahner in "Zur Hermeneutik eschatologischer Aussagen," *Zeitschrift für katholische Theologie*, 82 (1960), 155-56, on the need to clarify our theory of knowledge regarding revealed eschatological realities.

[27] ". . . the Church is not only the first of the works of the sanctifying Spirit, but also that which includes, conditions, and absorbs all the rest. The entire process of salvation is worked out in her; indeed, it is identified with her." H. de Lubac, *The Splendour of the Church* (New York, 1956), p. 24; see also the entire Chap. 6, "The Sacrament of Christ," 147ff.

[28] E. Schillebeeckx, *De sacramentele heilseconomie* (Antwerpen 'T Groeit, 1952), pp. 395-402.

[29] Cf. E. Schillebeeckx, "The Sacraments: An Encounter with God," *Theology Digest*, 8 (1960), 117-21.

[30] In this context, one might profitably refer to contemporary discussion on "tradition," as, e.g., W. Burghardt in his paper to the 1951 convention of the C.T.S.A.; cf. *Proceedings*, 6 (1951), 42-75, esp. 66-69.

[31] Cf. *Mediator Dei* (NCWC), 76-81.

FRANK B. NORRIS, S.S.

The Response of Faith in the Sacraments

Tridentine teaching has proclaimed that the work of justification begins with God's gift, to which man must respond by faith. This process is the pattern for the work of salvation. Since the sacraments are the salvific acts of Christ, they too are God's gifts to which man must respond by faith. This article serves as an introduction to the following one in which the sacraments as signs of faith are treated more fully.

Father Norris teaches theology in St. Patrick's Seminary, Menlo Park, California.

The church has a one-track mind. Fifty-two Sundays a year she proclaims the selfsame message to her children. True enough, she may stress now one, now another, aspect of that message. She may indeed formulate the message in different words. But in season and out, from Advent to new Advent, she proclaims one thing and one thing only: Redemption. God our Father, she never tires of telling us, has done the "impossible." Through Christ, our Lord and Savior, He has made us—sinful men and women— to be His holy People, His holy family. Left to ourselves we could do nothing but work out our own destruction. "But God, who is rich in mercy," St. Paul declares, "by reason of His very great love wherewith He has loved us, even when we were dead by reason of our sins, brought us to life together with Christ (by

This article was first published in *The Liturgy and Unity in Christ*, proceedings of the Twenty-First Annual North American Liturgical Week. It is reprinted here with permission of the Liturgical Conference.

grace you have been saved), and raised us up together, and seated us together in heaven in Christ Jesus" (Eph 2:4-6).

There is no more important truth to which the Christian Catholic Church must bear witness than this. We are a *redeemed* people, a people who have been rescued "from the power of darkness and transferred into the kingdom of God's beloved Son, in whom we have our redemption, the remission of our sins" (Col 1:13, 14). We are a redeemed people who have been ransomed from bondage "not with perishable things, with silver or gold, but with the precious blood of Christ, as of a lamb without blemish and without spot" (1 Pt 1:18, 19). We who once were no people are now God's people; we who had not received mercy now have received mercy (cf. 1 Pt 2:10).

Man does not save, man does not justify, man does not sanctify himself therefore. Salvation, justification, sanctification—these are God's gracious gifts to us. It is God who first had compassion on us when we were dead through our trespasses. It is God who made us alive in Christ Jesus. Christianity is not a fifty-fifty proposition, a sort of "gentleman's agreement" between God and man, to which each contributes his own share. We are not partners with God in working out our salvation. Rather we stand before Him as naked, indigent beggars, powerless to change our lot. And even when we have become His adopted sons through union with His only begotten Son, we still come into His presence conscious of our utter dependence upon Him for the continued grace of sonship; conscious, too, of the frightening potential for sin and evil that is within us yet and which is held back only by His saving power and strength. This, then, is the heart and soul of the Church's message of redemption. This is the gospel, the kerygma, the Good News which the Church repeats tirelessly over and over again for us her children. For really there is nothing else the Church can proclaim except the saving work of God in Christ. "In this is the love," St. John writes, "not that we have loved God, but that He has first loved us, and sent His Son a propitiation for our sins" (1 Jn 4:10).

If we have deliberately stressed the divine initiative in the work of man's salvation in . . . [an article] which is principally concerned with man's response to God, we have done so because of the tendency we have, in the actual living of our lives, to be less than keenly aware of the absolute priority and pre-eminence of God's action. In a way we are all Pelagians at heart. For we are forever prone to attribute spiritual growth to our vigorous efforts and good resolutions and to feel that basically a man can do a pretty good job of being a Christian if he once makes up his mind and really buckles down to it. Whatever we may think of the Horatio Alger legend in the economic or social spheres, let us disabuse ourselves of any notion that it has application in man's relationship with God. At every step of the way salvation is God's free gift: it is a grace.

And yet man is not totally passive. He must accept the gift of salvation that is proffered him. It will not be thrust upon him against his will. It is no surprise, therefore, to find the same inspired writers who underscore the primacy of God's action stressing with equal insistence the role of faith, of man's personal response, in the process of salvation. "For God so loved the world," St. John tells us, "that He gave His only begotten Son, that those who believe in Him may not perish, but may have eternal life" (Jn 3:16). And to the question put to Him by his countrymen, "What are we to do, that we may perform the works of God?" our Savior replied, "This is the work of God, that you believe in Him whom the Father has sent" (Jn 6:28, 29). And further on, in the same context, He adds: "Truly, truly I say to you, he who believes in me has life everlasting" (v. 47). We recall here, too, the peremptory words of Christ at the close of St. Mark's gospel: ". . . but he who does not believe will be condemned" (Mk 16:16).

There is no need to multiply instances of what is so patently an integral part of the Christian message. Man must respond to God's gracious gift. Truly we are saved through faith. St. Thomas, then, was merely summing up the Christian tradition of twelve hundred years when he wrote: "As the Fathers of old were saved through their faith in Christ who was to come, so are we saved through faith in Christ who has already been born and has suffered (for us)." [1]

Does, then, the crucial necessity for faith somehow lessen the pre-eminence of God's activity? Is salvation, after all, a fifty-fifty proposition? By no means! For the very response of man to God's overture of redeeming love is itself a gift from God. Doubtless we are here face to face with high and inpenetrable mystery, mystery which man's limited mind will never fully comprehend. Nonetheless the data of revelation are clear. In the sixth chapter of St. John's Gospel, in the very discourse wherein our Lord insists so much on man's response of faith, Christ Himself states categorically: "No one can come to me unless the Father who sent me draws him" (Jn 6:44). Our coming to Christ through faith— conscious and free human act though it be—is not to be credited to us but to God: ". . . unless the Father draws him." St. Paul, therefore, simply echoes the teaching of his Master when he tells us, "For by grace you have been saved through faith; and that not from yourselves, for it is the gift of God . . ." (Eph 2:8). Moreover God's action is not something done once and for all at the moment of our justification. No, at every instant of our Christian existence we are continually indebted to God for the faith that is in us. Here again St. Thomas bears eloquent witness to what is traditional Christian teaching. "Grace produces faith," he writes, "not only when faith begins to exist in the soul, but also as long as it remains in the believing soul. . . . For God continues without ceasing to effect our justification, just as the sun continues without ceasing to illumine the air." [2]

Here then, in brief, is the work of salvation: a work which is God's free gift from beginning to end, to which man "drawn by the Father" can nevertheless freely respond through faith. Where salvation is present, there the mysterious interplay of divine and human activity will be found.

It follows, then, that the sacraments of our holy Faith will be the sacred and effective signs of the full process of salvation. For it is through the sacraments that our Lord and Savior lives on in our midst, bringing to men and women of our and of every age the healing power of His triumphant passion and death. "That which, formerly, was visible in our Savior," St. Leo writes, "has now passed into the mysteries" [3]—that is, the sacramental rites of the Church. The sacraments will then be signs of God's redeeming love, of His cleansing and purifying love, of His forgiving love, of His strengthening and healing love. They will be before all else signs of God reconciling the world to Himself in Christ Jesus (cf. 2 Cor 5:19). But they will also be signs of our faith, of our response to the gift of God. In a word, the sacraments will be signs, full and effective signs, of our personal encounter with Christ. Far from being obstacles to the direct union of the Christian with his Redeemer, the sacraments are the very means of effecting that union. We recognize and acknowledge our risen Lord in the Breaking of the Bread. It is through the Eucharist and through every sacrament that Christ comes to us with outstretched arms and we go forth to meet Him through faith. The sacraments, on our part, must be deep and loving acts of faith. They must be the conscious and responsible acceptance of the free gift of God, which Christ without ceasing brings to us. It is by grace we have been saved through faith.

It is because the sacraments are signs of our faith, it is because they are acts of faith, that the New Testament writers can attribute our justification now to faith, now to baptism. "He who believes in the Son," Christ tells us, "has everlasting life; he who is unbelieving towards the Son shall not see life, but the wrath of God rests upon him" (Jn 3:36). Yet in the same chapter of that fourth Gospel, our Lord solemnly declares: "Truly, truly I say to you, unless a man be born again of water and the Spirit, he cannot enter into the kingdom of God" (v. 5). So, too, St. Paul. "If you confess with your lips," he writes to the Christians at Rome, "that Jesus is the Lord and believe in your heart that God has raised Him from the dead, you will be saved" (Rom 10:9). Earlier in that same epistle, however, he attributes our justification to the rite of baptism. "Do you not know that all we who have been baptized into Christ Jesus have been baptized into His death? For we were buried with Him by means of baptism into death, in order that, just as Christ has risen from the dead through the glory of the Father, so we also may walk in newness of life" (Rom 6:3-14). And to Titus he writes: "He saved us through the bath of regeneration and renewal by the Holy Spirit" (Ti 3:5).

There is no conflict or contradiction here. Our justification can be attributed both to faith and to baptism precisely because baptism is an act of faith and because faith itself embraces all that Christ has established as means for a personal encounter with Him.

When we say that the sacraments are effective signs of faith, we do not understand the term "faith" merely in the restricted sense of an act of man's intellect accepting as true what God has revealed, but rather in the richer and broader biblical understanding of the term. Faith for the writers of the New Testament means the acceptance by the whole man of God's invitation to loving union with Him in Christ. Concretely, it is the acceptance of the Person of the Word, made flesh for our salvation. In the language of St. Paul it is confessing with all of one's being that "Jesus is the Lord." It is the full commitment of a person to a Person.

That this is an intensely personal act needs no demonstration. And the sacraments are signs of that personal commitment to

Christ. But what must be brought out is that the faith shown forth
in the sacraments has also, and essentially, a corporate, an ecclesial
dimension. Christ came not to save isolated souls but to cleanse for
Himself an acceptable people (cf. Ti 2:14), to establish a new and
eternal covenant between God and man. The faith that we profess
in and through the sacraments is, above all, faith in the covenant
which has been sealed with the blood that speaks more graciously
than the blood of Abel, the blood of Jesus Christ (cf. Hb 12:24).
Each celebration of the Eucharist, in particular, is a rededication by
the individual and by the community to the terms of the new and
eternal Covenant. We read in the Book of Exodus that when the
covenant of old was sealed at Mt. Sinai, Moses sprinkled both the
altar and the assembled multitude with the blood of the sacrificial
victim and read the book of the covenant in the hearing of the
people. For their part the people cried out, "All that the Lord has
said we will heed and do" (Ex 24:7). So, too, when Christ represents his one, perfect sacrifice in the Holy Eucharist and sprinkles
us anew with his cleansing, out-poured blood, the sacramental rite
is not complete unless we too do our part and cry out with living
faith: "All that the Lord has said we will heed and do." The sacraments are acts of faith.

We are living in wonderful and exciting times for the Church.
Thanks to the patient and largely unrewarded work of many who
have gone before us, we today are able to reap the harvest which
they sowed with so much love and faith. In particular, we are
regaining an appreciation of the integral Christian message, which
for centuries has not been commonly shared by Christians. One such
area of renewed understanding is the doctrine of the sacraments. We
see the sacraments today as signs rich in content, eloquent in their
power to teach us and mighty in their power to bring us into personal contact with our Redeemer. But we cannot selfishly keep the
vision of what we have seen to ourselves. What we have learned in
secret we must shout from the housetops to others, to our Catholic
and non-Catholic brothers alike, so that at last all may be drawn into
a deeper knowledge and love of the unfathomable riches of Christ.

References

[1] *Summa Theologica*, III, q. 62, a. 1.
[2] *Summa Theologica*, II-II, q. 4, a. 4, and ad 3.
[3] Sermon, 74, 2; *PL*, 54, 398.

PETER FRANSEN, S.J.

Sacraments:
Signs of Faith

Modern sacramental theology insists on an existential emphasis. The saving action of God is always directed toward man, a free agent; salvation is never automatic nor magical, but is always connected with man's free response, his faith. In examining the role of faith in regard to the sacraments, the following article considers the nature of grace, the law of Incarnation, and the sacraments as symbolic activity.

The sacraments are seen as possessing efficacy from faith; the faith of the Church and the faith of the man receiving the sacrament. Father Fransen insists that it is by means of the "faith of the Church" that it is possible to avoid that allegation raised against the Catholic concept of sacraments, namely, that they represent a species of magic.

Father Fransen is a Belgian Jesuit who after a period of teaching in the Belgian Congo has lectured at several American universities in recent years.

An interesting renewal in the theology of the sacraments is presently occurring in Europe, especially in the Low Countries. This renewal had its origins in the study of the New Testament, and in historical studies dealing with the theology of St. Augustine, St. Thomas, and other medieval writers and of the Council of Trent. It was stimulated by the popular success of the liturgical movement in Germany and in France, and the urgent pastoral needs of the Christian people, especially in the large cities, after the last war. We would

This article was first published in *Worship*, December 1962. It is reprinted here with permission of the copyright holders, the Order of St. Benedict, Inc.

like to give an insight into the fundamental positions of this sacramental theology—its primary motives and perspectives, its practical conclusions—which is now spreading quickly among west-European theologians and countries.

We would have liked to refer our readers, for every important point we have to make, to the abundant literature which can be found in French, German, and Dutch, in many reviews, and in important books. But . . . [circumstances made] this utterly impossible. Therefore we decided to forego all footnotes, and merely mention, wherever this might be useful, the name of the author who has specialized in a given subject.

The Problem

And first of all, is there any real problem? What was wrong with the fairly common and seemingly undisputed doctrine of the manuals published in the last century?

There is indeed a double problem—dogmatic and historical.

Reading the New Testament, we cannot avoid being impressed by the primordial emphasis on faith as a means of salvation. This "faith," whose absence moved Christ to complain so frequently and insistently, and which St. Paul so passionately defended against the legalistic religion of the Judaeo-Christians, had a wider meaning than it has now.

By "faith" the New Testament expressed the free and definitive dedication of our life to Christ in the unconditional acceptance of His message of redemption—the "kerygma," the "Gospel," or "the Word," as it was called—and of the way of life exemplified in Himself, which the New Testament and especially St. John call the "Truth." In short, the biblical meaning of faith had an even richer content than our technical notion: it was "*fides charitate formata*," faith perfected by charity. This was acknowledged also by St. Thomas.

Scripture, of course, knows more requirements for our salvation in Christ: baptism, the "Gift of the Spirit," membership in the Church, the observance of God's commandments, and charity. But there can be no doubt at all that faith is the first demand of Christ, uncontested and incontestable.

This primacy of faith was affirmed by the Council of Trent in Chapter 8 of the Decree on Justification:

But when the Apostle says that man is justified "through faith" and "freely" (Rom 3:22, 24), those words must be understood in the sense that the Catholic Church has always continuously held and declared. We may then be said to be justified through faith, in the sense that "faith is the beginning of man's salvation," the foundation and the source of all justification, "without which it is impossible to please God" (Heb 11:6). [Denz. 801, as translated in *The Church Teaches* (St. Louis: 1955), n. 565; henceforth quoted as *TCT*.]

And although this was clear enough, many Fathers of the Council insisted mentioning "faith" again in the important Chapter 7 "On the Nature and the Causes of the Justification of the Sinner":

The instrumental cause is the sacrament of baptism, which is the "sacrament of faith," *without which* [in the Latin text there is no doubt about the meaning of this relative particle, since it reads "*sine qua,*" referring to the feminine word "*fides,*" and not "*sine quo,*" which could have referred to the masculine word "*baptismus*"] no one has ever been justified [Denz. 799; *TCT*, n. 563].

Indeed, before the Council of Trent there had never been any doubt about the primordial role of faith. Medieval theology took its origin principally from commentaries on the Bible or, at least, on selected texts from the Bible, which were assembled according to special themes in the so-called *catenae*. But even later, when theologians switched to commentaries on the famous Sentences of Peter Lombard, and started the *Summae*, the primacy of faith was so universally held among all schools of scholastic theology that the sacraments, and especially though not exclusively, the sacrament of baptism, were called "the sacraments of faith," a designation of which Trent was to give us one of the last examples in the above-quoted sentence.

Nevertheless during the discussions of these chapters at Trent, one can detect a definite feeling of uneasiness among certain bishops and theologians. Not that they disagree with the common doctrine, but since Luther had sewed "*sola fide*" on his banner of rebellion, they saw no point in stressing his position by emphasizing this doctrine, which after all was denied by nobody.

Systematic theologians all too easily forget the fact (which is so well known among scholars in the field of Tridentine studies and which, for that matter, has been more than sufficiently proved from the study of the Acts of the Council) that the assembled Fathers never intended to delineate a *complete* exposition of the doctrine of justification, and even less so of the doctrine of the sacraments, to which less time and study were devoted than to the wording of the decree on justification. Rather, quite explicitly and consciously, they aimed only at condemning the heretical positions of the Lutherans and the Calvinists, deliberately dropping whatever question, however important, was still under discussion among Catholic theologians.

The positive Catholic doctrine proposed in the decrees and canons is therefore only the *necessary minimum*, in opposition and contrast to the heretical positions of that time.

After the Council of Trent this fear of a possibly misleading stress on faith remained. At the same time the theologians, who had access only to the final official text of the decrees, published in 1563 (since the minutes of the discussions were, according to Canon Law, safely kept in the archives of the Vatican), were driven by the psychological laws which, whether we like it or not, govern every passionate stage of controversy, into hardening and narrowing their own positions, precisely in reaction against the Reformers' "*sola fide.*"

The same thing happened in the case of the doctrine concerning the Church, where too much emphasis was laid upon the hierarchical structure of the Church, so that other equally essential aspects almost disappeared from ordinary teaching, in the catechisms and the manuals of theology.

In the case of the doctrine of the sacraments, this evolution in theology was endangered by the fact that the common theology of those days was strongly influenced by Nominalism, as it was later to be influenced by rationalism and Cartesianism. Nominalists claimed that "*de potentia absoluta,*" that is, as such, philosophically, as a matter of essential and internal necessity, man could be saved without habitual grace and without faith, because they emphasized in their philosophical system the absolute freedom of God, which could not be limited by any necessity whatever, either in or outside God. If either faith or grace was in fact demanded, this was only "*de potentia ordinata,*" that is, in this given economy of redemption. And by so doing they remained within orthodoxy.

In the teaching on the sacraments this philosophical and theological bias, together with the urge for controversy, hardened the notion of "*opus operatum.*" Even before the Council, the Nominalists had stated that the only requirement on the part of the subjects receiving a sacrament was the "*non positio obicis,*" that is, not to place any obstacle to the influx of grace. In practice this simply meant that they must be free of mortal sin, which was, incidentally, defined by its mere juridical relation to its punishment, expressed in a divine decree. That was all! And so they laid the foundations for the later "mechanical" interpretations of the *"opus operatum,"* and certainly influenced those quasi-magical practices in the Church of the fifteenth century which started the Reformation.

As a matter of fact, it was this nominalistic definition of the efficacy of the sacraments which was accepted by the Council in canons 6 and 8 (Denz. 849 and 851; *TCT*, nn. 670 and 672) of the decree on the Sacraments in General. The Nominalists constituted the majority at the Council. However, this definition could safely be stated as *a minimal* condition, in itself wholly orthodox, *on which all could agree.* Once again the Council refused to enter into the discussions carried on by the scholastic theologians before Trent; it was primarily concerned, in the wording of both these canons, with condemning the heretical position that the sacraments "are only external signs of grace or justice received through faith" (Denz. 849; *TCT*, n. 670). But unfortunately, after the Council, this canon became *the* exhaustive definition of the *"opus operatum,"* of the efficacy of any sacrament.

The contrary notion known as *"opus operantis,"* that is, through the personal devotion of the subject receiving a sacrament, was developed into a completely separate and distinct notion. One could receive "sacramental" grace through the efficacy of the sacrament itself, and "other" graces, whatever these might be(!), *"ex opere operantis,"* that is, by one's own devotion and piety in receiving the sacrament.

This was never dreamed of by St. Thomas or any theologian of his time. For them *"opus operantis"* was essentially related to the *"opus operatum,"* as *the personal aspect* in the justifying process of any sacrament, that aspect by which a free and responsible person accepted God's grace conferred by the sanctifying efficacy of the sacramental rite, that is, by virtue of the *"opus operatum."*

In connection with this St. Thomas developed a parallel of his own which might be called "existential."

In so far as a given sacrament was truly the visible presentation and manifestation in the Church of the "power of Christ's passion," it possessed its own "sacramental truth," the *"veritas sacramenti."* But as soon as the person receiving a sacrament accepted it *in faith and charity,* of course by virtue of "the mysteries of Christ's flesh," contained in the so-called *"opus operatum,"* St. Thomas said it had acquired its "final truth," the *"veritas simpliciter."*

Therefore "faith" entered the very structure of every sacrament, not of course in the Lutheran sense of the word, but as the necessary personalist complement in any process of sanctification and justification. We are saved as free persons, and not automatically, nor, which would be worse, magically. In other words, as Father Schillebeeckx expressed it so well, the sacraments can never be an excuse for loving God less!

But we must admit that the later controversies of decadent scholasticism on sacramental causality brought the idea of a sacrament, as it was taught in the catechisms and pulpits and as it was carried out in the practice of so many Christians, dangerously close to a "magical rite." This was especially true when grace was detached from its normal source, God's indwelling (which then became only a "formal effect" of created grace!), and was viewed as only a "created habitual entity or quality, infused into the soul." It never actually did become "magical" however, because the administration of the sacraments was always observed in obedience to Christ, who instituted them and gave them to the Church.

As a matter of fact, especially in regard to the sacraments of the Eucharist and penance, the existential attitude of many Christians remained far better and more orthodox than their own ideas about it, for the simple reason that it was never forgotten, even in teaching children, that, according to the pregnant formula of St. Augustine: "Peter baptizes, Judas baptizes, it is Christ who baptizes. A drunk, a thief, a man of sinful habits baptizes, once again it is Christ who baptizes." And this is the real and the full notion of the *"opus operatum."*

The Answer

Basic Principles

The renewal of the theology of the sacraments is inevitably related to the reorientation of many other aspects of theology. Truth is one. Once we touch a part of it, everything has to be reconsidered. In this short article we can only touch upon a few points which seem of greater importance. But as we can discover in the many books of Otto Semmelroth, H. Schillebeeckx, and K. Rahner, three of the best modern theologians in sacramental theology, these new sacramental perspectives shed light upon the whole of theology.

THE NATURE OF GRACE. Grace is, by its very nature, not *only* "a created entity or quality, infused into the soul"—a simplification which was likewise induced by the reaction against the Lutheran doctrine of *external* justification—but grace is, according to the language and the doctrine of the New Testament, fundamentally and primarily God Himself, the so-called "Uncreated Grace." St. Augustine once again expressed this in his incomparable way: *"Because* You loved me, You made me lovable and capable of love."

Since the last war it has become the more common teaching among the theologians of grace, that the indwelling of the Holy Trinity is the unique foundation of any grace; created grace is only a subsidiary, partial and limited, though a very real aspect in this sublime mystery of the creative Presence of God in us. It is the result, the fruit of, and the bond with this divine and active Presence of the three divine Persons in the soul.

But, if this is true, the sole valid explication of the efficaciousness of the sacraments is the efficaciousness, not of an impersonal instrumental cause producing a certain amount of created grace in us—we cannot avoid thinking of a slot-machine! So sorry!—but primarily the personal efficaciousness of the Indwelling Trinity itself. It is "Christ who baptizes," the Christ, eternally sent and given to us by the Father, and continuously realizing His own work through the power of the Holy Ghost. Here again we rediscover a very old and rich tradition of the Church, expressed in the liturgical praxis of the "epiclesis," the solemn prayer of the Church to the Holy Ghost who reaches us in every sacrament, and who sanctifies us according to the Image of the Son, unifying us in faith and charity through the Son with the Father, the origin and the end of all graces.

THE STRUCTURE OF INCARNATION EXPRESSED IN THE DIVINE ACT OF REDEMPTION. Christ did not redeem us by the mere amount of His sufferings, accepting in our place and name a so-called "cosmic law," that whoever had enjoyed sinful pleasures should suffer for it. The only true redemption is the conversion of hearts in faith, charity, and repentance. Here again we meet the central theme of this article.

Therefore Christ entered into this world, our world of sin and sinfulness, became a man and, in that quality, became what we ourselves should always have been from the beginning of creation according to the heart of God: the true Servant of the Lord. He saved us through His own obedience and love, "even to the death on the cross," and therefore He "received the Name which is above all names" ("name" in semitic language means reality!), that is, "the Lord."

It is through this mystery of final obedience and love that He merited for us to be, as He was, servants in the Servant and adopted sons in the Son (according to the beautiful formula of E. Mersch, the theologian of the Mystical Body); that is, that we, "through Him, with Him, and in Him" should accept our life and death from the hands of God in the same spirit of total obedience and love. Incidentally, let us not forget that St. Paul frequently speaks of our "obedience of *faith*"! Such is the mystery of grace expressed in terms of our historical redemption.

By sending us His own Son in the power of the Holy Spirit, the eternal Father "made us into His own people" and "inheritance"; He "acquired us for His own as a chosen people." As Father Stanislas Lyonnet has shown in so many articles, this is the real meaning of the words "redemption," "salvation," and so forth, in the Bible. Therefore this act of redemption is at the same time essentially connected with the foundation and the deepest nature of the Church, as God's chosen people on earth, as the visible place of His divine and saving Presence in this world. The treatises on grace, redemption, incarnation, and on the Church are thereby centrally connected with one another.

In this act of incarnation and redemption we find an essential structure which pervades the whole economy of salvation. Fundamentally and primarily we have the *descending* movement—sometimes called, less happily the virile line—of the Father, establishing His divine and saving Presence through His Son by the power of the Holy Spirit. In this aspect of redemption the essential primacy of God in any grace becomes manifest, this essential primacy which shall have to find its final and conclusive expression in a religious notion of the "*opus operatum.*"

Then there is the complementary, the subsidiary, and nevertheless necessary *ascending* movement of love and obedience in faith—sometimes called, with more success, the bridal line—in which we all, patterned on the Image of the Son and with and through Him, by the power of the Holy Ghost return to the Father, the origin and the end of all graces and of all salvation. It is in this so-called "bridal" movement of dedication and personal devotion that the proper place of "faith" in the sacramental mystery should become clear and evident.

We do find this structure in Christ Himself, the living Tabernacle of God, His Shekinah, descended from the Father and, at the same time, the perfect Servant of the Lord in His act of final dedication and love. Therefore Christ is rightly called the *Fundamental Sacrament*.

The Church is the Body of Christ and the Temple of God, and therefore the visible "sign set up before all nations" of this descending Presence of God. But, as the Bride of Christ, she is also united with Him in this movement of ascending obedience, love, and adoration. Therefore the Church nowadays is truly called the *Primordial Sacrament*.

If this is true, it is but normal that every sacrament should express the same dialectical movement, descending from God to us (the aspect of the *"opus operatum"*), and ascending through corporate prayer (the proper dogmatic role of liturgy as confession of faith) in faith and love back to God again (the aspect of *"opus operantis"*).

THE PHILOSOPHY OF SYMBOLIC ACTIVITY. It is necessary to enter into a more speculative problem, the philosophy of the symbolic activity. This philosophy has been especially developed in the Low Countries, although one could find related thinking in many other places, even among non-Christians and non-Catholics. The philosophy of the symbol is remarkably actual.

The classical notion of "sign," as used in our manuals of sacramental theology, was derived by the medieval scholastics from a small philosophical work of St. Augustine: a sign is something which, once it is known, leads us to the knowledge of another reality. This is in fact a very poor philosophy of "sign," or, as we from now on prefer to call it, symbol. It is quite useless. The medieval authors did not know that they could have found in St. Augustine's fascinating doctrine of the nature of *"sacramentum"* and of *"mysterium"* a more appropriate definition and much richer perspectives of thought.

Sacraments are never things, they are not "something." They are, as everybody can see who leaves his books and enters a church, an action, a *liturgical action* in which different persons exercise their own activity. They are symbolic activities of a special kind, that is,

ritual and ecclesiastic. Their symbolism finds its final and full meaning in the religious community in which they are performed, that is,
in the Church, simply because they are essentially "corporative"
symbols of a religious community. Therefore the *minimal*—not the
normal, by any means!—condition for a valid administration on the
part of the minister and on the part of the subject is to do and to
intend what the Church intends to do and to give in the name of
God.

The nature of any symbolic activity is grounded in the particular nature of man, as an embodied spirit, as a person. Man knows no
other form of activity. For him there cannot be any other. In every
act, even in silent thought, there is always a visibility, however tiny
and slight it may be, which manifests a deeper invisibility, and expresses it in the very act in which this deeper invisibility, which is
the acting person, realizes itself.

We have neither time nor space to enlarge upon this subject. We
would like, however, to stress a few important points which matter
greatly for a proper interpretation of the doctrine of the sacraments.

The more this invisible source of activity, which is the person,
lends sense and meaning to this visible manifestation of itself, the
richer the human activity is. On the other hand, the more our visible
activity keeps to its very nature of expressing our invisible intentions, the more faithful it is to its own nature of being a symbol, the
truer it is. Here again we find the thought of St. Thomas. This is
what the French call our "authenticity," and what we could call
our human honesty and sincerity.

This principle is very important indeed for any performance of
a given liturgical action. The minister and the assembled members
of the community, each in their way and according to their vocation representing the living Church, together with the subject receiving the sacrament have to express by their reverence, their
external piety, and their real religious attitude *the truth* of what is
happening: the truth of the invisible mystery in which God descends
to us and we return again to God in faith and charity. Every performance of a liturgical action lacking reverence and decency—in
the hurried Latin formulas we mumble or jabber, the indecorous
gestures we adopt, the matter-of-fact indifference we assume since
(as we say) everything is secured by the "*opus operatum*"—even
if it cannot touch the fundamental "truth" of the sacrament, its

"*opus operatum*," does endanger and threaten seriously by its very inauthenticity "the final truth."

This is the *dogmatic* foundation of any serious liturgical movement, which is not, as many still think, a special hobby for esthetes or for archeologists; what is at stake is this authenticity, this naked honesty of our life of faith expressed in the liturgy of the sacraments.

There is another point we would like to make. *Every symbolic activity possesses its own efficacy,* precisely because it is an activity. If there is any difference in efficacy, this cannot be caused by the nature of the person who is at the origin of this activity. Christ, real man and real God in the unity of one divine Person, acted as we do, according to the laws of symbolic activity, expressing in words and gestures His invisible divine intentions and actions. But because His humanity was united with His divinity in the mystery of the hypostatic union, His human symbolic activities possessed a divine efficacy. We are only human, and yet our symbolic activity possesses a very limited though real efficacy.

The important consequence of this is that, for the theology of the sacraments, we do not have to look for a second notion to explain sacramental causality, which could supplement our all too-limited, narrow, and rationalistic notion of a "sign." If the "sign," as such, acts only insofar as it brings us further *knowledge* of its meaning, then we must indeed supplement this static notion of the "sign" with a more dynamic notion of "instrumental cause." In the unity of his person every man, and this includes Christ too, each according to his own dignity and power possesses in and through his symbolic activity both the symbolic manifestation of what he intends to do, and at the same time and *in the same movement,* the realization of his symbolic activity.

In the matter of the sacraments, there is one serious objection against the universal application of this principle, which has been brought up several times by Father Schillebeeckx. He accepts our application of symbolic activity to Christ, because in Christ, as we said, there is a real unity of the Person, expressing itself in His human activity. But the minister of the Sacrament is not God. One can therefore never say that the minister's visible sacramental activity in the liturgy could possess the efficacy of God.

This, of course, is indubitably true. But the question is whether the unity of the Church with Christ, as His Body—and the minister is nothing else than the ordained deputy of the Church, the representative of the Church acting in him and through him—is not a unity which, even though it differs completely from the hypostatic union, would appear sufficient to constitute a true symbolic activity with divine efficacy. Not that the Church would receive, and keep and dispose for and by herself of the power of God—a position which Protestants often think we defend. But as the Body of Christ, and therefore as His living visibility on earth, always and inseparably united with her Head, who acts in her through His own Spirit in the name of the Father, she seems to be sufficiently united with Christ to perform in her liturgy such a symbolic activity; in other words, through this divine and ever active Presence in her, her activity acquires really, and yet never as separated from its divine Source, a divine efficacy.

This is of course a unique case for which we have no other parallel in human life. But if the unity of the Church with Christ her Head means anything at all, this unity must be more intimate than what Schillebeeckx seems to accept, although of course it never approximates the hypostatic unity.

By these considerations we are only trying to view the Church, consequently and fully, as the Primordial Sacrament of God's Presence in this world. If our line of reasoning is correct, we could henceforth dispense with the notion of "instrumental causality," which, as it seems to us, has done so much harm, and is doing so still. We concede, however, that the notion of "instrumental causality," so long as it is correctly explained, would seem to be the key concept in this chapter of sacramental theology *if* we choose to think in scholastic and aristotelian categories. We merely affirm that there are other ways of thought which might enable us to come nearer to the *personal* mystery contained in every Sacrament.

If the sacraments are essentially activities, they belong essentially to persons. They contain the mystery of *real personal encounter* between the descending mystery of God's mercy and the obedient faith of the sinner, within the Church as a living community of persons, represented in a personal way by the minister of the sacrament. He presides at the liturgical action, as a responsible person, in the name of Christ; and in this he is representing both the descending Christ of our salvation and grace in his symbolic actions of benediction and consecration, and the ascending Christ of our faith and charity in the fact that he leads our corporate prayers in the liturgy. In his "representation," as a sacral function within the Church, both movements of grace find their mutual and reciprocal completion.

There is finally a third point we think could be of importance. It is taken from the phenomenology of any human symbolic activity. When we consider the evolution of any symbolic activity, we discover two important laws: the law of appropriation and the law of extension.

When the invisible meaning and content of a given symbol is too rich to be expressed satisfactorily in that particular symbol, we see how human nature looks spontaneously for more symbols, integrating them in the initial symbolic activity in accordance with its fundamental meaning and intention. Every symbol, especially when it is expressing a rich and full meaning, tends to transcend itself by appropriating in this movement other symbolic activities in the desperate effort to equal what must ever surpass any full expression.

We discover the same evolution in the history of the liturgy. It witnesses to this effort of the Church to manifest more deeply and with greater power of suggestion what forever shall transcend its expression. Such has been the case, for instance, in the development of the liturgy of the Mass, or of ordinations.

There is an important consequence to this. It is philosophically and liturgically, and therefore theologically, unsound to depreciate any liturgical symbol which the Church has added to the initial symbol given us by Christ or established by the Church in the Apostolic Age. It is also unsound to consider whatever symbolic actions do not belong to the "form and the matter" of the sacrament, that is, to their "valid" administration, as "mere ceremonies." They belong to the very structure of the sacrament and, even if they can be changed, adapted, abolished, and omitted in case of necessity, *when they are performed*, in the very act of the liturgical action, they do belong to the integrity of the sacrament and they share in its divine dignity and meaning. This is also very important for any theological foundation for the liturgical movement.

The law of extension is also quite interesting. Every symbol, which from its fundamental meaning and content possesses a central importance in life, tends to extend itself in similar, although only analogical, symbolic actions. In this way the central mystery of the eucharistic Sacrifice, as the Church's supreme act of worship, has *de facto* extended itself over our whole life: through the conventual office in the choir of an abbey, through the breviary, through such celebrations as Benediction and procession with the Blessed Sacrament, through adoration of the holy Sacrament and devotion to the Real Presence.

This has further significance for our Christian life. These "extensions" of the Mass, if we want to accept them for what they really are, have to remain related to their original source and background, that is, to the eucharistic Sacrifice itself. They must not be allowed to develop outside this mystery, and sometimes against the very meaning of the Mass, as when devout persons insist on going to Communion before the Mass in order to have the whole Mass as a prayer of thanksgiving! Whatever valid meaning these eucharistic practices have, they possess as further expressions and actualizations of our faith which has been fortified and nourished in the Mass.

On the other hand, precisely because they are extensions of this central Mystery of our faith, it is again unsound, unwise, and unrealistic to despise them on the ground, for instance, that in the time of the apostles there were no eucharistic processions at all. These practices can of course be reformed, adapted to our modern conditions of life; they must certainly be purified. But to depreciate them is fundamentally a denegation of our human condition, and of the rich and full respect for humanity involved and manifested in the mystery of Incarnation, as realized and continued in the Church and in her life.

This same law of extension should thus enable us to construct a more acceptable theology of the sacramentals of the Church; for they are precisely nothing else than the full extension over our whole life and human condition of the sacramental reality established in the Incarnation, and continued in the Church. Therefore they also belong to our full expression and confession of faith in the God of our salvation, manifested in the manifold forms of benediction and consecration.

A SHORT NOTE ON METHODOLOGY. During the last centuries the manuals of theology got used to a method which, it seems to us, is completely wrong. To establish the nature and structure of a sacrament, they started, or at least they considered primarily, the liminal cases in which a given sacrament could still be said to be valid. In studying baptism, they narrowed their subject to infant baptism. In studying penance and extreme unction, they considered the fact that the Church permitted the anointing and the absolution of an unconscious man, and so on, forgetting that in those cases the Church does not define a dogmatic truth but acts according to what is called "sacramental tutiorism." This is a completely wrong approach.

To study the nature of these living realities which are called sacraments, we have always to build our theory on the firm basis of a study of the administration of the sacraments *to adults*. That is whom they are meant for in the first instance. The extraordinary cases have to be explained, as the laws of Logics impel us to do, formally as extraordinary and liminal cases, not as normal. When studying humanity, one does not chop off every part of the human body which is not absolutely required for life—ears, nose, lips, arms, and legs, and if necessary, the appendix, a part of the lungs and the kidneys—and then begin one's description of what a man should be, in the supposition that one is now indeed confronted with whatever "validly" belongs to this humanity!

Space does not allow us to explain how then we interpret the extraordinary and liminal cases in sacramental practice; but we refer our readers to an article in . . . [an] issue of the *Zeitschrift für katholische Theologie*, 84 (1962), 401-26, in which we present our theory in greater detail, particularly as applied to confirmation.

Sacraments, Signs of Faith

In the paper "Faith and the Sacraments," which we read before the Aquinas Society at Burlington Hall in London in 1957, and which was subsequently published by Blackfriars in pamphlet form, we quoted the most important texts of St. Thomas in this matter. There is a central principle which we stated in the first part of that essay: "*Fidei efficacia non est diminuta, cum omnia Sacramenta ex fide efficaciam habent.*—The efficacy of faith [for salvation] is not diminished, since all the sacraments possess an efficacy from faith" (*In IV Sent.* d. I, q. 2, a. 6, sol. 2, ad 3). There is however a double "faith" involved in the efficacious process of the sacraments, the "faith of the Church," and the faith of the subject receiving the sacrament.

THE FAITH OF THE CHURCH. This most important notion has practically disappeared from our treatises on sacramental theology, although it was common doctrine among the different schools before the Council of Trent, not only among the Thomists, but also among the early and later Franciscans, the Scotists, and the Nominalists (see our paper *Faith and the Sacraments*, pp. 15-17).

This notion is, however, of fundamental importance if we want to avoid, as we decidedly must, any suspicion or danger of mechanical interpretation and magic. For it is this "faith of the Church" which determines the real meaning of the sacramental rite (*Summa theologica*, III, 64, 9, ad 1). Philosophically any religious symbol receives its meaning from the religious community in which it is used. This also happened in the Church, but under the guidance of the Holy Spirit, and in faithfulness to the initial institution of Christ—whatever the theological opinion we may hold in regard to the nature of this institution, whether it was a specific or what we now call a "generic" institution.

The ritual of any sacrament, that is, the things used, such as bread, wine, and oil, the gestures, and the words, grew within the Church as the expression in symbols and words of what the Church believed this sacrament was instituted for by Christ according to the Apostolic Tradition, keeping the "deposit of faith" as a sacred inheritance. This corporate, often anonymous, work of popes, bishops, councils, and simple priests and monks, this tradition of a living community in the course of centuries established, according to the law of appropriation we have explained, the sacramental rites we possess today, and handed them down as a sacred tradition in the *Pontificalia* and the *Ritualia* of the Churches in East and West.

In this sacred liturgy, the liturgical prayer—for the love of God, let us never forget that the sacramental liturgy is in the first instance a prayer!—the so-called "words of the sacraments" do possess a predominance, wherefore they are called "the form of a sacrament," insofar as they determine precisely and finally the real divine meaning of the various and, in themselves, ambiguous religious symbols. Since they actually were formed and prompted by "the faith of the Church," this "form of the sacrament" was called in patristic times the "word of faith," in contradistinction to "the elements," a terminology typically Augustinian.

But there is a more existential aspect to the role of the "faith of the Church," that is, during the actual celebration of any sacrament. The sacraments are not "things," of which the Church can dispose at her own will and pleasure. In other words it is not enough to accept an initial institution by Christ, whether generic or specific, to escape suspicion of magic.

Every sacramental act is ever and again a new miracle of God's mercy, descending from the Father in the Son through the power and the efficacy of the Holy Spirit. The Church acknowledges this in all sacramental acts, inasmuch as they contain essentially prayers addressed to God, in and through which the Church receives, *every time anew*, the supernatural meaning of the sacrament and its supernatural efficacy and content.

Magic, on the contrary is a degradation of authentic religion in which man thinks he can dispose *by his own initiative* of any divine power by means of a formula which is thought to have the virtue of acquiring and mastering a certain amount of divine power as soon as it is fully and correctly pronounced. Black magic is exercised against the will of God, and white magic is considered to be practiced, more or less, in accordance with God's will and intention.

If we retain a rather mechanical interpretation of sacramental causality, and even if we accept (as without doubt we do) the initial fact of Christ's institution, I am afraid we don't fully escape the accusation of "white magic." For there is always the final initiative which seems to remain in the hands of man, and it is he who decides, in last instance, whether and how he shall use it.

This cannot be accepted as an orthodox interpretation of sacramental efficacy. It is significant that as soon as our laymen acquire a certain religious maturity in faith, they spontaneously refuse to accept it, and rightly so. The notion of the "faith of the Church," as a necessary component and aspect within the redemptive process of any sacrament, is the only real answer. The "faith of the Church" relates and "connects" this sacramental act "with the power of Christ's passion," as was commonly said before the Council of Trent. We prefer to say: the "faith of the Church," expressed through the symbolism of the liturgical prayer, relates and connects the actual sacramental dispensation with the living and creative Presence of the Holy Trinity in the Church.

THE FAITH OF THE SUBJECT. We have prepared this final conclusion in the light of the several basic theological expositions presented in the earlier parts of this article. St. Thomas, almost as if he were presenting the Lutheran heresy, stated the fundamental principle in this matter very clearly: "*Per fidem igitur iustificatur homo, non quasi homo credendo mereatur iustificationem, sed quia dum iustificatur credit.*—And therefore man is justified by faith, not in the sense that he merits his justification by his act of faith, but in so far as he being justified does believe" (*Summa theologica,*

I-II, 114, 5, ad 1). And elsewhere he explains the meaning of this "act of faith" within the divine act of sacramental justification and sanctification: *"Requiritur voluntas qua intendit vitae novitatem, cuius principium est ipsa susceptio Sacramenti.*—And the will is required by which he intends this newness of life [that is this justification and sanctification through faith and charity], the source of which is the actual reception of the sacrament" (*Summa theologica,* III, 68, 7 c).

The dogmatic principle of this is very simple. We are justified and sanctified *as free and responsible persons;* and this free acceptance in faith belongs essentially to the process of any infusion of grace, and therefore also of any sacramental grace.

If Karl Rahner rightly distinguishes in every grace, whatever it may be, the aspect of "offered grace" and of "accepted grace" (which latter is the same grace, insofar as it is freely accepted in faith by virtue of God's sanctifying activity, the ever-living source of "offered grace"), St. Thomas approaches the same truth from a slightly different perspective, when he says that in faith the "truth of any sacrament" acquires its "final truth" by virtue of the sacramental efficacy. That is why we said that *"opus operatum"* and *"opus operantis"* are reciprocally related and dialectically opposed notions, in which, however, the *"opus operatum,"* that is, the divine indwelling in the Church, obviously possesses a predominance, deriving from the essential primacy of God in every movement of grace.

THE SACRAMENTS AND THE PREACHING OF GOD'S WORD. Space does not permit development of the many practical consequences of this outline of renewed sacramental theology, in which we did nothing else than recall the old tradition of the Church, translating it, where necessary, into more modern language. This is the real dogmatic foundation for any serious liturgical movement truly meriting its name. We have the choice indeed, as in the case of holy Mass, between a curious ceremony in which the priest somewhere in front of the church is mumbling a lot of unintelligible words amidst distracting images and burning lights of different colors— a kind of voodoo, but stiff, respectable, and restrained, for the use of white people—or a corporate act of the living "people of God," of a real community whose every member according to his proper state and vocation participates in the most solemn prayer of adoration, thanksgiving, and praise which Christ has bequeathed to His Church.

But there is also another aspect of theology which has been touched by this renewal of sacramental theology: the theology of the preaching of the Word. Many articles and books are now being published in Europe on this subject.

Not only does the preaching of the Word of God show similar, though analogical, characteristics to the more central sacramental activity of the Church, insofar as the invisible Word of God reaches us through the audible word of the Bible and of preaching, but sacrament and word are in the Church intimately related to one another. There is no sacrament without the announcement of the Gospel of salvation, and there is no real preaching of the Gospel which does not prepare, accompany, and perfect the sanctifying activity of the sacraments. This Word of God, publicly announced in the administration of the sacrament, or in connection with its dispensation, feeds, guides, and nourishes our faith.

JOHN D. GERKEN, S.J.

Dialogue Between God and Man

The Tridentine doctrine that the sacraments confer grace *ex opere operato* has sometimes led the unthinking to ignore man's role in the reception of the sacraments. Moreover, the fear that a non-Catholic concept regarding the efficacy of the sacraments might be accepted has led some writers to ignore the part played by the recipient. In the following article, it is possible to see that Christ's sacraments always involve the recipient in a dynamic fashion. In keeping with the traditional adage, "Whatever is received, is received in a manner proper to the recipient," the author insists that the man receiving the sacraments engages in a dialogue with Christ through the Church. A man's action in receiving the sacrament is a response, similar to a reply given in a spoken dialogue.

Father Gerken teaches theology at John Carroll University, Cleveland, Ohio.

The title *Dialogue Between God and Man* as a part of The Liturgical Conference's theme, Bible-Life-Worship, is a confession and a promise. It is a confession that there is a dialogue, that it is related to scriptural studies, and that this relationship is quite important for our worship. Secondly, the title *Dialogue Between God and Man* promises to explain the relation between the Bible and dialogue and thereby gives us deeper understanding of wor-

This article was an address given at the Twenty-second Annual North American Liturgical Week. It was first printed in the proceedings, *Bible Life and Worship*. It is reprinted here with permission of The Liturgical Conference.

ship. The promise seems to say: Once you have seen the relation between the Bible and dialogue, you will read the Bible more and will become more involved in dialogue.

I am quite convinced that this confession and promise are true and important. But at the same time, I feel that the topic and theme suggest that there is a hidden unity between the Old and New Testaments, that there is a gradual progression in dialogue toward Christianity, and that this unity and progression can be made manifest by scientific exegesis. All that is really needed is a scholar who has the time to investigate it and write it up. If the theme and topic seem to promise you this, then I think we have a false promise. And this . . . [article] will not try to fulfill it. Rather my remarks will call attention to the real problem of making the Bible useful in the dialogue; then my remarks will be devoted to dialogue and sacramental life.

The Problem of the Unity of the Old with the New Testament

We are all aware of God's speaking to man through Abraham, Moses, David, and the prophets. We are aware that, except for the Servant Poems of Isaia and a few scattered references to the Messiah, there is very little in the Old Testament that suggests Christianity. This awareness is a disappointment, but a fact that has to be lived with; it is a fact that ought to be appreciated in some detail if our understanding of dialogue is to be solid. The details of which I speak are these:

First, the religious significance of the Old Testament for the New is still a problem for the exegetes. It must, therefore, be a problem for us. Secondly, the exegetes disagree as to how this significance is to be found. Some, impatient for the spiritual insight, would have us return to the spiritual exegesis of Clement and especially Origen.[1] Others favor the use of the fuller sense (*sensus plenior*) of scripture to understand this unity; and then there are those who hold that the only way to solid understanding of that unity is through the very hard and tedious work of literary and historical criticism. This disagreement tells us not only that there is a problem, but that most likely this problem will be with us for a long time. Our ignorance is going to cause us pain and inconvenience.

While we possess our souls in peace and wait for this problem to be solved, I think we can use the Old Testament very profitably in our personal dialogue with God. We should read it and see in it the fundamental religious truth, namely: "This is God's world. He has started salvation history, He has permitted sin and death, He alone can save us from them and from ourselves." We should see again and again in the dialogue between God and the Hebrews the futility of human wisdom, human power, human legislation to cage man's malice, to save him from himself. When the Old Testament turns us from trust in our own plans and makes us honestly ask God's help and mercy to see and to do His will, then it has proved itself a truly Christian book; it has prepared us for Christian dialogue.

Dialogue-Church-Sacraments

The term *dialogue* is, I believe, the key to understanding the Church and the sacraments and, consequently, gives us the insight into the problem of personal and social holiness. *Dialogue*, as I shall use the term, is not restricted to words—God's word to man and man's to God. Any human gesture participates in dialogue. Therefore any visible manifestation of God's mind, any visible manifestation of what goes on in the heart of man participates in dialogue.

The Church and Sacraments are constituted by dialogue.[2] And it is dialogue and the degree of involvement in it which determines the holiness of the Church today.

The Church

We find dialogue in the very constitution of the Church. Jesus came to us from the Father and asked: "Do you accept Me as the Son of God, the way, the truth, and life, as salvation for you from sin and from death?" Until there was an answer from man there could be no Church. There could be no visible manifestation of saving grace (that is, actually effecting salvation this instant) until man answered. Up to and including God's addressing man in Jesus Christ, there was only the visible manifestation of God's intention to bestow life, but there was no visible manifestation of that life *as bestowed on man*, no manifestation of salvation as effected. But when the apostles and disciples said Yes to Jesus and visibly joined themselves to Him by some action, then the saving grace of God, always at work in their hearts, triumphed and achieved to a greater or lesser degree the maturity it was intended to achieve. Only when these men accepted Christ and His plan for them to be the authoritative carriers of His message to mankind, only then do we have the Church, the primary sacrament, the primary visible sign of grace. Note well: The Church as the proto-sacrament is the visible manifestation and continuation of the fact that God in His Son Jesus Christ has interfered in the apparently natural process of history which courses in ignorance, confusion, despair and terminates in the nothingness of death. The Church shows that God has interfered and also that His interference is efficacious; for this interference has produced a knowledge which destroys the radical confusion of the natural man. It has produced a hope which puts order and purpose into this "natural life." It has produced peace among men, or more accurately, a love which unites them. This certitude which is faith, this purposefulness which is vital hope, this peace which is charity are the visible and mature manifestation of grace or salvation. Thus the group gathered around Christ or historically united to Him are the visible manifestations of God saving and man being saved; the Holy Church—that is the primary efficacious sign of grace which effects what it signifies by signifying what it effects, namely salvation, union of helpless man with God. Therefore, if we are to make progress in the way of personal and social salvation, we shall make that progress insofar as we are involved in a Yes to Christ and His providence in our lives.

Baptism and Dialogue

When the apostolic Church carries the message of salvation to man sitting in darkness, that man has met something for which he has been made, and he is therefore in a situation of serious personal decision. He may take a long time to decide—as has happened with converts through the centuries. But all that time, he is working within the condition of God's serious and operative salvific will. When in his heart he surrenders to God, salvation takes place, but is not manifest. It increases and matures when the secret of his heart becomes manifest in the presentation of himself to the Church and the Church's accepting him. This presentation and accepting constitute the visible sign of grace which we have come to call the sacrament of baptism. In that instant God's intention to save, which grew in visibility with the preaching of the Word, now matures to effect more completely and manifest, as is proper, the salvation intended.

Confirmation and Dialogue

It is not difficult to see dialogue in the sacrament of confirmation because confirmation is the continuation of the sacramental process of baptism and is thus the continuation of the dialogue of baptism. We can appreciate this fact better if we recall that our practice of confirming is a bit different from that of the early Church. With us it is customary that a great interval be between baptism and confirmation. In the beginning it was not so. In fact, at the outset it is hard to separate the sealing with the Spirit from the washing with water.[3] And we cannot say that the word *baptism*, as it occurs in the Fathers before the Donatist heresy, always refers to baptism of water. Further we have scripture evidence that the Spirit was given at baptism; we have an indication that when the Apostles were called or sent "to give the Spirit," it was not the Spirit which completed the rite of initiation, but the Spirit of tongues and prophecy.[4]

The point I wish to make with these references to scripture and tradition is this: Baptism and confirmation are closely allied in reality, and so there is no difficulty in seeing how confirmation is constituted by the dialogue between man and Christ in His Church. For the man who has said Yes in his heart to all that Christ stands for is already justified and led by the Spirit of God. But when he manifests—as he must if he is to be consistent with the law of life in his heart—this whole-hearted acceptance, he is manifesting his desire to receive the Spirit of God. When the Church seals him with the Spirit, the grace of God in him achieves a maturity it did not and could not have before. God's grace as sanctifying action is seen in the action of the bishop; God's grace as sanctity received is seen in the faith and love of the one confirmed. He is seen as one led by the Spirit to walk in newness of life and not according to the law of the flesh which leads to death.

Eucharist and Dialogue

It is quite important that we distinguish the real presence of Christ from the efficacious sign of grace which is the sacrament of the Eucharist.[5] Human activity is not needed to sustain Christ's real presence, but it is needed to constitute the effective sign of Christ establishing and nourishing charity toward God and men among men. When the priest receives the Eucharist and then turns and gives Christ to men and women and children, in that historical situation the effective salvation of God (grace) reaches a high point of maturity and visibility. For then there becomes apparent for all to see that this group believes in Christ, is one in Christ, and—because it is celebrating the death which conquered death—is willing to let the world pass in order that it may possess the life which transcends the vain promises of purely human life. That scene, obviously, is the effective and visible manifestation of salvation among men, the sacrament of the Eucharist.

But note, the visible action (or response) of men operating under the influence of grace is necessary for this sign. If they are not present, the efficacious sign of grace does not exist. It always exists where there is Mass, for man, a priest, is there. But, and this is important, there are degrees of visibility and sacramentality.

Penance and Dialogue

All sin, even the most hidden sins of weakness, rebellion, and hatred, is radically divisive. It separates us from God and good men. If the secret sinner is loyal to the law of sin which he has embraced, he can only progress toward a visible manifestation of his real and self-inflicted ostracism. He will leave his Church, his wife, his friends; he will not trust anyone nor be trusted as he matures in loneliness and approaches the inevitable and frustrating defeat of death. But when this truly bad person responds to God's call, renounces the law of sin, and chooses God above all things, then God's life is secretly triumphant in him. But that justifying grace matures when it gets into his actions and brings him back to the unity of his fellow believers by the official welcoming judgment of the absolving priest. He is visibly reconciled and united to the community of the saints. Note again, the personal action of man—his part in the dialogue—is necessary for this sign of forgiveness, sign of reconciliation, for this one sign of reconciling and being reconciled. This visible reconciliation is the efficacious sign of salvation called the sacrament of penance.

Extreme Unction and Dialogue

In the situation of death when human wisdom, human power, and human hope are manifestly about to be vanquished, when the world becomes confused and embarrassed and stammers in its helplessness, the confident Christ comes in the ministry of His Church to address the believer: "You are mine," He says, "if you want to be, if you want Me, if you are willing to commend your life, as I did mine, to the Father." When the believer accepts Christ, when he says Yes to Christ, there is again the visible efficacious sign of salvation—Christ through His Church in His minister and member triumphing over death. Of course, Christ's grace was already triumphant in the member's heart to a degree, but now, joined to the action of the priest, it necessarily becomes visible and reaches its full maturity.

Holy Orders and Dialogue

The sacrament of orders verifies this dialogue in a way similar to that of confirmation and baptism. For here, too, the individual has been moved—and usually for a long time—by the grace of God to a desire for office in the Church. The office he desires is that of preaching the Word, receiving the results of his preaching into Christ's Mystical Body, sustaining that life with the Body of Christ, reminding those people of Christ's redeeming death with his Mass, and, should those entrusted to his care leave the fold, he desires the office of reconciler that they may be brought back to full union with the life-giving Body of Christ, His Church.

The candidate for the priesthood answers the call of Christ in the bishop and is effectively received by Him into the ranks of the officers of Christ's life-giving Body. This reception is constituted by dialogue: The candidate saying "I want this office," and Christ in the bishop saying "I give it to you." This dialogue is the sign of grace, the visible manifestation of God sanctifying and the man being sanctified—the sacrament of orders.

Marriage and Dialogue

Matrimony doesn't manifest dialogue in the same way as the other sacraments do. In the other sacraments the officers of the Church address the layman (or outsider) and await his response. From this human confrontation of acceptance and bestowal there results the visible sign of salvation. But here the dialogue is not between layman and officer, but between two Christian (!) laymen.

We might get the idea, especially since we have no word of Christ on the institution of this sacrament, that really we have no visible sign of grace here, but only a natural institution that the Church has arbitrarily subjected to her discipline. One might be tempted to conclude that there is nothing ecclesiastical and therefore nothing sacramental about marriage at all, that it is strictly a private affair among people who happen to be Christians. Nothing could be farther from the truth.

Marriage is constituted by dialogue, is thereby a visible sign of grace, and is necessarily ecclesiastical. This is not too difficult to see if one but contrasts the law of Christ with the law of sin and death. Sin and death persuade men to be selfish, to refuse to make the self-surrender required by marriage. Sin says: Live for yourself, for you really can't trust anybody. Death says: Live for yourself, tomorrow you die. But Christ's law, which is operative among men by means of the Church and in all men by the fact that they *are* ordered to Him and *are* in a Christian order of salvation, persuades man to deny that death is the end of *this* human existence, to deny that sin is absolutely invincible. Christ's law—whether recognized as His or not[6]—persuades them to embrace a life of self-surrender. His law says: Hope, live for one another, lay down your life for one another even though there is the fact of sin and death. Consequently, anyone who embraces *such* a life is a believer. For only belief makes such a life reasonable. Marriage, is therefore, a profession of belief, a sign that self-surrender is reasonable even though sin and death abound; it is a sign that sin and death are overcome—at least in germ—by the very fact that this life of self-surrender has been entered upon and in some degree has been realized.

This sign is naturally ecclesiastical, for the Church means: That group of believers in the Christian triumph over sin and death.[7] Since marriage is by nature a public, social act, it is natural, that this public act take place in a public situation of Christian belief. It is no accident, no bit of caprice upon the part of the ruling Church, that marital love terminates in marital vows before the Church's officer and is closely joined to the Mass. For the Mass is that act which most shows and thereby augments Christian vitality, that is, belief and love of a good that exceeds the vain promises of nature. For the reasonableness of the marital vows are founded on and derive their power over sin and death from Christ's death and from union with Christ and His brothers. He has promised hope, victory over sin and death; consequently, the very dynamism of Christian marital love seeks visible expression of itself as Christian. The Mass is the best place for this and consequently the only proper place for it, for in this visible expression of marital love it achieves the maturity and fulness that is proper (not just convenient) to all grace that comes from the Word made flesh.

I do not doubt that there are many questions in your minds regarding this explanation of marriage as a sacrament and as dialogue. Marriage before the Old Testament times? Marriage before Christ? Marriage among present-day heathens? Exceptional cases of marriage of Catholics before two witnesses, and so on? But I really believe that those difficulties find their solution in the application of the three following principles: (1) The grace of Christ was and is operative (but not visible as such and therefore not sacramental) both before and after Judaic and Christian revelation. (2) There are degrees of sacramentality or visibility of grace: for example, the sign that is had when two Catholics exchange marital vows before two witnesses alone does not have the same degree of sacramentality as in the normal Church wedding, although it is nonetheless a true sacrament. (3) As in all sacraments and questions of justification, so especially in this situation where the fact of personal responsibility is two-fold, our certitude about the validity of particular marriages—whether before or after Christ—is quite limited. In other words, certitude about the law is far greater than certitude about the correct application of the law.

Conclusion

The purpose of this . . . [article]—as I understood it—was to make manifest to you the reasons why Christian dialogue is important. I feel that it should be evident from the fact that dialogue is a Yes to Christ and a No to human power, a No to self, that dialogue is the very essence of Christianity. If we realize this, I am sure that we shall be more concerned about the *personal* quality of our religious acts; we shall be quite concerned about wanting God's will, about believing that God is the one—not ourselves—who will save us from the downward drag of human nature. And though I have said relatively little about the Bible, I feel that even that little is quite important, namely, that we have to suffer from our own ignorance of the unity of the Old Testament with the New, and yet can use its obvious lessons on the transcendence of God and the inconstancy of man to stir up our faith and love to the point of a most profitable meeting of Christ in the sacraments and to the point of becoming most *active members of that people in whom God's grace is manifest*—the Holy, Visible Church.

References

[1] J. L. McKenzie, S.J., "Problems of Hermeneutics in Roman Catholic Exegesis," *Journal of Biblical Literature*, 77 (1958), 197-204, esp. 201. Cf. also his review of de Lubac's *Histoire et Esprit* in *Theological Studies*, 12 (1950), 363-84; also his note "More on Benoit" in *Theology Digest*, IX (1961), 66 and 126; further, "The Old and the New" in his *The Two-Edged Sword* (Milwaukee: Bruce Publishing Co., 1956), pp. 295-308, esp. 305-308. Further literature on the problem of the unity of the Old and the New in Joseph Coppens' *Les Harmonies des deux Testaments* (Tournai-Paris: Casterman, 1949); then Raymond E. Brown's *The "Sensus Plenior" of Sacred Scripture* (Baltimore: St. Mary's University, 1955).

[2] Karl Rahner, S.J., "Personale und Sakramentale Froemmigkeit," *Schriften zur Theologie*, *II*, 2 (Auflage: Benziger Verlag, *Einsiedeln*, 1956), 132: "The sacrament takes place thus in an historical dialogue between Christ-Church on the one hand and man on the other; the two parts of this dialogue are the constitutive sign of the one grace of Christ and His Church, which is effective in this moment." This makes the personal action the material cause of the sacramental sign. This idea can be found in many places of Rahner's work.

[3] Dom Gregory Dix, *The Theology of Confirmation in Relation to Baptism* (Dacre Press: Adam & Charles Black, 1940), p. 14: "First, we, with our modern presuppositions, naturally tend to see in this *two* rites in succession, 'baptism' conducted by a Presbyter followed at once by 'confirmation' conducted by the Bishop. Yet the ancient title of the whole account, which (though probably not from the pen of Hippolytus himself) is certainly early, is simply 'Of the

Paradosis of holy baptism.' In the same way Origen, to take an example from the East, summarises the whole Initiation rite by 'we have all been baptised in visible waters and in visible chrism' including the whole rite under the one word 'baptism.' This remained common until the later fourth century."

⁴ Rahner is of this opinion as is evident from: "For though there was certainly a confirmation in Samaria, nonetheless one does not get the impression that there was something lacking in the 'baptism' in Jerusalem. Here they receive the Holy Spirit in that they are cleansed from sin in baptism and as believers are incorporated into the new people of God on whom the Holy Spirit has been poured out. It is thus that He reaches everyone who has become a member." *Kirche und Sakrament*, 46.

⁵ Karl Rahner, S.J., "Danksagung nach der hl. Messe," *Geist u. Leben* (1959), p. 185: "For the sacramental sign which increases grace is not the presence of Christ as such, but the *eating* of the Body of Christ."

⁶ This may strike the reader as a bold statement, but I do not believe it is any bolder than the one made by Pius XII when he spoke of non-Catholics as being related to the Mystical Body of the Redeemer by a certain unconscious desire and resolution (*quandoquidem, etiamsi inscio quodam desiderio ac voto ad mysticum Redemptoris corpus ordinentur*) in *Acta Apostolicae Sedis*, 35 (1943), 243. The Holy Office in its letter to Archbishop Cushing [Cf. *The American Ecclesiastical Review*, 127 (1952), 307] did not nullify this statement when it insisted that the unconscious desire had to include faith and charity to be supernaturally effective. All theologians had to hold that. But by recalling these facts, the Holy Office thereby stressed the problem of explaining how such an unconscious desire could be supernatural.

⁷ Once married non-Catholics enter the Church, it is not necessary (or possible) that they "re-marry" in order that their union be a visible manifestation of grace (a sacrament). For marriage (*in facto esse*) within the community of the faithful is, because of the law of life of that community which permeates marriage, a grace-filled union. Yet this union can and perhaps should (*ex decentia* and subject to Church legislation) become more ecclesiastical through the granting of the nuptial blessing to the newly converted couple.

CYRIL VOLLERT, S.J.

The Church
and the Sacraments

The sacramental economy of the Church is based ultimately on St. Augustine's statement, "There is no other sacrament of God than Christ." In the following essay the relationship of God, Christ, Church, and sacraments is examined. This analysis shows that a clear understanding of sacraments demands an understanding of the meaning of Christ's Church—the "people of God" of the New Dispensation.

Father Vollert is Professor of Dogmatic Theology at St. Mary's College in St. Marys, Kansas.

At the present stage of development of sacramental theology, theologians seldom speak of the sacraments without speaking also of the Church. They are perceiving with increasing comprehension that the mystery of the Church and the mystery of the sacraments may not be separated, even in thought. Our question is this: How is the sacramental system as a whole and how is each of the sacraments related to the Church?

The two great mysteries, Church and sacrament, should illuminate each other. Our understanding of the Church deepens when we ask what the sacraments are, and our understanding of the sacraments increases when we reflect on what the Church is. The faithful in general and also many theologians, particularly in the past, have not had a very clear idea of the relationship between

This paper was first published in the *Proceedings of the Eighth Annual Convention of the Society of Catholic College Teachers of Sacred Doctrine*. It is reproduced here with permission.

the Church and the sacraments. Every Catholic knows that the Church has the power to confer the sacraments, because Christ who instituted the sacraments entrusted them to the Church. But that is about all that is grasped concerning the relationship between the two. The sacraments are conceived as means of grace for the salvation of the individual (which is true) and nothing else (which is short of the truth). When the sacraments are envisioned in such a way, the Church appears only as administrator of these channels of grace for the individual's benefit, as a purveyor of heavenly treasures. To receive these treasures, the people turn to the sacraments; as soon as they have been given their share they depart, and think no more about the transaction.

If we wish to gain a more adequate knowledge of this relationship, we must start out by regarding the Church precisely as the Church of the sacraments; that is, we must move from an understanding of the Church to the sacraments. And after that we must come to a realization that the sacraments are the proper activity of the Church, thus proceeding from a consideration of the various sacraments toward a more profound knowledge of the nature of the Church.

We all know that to be a Christian means to believe in Jesus Christ and to belong to the Church He founded. The Church organizes its whole life around the Mass, and its edifices guide the attention of its congregations toward the altar and the tabernacle. We are incorporated into the Church by the sacrament of baptism. As members of the Church we offer the Eucharistic sacrifice, receive Holy Communion, and are granted sacramental pardon of our sins. A man becomes a priest of the Church by the sacrament of Holy Orders. When a Christian man and woman found a home, they inaugurate their life together by the sacrament of matrimony. At the approach of death we make ourselves ready by receiving the Last Sacraments. Clearly, the sacraments occupy a predominant place in the Church; they set the pattern for every normal Catholic life. Therefore it is important to situate the sacraments correctly in the aggregate of the activities of the Church.

Fortunately the vigorous upsurge of the theology of the Church during the past three or four decades furnishes an excellent basis for a renewed study of the sacraments, enabling us to apprehend the sacraments as vital functions of the life of the Church. Recent concentration on ecclesiology creates an intellectual climate favorable for promoting a more lucid appreciation of the sacraments as acts of the Church that involve the cooperation of the whole Christ, head and body, the hierarchy, and the faithful.

Too often the sacraments have been regarded from an excessively individualist point of view; they have been reduced to the status of instruments of grace meant to procure the individual's salvation. The sacraments are more than that; they are prolongations of Christ's activity in the Church, designed by Him to associate His members in His own redemptive mission and to empower them to work with Him in constructing the Kingdom of God. Unquestionably the sacraments are instruments of grace that unite the recipient with God. But this union with God is brought about in the measure of our activity among the new people of God, in the body of Christ. Fellowship with the Savior creates new bonds among men; the believer who has been incorporated into the Church can and should collaborate in building up the community of love that is based on Christ.

Jesus Christ, Primeval Sacrament of God

When Jesus Christ founded the Church, what He organized into a hierarchical, juridical society was not an amorphous mass of individual men in need of salvation, but the "people of God." The eternal Son of God, who is also the Son of Mary, a daughter of Adam, has become one with us, not only in nature, but also in race. He belongs to the one mankind, which is more than a conglomeration of many individuals; it is a real unity, as is plain from the descent of all men from the one Adam. In our father Adam we were elevated to a supernatural end. In spite of sin which has marked every stage of our history, God maintains our supernatural calling because the man Jesus is a member of our human family. God sees us all as brothers and sisters of His incarnate Son, as His own people with whom He contracted a new and eternal covenant. By the coming of the Word that was made flesh into the history of mankind in unity of race, our people is the consecrated people of God. Through the Incarnation the whole of humanity was radically taken up to salvation in this member of our family, Jesus Christ. The moment the Logos assumed a human nature from the one mankind and in union with it, our redemption was assured. Because Christ is one of us, the world is reconciled, in principle, with God;

because of Him the grace of God appears in place and time. Christ is the sign of God's redeeming grace, which in Him comes to manifestation and is definitively given to the world. He is the great primeval sacrament of God; and St. Augustine goes so far as to say: "There is no other sacrament of God than Christ." [1]

A sacrament is a sign that signifies and conveys God's gift of love to men. That is why Christ is the sacrament *par excellence*, the supreme sign of God who is love and source of all grace. The Savior is the visible appearance of God's redemptive love and our one access to salvation. For the contemporaries of Jesus, encounter with Him was an invitation to encounter with God, because this Man is personally the Son of God. We who come later cannot encounter Him in the same fashion; in His visible form He has departed from our midst. But the sacraments of the Church bring us into living contact with the eternally living Christ. Consequently the sacraments of the Church stand on a Christological foundation. They sacramentalize Christ's redemptive work and apply it to us. "What was visible in our Redeemer," in the words of Leo the Great "has passed over to the sacraments." [2] To clarify the Christological basis of the sacraments, we have to examine their ecclesiological dimension.

The Church, Sacrament of Christ

The man Jesus Christ is the sign of redemption—a sign that contains and conveys the reality which is signified. But up to the Parousia this heavenly sign remains invisible to us men on earth. That is why the Redeemer has given it a visible prolongation, the visible Church. As Christ is the sacrament of God, the Church is the sacrament of Christ. As the actions of the earthly Christ were the actions of God performed in a human way, so the actions of the Church are the actions of the now invisible Christ permanently carried on in visible form. Thus the Church is the perfect living sacrament of Christ whose redemptive Incarnation it announces and communicates.

What we ordinarily call the seven sacraments must be situated in this larger sacramental society that is the Church. For a sacrament is primarily and basically a personal act of Christ Himself, performed through the earthly visibility of the Church. As Christ still acts invisibly in His glorified body in heaven, so He acts visibly in and through His earthly body, the Church; the sacraments are personal saving acts of Christ which take the shape of visible acts of the Church.

In the encyclical *Mystici corporis*, Pius XII sums up all Catholic tradition when he says that it is Christ who baptizes, who absolves, who sacrifices.[3] Christ is really and personally present in the Eucharist; yet He is present also in the other sacraments, by reason of His act of redemption that is ever operative. Christ Himself is present in both cases, although the foundation of His presence is different. In the Eucharist He is present by the power of transubstantiation; in the other sacraments He is present under a visible sacramental form by the power of His continuing act of salvation. Since the human body of Christ is now glorified, the sign of the life-giving act of salvation accomplished by Him has become invisible for us; nevertheless His body is mysteriously prolonged in a visible, earthly shape, that is, the sacramental Church, which is His body. When we say that a sacrament, sign of grace, confers the grace it signifies *ex opere operato*, we ultimately mean that in that sacrament we have an act of Christ performed in the Church. What Christ on earth did alone in objective redemption, on our behalf and in place of all of us, that He now does in the sacraments for those who receive them and, in the Eucharistic sacrifice, for all men, that all may be brought into union with the people of God, the holy Church He has acquired.

Sacramental Structure of the Church

As the projection of Christ in the world, the Church is the great sacrament, origin of the sacraments in the usual sense of the word, and has its sacramental structure from Christ. This truth involves the consequence that whenever salvation is offered and imparted to any man, that man enters into some relationship with the Church. Such relationship may vary enormously in grade and intensity, but cannot be totally lacking. There can be no instance of salvation where the person saved can say that he never had anything to do with the Church. Whoever finds salvation, finds it in the Church. The person concerned may never have even heard of the Church; yet the redemptive grace of which he is the beneficiary implies a true relationship with the Church and its sacraments. This does not mean that every reception of salvation from the Church is invariably a reception of a sacrament in the technical sense. But where the

Church in its official, social capacity and activity confers saving grace, there we have sacraments in the proper sense. Without the Church, no sacramental act is possible.

To understand this truth, we must have a correct notion of the Church. In the present context the Church is the community of the faithful, the new people of God, the society of all who are called and received into God's Kingdom. Indeed, it is the very Kingdom of God, socially and hierarchically organized, of this final phase of earthly history, the Kingdom in which Christ exercises His kingship, in which He distributes the goods of the new salvation.

This new community of God is a body, the mystical body of Christ Himself. One and the same Holy Spirit who fills the God-man unites the citizens of the Kingdom of God with Christ and also with one another. They all have the Spirit of Christ in common, so that we rightly speak of the Holy Spirit as the one soul animating the one body of Christ. Jesus Christ is the head of this body and as such uninterruptedly sends His Spirit into it to guide and sanctify it. At the same time He selects various members as definite organs of the body and appoints them to the functions and services that correspond to the offices they have received. Thus the Church is a social, supernatural community of salvation and a hierarchically structured body, in which the many organs and members exercise differing powers.

This Church, Christ's mystical body, is visible. Everywhere it manifests its mission and its task, the bringing of salvation to all mankind. It sanctifies and saves its members, and through them reaches out to those who are still to be saved. Accordingly it is a sacramental organism of salvation, for in its visible form it signifies grace and confers grace.

Since Christ, head of this sacramental organism of salvation, is incessantly active in it and at every instant sends His Spirit into the whole body and its individual members, we fittingly regard the Church as the ever-living and ever-acting Christ.[4] The Church does nothing that Christ does not accomplish along with it; all its sacramental actions are His actions. He sends His Holy Spirit into the acting organs of His body in order that, filled and moved by Him, they may perform the actions that signify and impart grace.

Thus the power and efficacy of the sacraments are grounded on the fact that they are saving acts of Christ continuing to act in the

Church through His Spirit. That is why these acts are never empty; they are always full of the grace they signify.

But only the qualified member of Christ's mystical body is empowered to perform the saving sacramental act. Baptism seems to be an exception; but it is only an apparent exception. The Church cooperates even in the baptism administered by an unbaptized person. To act validly the minister of the sacrament must in some way, deliberately or obscurely, explicitly or implicitly, relate himself to the Church, if only by having the intention of doing what the Church does. Thus there is no sacrament apart from the Church. If a person does not have grace from the Church, he does not have it at all.

The life of grace is conferred when Christ sends His Holy Spirit. Hence it is always Christ who in the Spirit accomplishes the sacramental activity of the Church. As the Church is never active without its organs and members, so it is never active without Christ. Through the Church and its qualified members Christ Himself carries on His redemptive activity for the consecration of the world and the salvation of mankind. The sacraments are unthinkable without Him and without the Church.

Sacramental activity imparts grace because it is a saving activity of the Church that is united to Christ and is filled with His Spirit; indeed, it is the activity of Christ Himself. This activity unfailingly reaches its goal, unless a man refuses its power. Christ's action is never without issue. The same is true of the sacramental activity of the Church. Because Christ Himself performs this sacramental activity through His Church, the sacraments achieve their effects *ex opere operato.*

The sacraments, accordingly, are by no means incidental or occasional in the Church. They are activities essential to its life. The Church is not static; it is vitally dynamic. If we wish to enhance our knowledge of what the Church really is, we must see it as energetically operative in the vital functions that are the sacraments.

Sacramental Life of the Church

In undertaking a brief survey of the seven sacraments in relation to the life of the Church, we shall do well to begin with the Eucharist. For the Eucharist, as sacrifice, is the converging point of

the Church, the sacrifice in which Christ constantly renews the
covenant of God with His people; and Holy Communion is the
fraternal repast at which Christians of every race and nation are
nourished on the same Bread of Life to perfect their unity as one
body of Christ. The other sacraments all have their finality in the
Eucharist; they prepare for it or are in some way referred to it.
After the Eucharist come baptism and confirmation, the two stages
of Christian initiation that orient the recipient toward the Eucharist.
Next come the two medicinal sacraments by which Christ through
the Church provides remedies for the sins of Christians and for illness, the penalty of sin; these are penance and extreme unction. Last
come the two functional sacraments which define a special way of
serving the Church; the sacrament of holy orders perpetuates the
priestly ministry of the Church, and matrimony consecrates husband and wife in the responsibility they take on of procreating and
educating children for the Church.

The Eucharist

The reason why the Eucharist is numbered third in the traditional
list of the sacraments is its position in the ancient ceremonial of
Christian initiation. The catechumen admitted into the Church had
to receive baptism and confirmation before he was allowed to take
part in the Eucharistic sacrifice. But from the point of view of the
Eucharist itself and its supreme importance in the life of the Church,
it occupies the very first and highest place, because in it Christ in
person gives Himself to the Church as the foundation of the
Covenant, as center and source of Catholic unity, as Bread of eternal
life. The Eucharist is *the* great sacrament, and we indicate our grasp
of this truth when we call it the "Blessed Sacrament." Because of
what it is and what it does, it is out of series; we may not put it on a
par with the rest of the sacraments. This is clear from the real
presence of Christ in the Eucharist, and from the fact that it is not
only a sacrament but a sacrifice.

The relation of the Eucharist to the Church is quite obvious. Our
faith informs us that the Mass is so truly the sacrifice of the Church
that even the so-called "private" Mass of an isolated priest is always
the sacrifice of the entire Church; and Communion is a deeper insertion into Christ's mystical body. Reception of Christ's mystical

body in Communion assures us the grace of Christ because this common eating of one Bread is the effective sign of a more penetrating and more vital membership in the body of Christ that is the Church.

A most important consideration is the fact that the words of consecration are the words of the new and eternal covenant that was concluded in the blood of Christ. These words of covenant are the words by which Christ is made present in the Eucharist. Therefore He is present precisely as the foundation of the covenant between God and men, hence as the source and bond of the unity of the Church. Because He gives Himself ever anew to the Church in the very act in which He, the high priest, offers Himself to the Father as victim of the redemptive sacrifice, and because He is present in the Church in sacramental accessibility, the Church itself exists. And when the Church gives the body of Christ to a Christian in Holy Communion, it makes that person an ever more perfect partaker of the unity and love of the holy covenant of God with His people, and so fills him with all grace.

Sacraments of Initiation

Baptism

Not much has to be said about baptism; its relationship with the Church is evident. Every instructed Catholic knows that baptism is the sacrament of incorporation of men into the Church as members of the mystical body. Membership in the Church is the effect primarily signified by this sacrament of Christian initiation, and brings with it all the other baptismal effects. In the New Testament, as formerly in the Old Testament, the beneficiary of salvation is always, in the first instance, the people, the Church as partner in the covenant with God; individual men receive grace as members of this people of promise. So powerful is this effect of baptism that even when a baptized person, as Pius XII teaches in the encyclical *Mystici corporis*, is no longer an actual member of the Church, because he is a schismatic or a heretic or an apostate, nevertheless the baptism he has received orients him to the Church in a way that is not verified in a nonbaptized person, even though the latter, by reason of union with God in perfect charity, may be living in sanctifying grace.

Confirmation

Relationship of the sacrament of confirmation with the Church is not hard to detect. Confirmation gives the Holy Spirit in view of the vast mission of Christ that is carried on by the Church—the mission of worship, intercession, sacrifice of reparation, and the apostolate. This sacrament presupposes baptism, in which the Holy Spirit communicates Himself as principle of supernatural life, of radical union with the incarnate Son of God. Confirmation is the sacrament that incorporates us into the mystery of Pentecost, the laying on of hands for imparting of the Holy Spirit for the mission that is to transform the world by empowering the members of the Church to be witnesses of God in the world, testifying that God does not abandon the universe to the nothingness of its sin, but redeems, saves, and transfigures it.

When we describe confirmation as the sacrament of strength in the faith and of witness to the faith, we may not understand this only in the sense that by confirmation the Christian receives the grace, by the power of the Holy Spirit, to preserve his faith in a world that is hostile to the faith. By confirmation the Christian is raised to spiritual adulthood and is sent out on an apostolate befitting his position in the Church. This is not merely an apostolate of defense of the Church, to maintain and save it in anxiety, but is an apostolate assigned to the Church to save the world. The grace of confirmation is indeed a grace given to the individual concerned with saving his own soul; but it is also, and particularly, a charismatic gift, that is, a gift which is rich in blessings for others, to cooperate in the mission of the Church for the salvation of all men. Thus confirmation is the sacrament of the apostolate of Pentecost, the apostolate of witness, as activity of the Holy Spirit through the visible activity of adult sons of God in the Church.

Medicinal Sacraments

Penance

Sin has two distinct but inseparable aspects. When a person commits a grave sin he turns away from God by a deordinate attachment to creatures. Such is sin essentially—for anyone, whether Christian or pagan. But for the Christian sin also has an ecclesiastical dimension. The Church has the task of manifesting the victory of grace and the inception of the Kingdom of God. Sin cannot be a matter of indifference to the Church of Christ. The Church must react against sin, by which a member of the salvation community sets himself in opposition not only to God but also to the Church, seeing that the Church is the basic sacramental sign of God's grace. That is why the Church removes the sinner from itself by some form of ejection, which is not indeed excommunication in any sense, but in our day, for example, consists in exclusion from the Eucharistic table. The consequence is that the sinner cannot be regarded by God as pertaining to the holy community in the full sense of enjoying all its rights and privileges, and that he cannot, as long as he clings to his sin, share in the salvation which God bestows on men in the Church of Jesus Christ.

Thus the sinner places himself in a false situation respecting both God and the Church; his sin excludes him from the salvation of the Covenant and makes him unworthy to take full part in the sacrifice of the Covenant by reception of the Eucharist. Therefore he must in repentance return to favor with the Church and with God by submitting to the judgment and requirements of the ministers of the Church. If the Church imparts sacramental absolution and so releases the sinner by restoring him to full peace with the Church, then God too regards him as really again a member of the salvation community in good standing, and so forgives his sins. Reconciliation through the Church is also reconciliation with the Church and so with God, for reconciliation with the Church is the efficacious sign, the sacrament of reconciliation with God in Christ.

Extreme Unction

A Christian is seriously ill, and death is more than a remote possibility. He knows that he has often offended God during his life, and that his fidelity in serving his Creator has been marred by many lapses. The hour approaches for rendering an account of his stewardship. Can he really expect the reward of eternal beatitude, or will temporal death lead to the dread second death? In his crisis he calls on the Church to come to his rescue. And the Church responds. The priest comes, official representative of the Church, hears the sick man's confession and imparts sacramental absolution. The priest anoints him with the holy oils, sign of exorcism and consecration. The action of the Church with its prayer and sacramental anointing restores peace and hope; Christ, far from abandoning His member who has fallen ill, comes to save him from all assault. The sick man can calmly and trustfully await the issue of his illness.

Thus the Church, in its official capacity, stands at the sick bed and takes its part in the drama of death, which on the human level is so stark a solitude. A Church that could not or would not do this would not be the Church of eschatological hope. The relationship between the Church and the sacrament of last anointing is clear, both in the sick man himself who, as a baptized member of the Church, receives this anointing, and in the action of the Church, which comes to the aid of its member in urgent need and shows itself in solidarity with him. The Church is the earthly representative of Christ's redemption that has triumphed, not only over sin, but also over death. Extreme unction is the act of the Church that conquers death, to the benefit of a Christian who is gravely ill; it is a sacrament that, in some cases, heals illnesses, or, if in God's providence death should climax the illness, gives the future life that follows death.

Functional Sacraments

The two sacraments referred to as "functional"—for want of a better name—sanctify the recipient with immense spiritual riches, but they do so by equipping him for special functions in the Church. They confer on him charge over souls and confide to him responsibility over a part of Christ's flock. A man is not a priest mainly for himself but for the Church. A man is not a husband and a woman is not a wife primarily for themselves but for the home, for each other, and for the children to whom they give life and whose human and religious development they must direct. A man is a bishop or a priest to assure the spiritual vitality and religious government of the Catholic community. A Christian is married to procure the human continuity of the Church, to consecrate to God the transmission of human life among the Christian people of the earth.

Holy Orders

The relationship of holy orders to the Church is readily perceptible. Apostolic office, the ecclesiastical episcopacy, is required by the very existence of the Christian community. The people of God is built up on sacrament and word. Christ has entrusted the hierarchic leadership of this people of God to the apostolic function, which possesses authority to govern, the charism to proclaim God's word, and power to sanctify in the Church. The ordinary priesthood is an auxiliary sacerdotal corps assisting the apostolic or episcopal body.

The highest power conferred by sacerdotal ordination is exercised in the celebration of Mass. This central act of the Church is a divine gift bestowed on the whole Church, a sacrifice offered to God by the whole Christ through the priest. At the altar the priest represents God and Christ in the presence of the entire Church, as he also represents Christ and the entire Church in the presence of God. Day after day the Mass makes the redemptive sacrifice sacramentally available to the people of God and communicates the sacrifice of the High Priest to His mystical body.

Matrimony

In its visible form the Church manifests itself not only as mystical body of Christ, but also as spouse of Christ. Matrimony is an image, an echo of the love between Christ and the Church, as St. Paul attests in Ephesians 5:32. Christian marriage and God's covenant with mankind in Christ are not merely capable of being compared to each other by us, but in themselves display so striking a likeness that matrimony objectively represents the love of God in Christ for the Church.

If we ask why and in what sense the marriage contract between Christians is a sacrament, a sign efficacious of grace, we can clarify the question by situating the Christian home in the life and mission of the Church: what is its function in the mystical body of Christ? It is the basic cell of the Church, the minimum human society in which Christian life normally develops. True Catholic families are the foundation of the human and religious vitality of the Church.

When a Christian man and woman marry, they give to each other the right and the mission to procreate and educate new Christians. Such mission and power come from Him who is the head of the Church, source of its life, its divine Spouse. By espousing the Church at the price of His blood, Christ has made the human marriage contract a Christian marriage sacrament. Thus Christian conjugal love is raised to the rank of a sacred sign. By giving themselves to each other, the Catholic husband and wife express Christ's love to each other by their own conjugal love.

Each day death takes from the Church some of its members, who accordingly must be replaced. The sacrament of matrimony fills up the void. But its function does not stop there. In the home the Christian family forms on a tiny scale what the Church is on a grand scale; the family is the basis of every society, religious no less than civil. By assuring the continuation and circulation of grace to ever new generations, married couples perform an indispensable service for the building up and the vitalizing of the Church.

Theologians who have been writing on the subject of the relationship between the Church and the sacraments these latter years seem to be in accord that the first effect of each of the sacraments (the *res et sacramentum*) is a new and specifically different form of union with the Church. The sacraments join us to Christ in grace because they place us in contact with the Church; they insert the recipient, in a way that varies in manner, depth, and finality with each sacrament, into the mystical body of Christ.

When we study the sacraments we also study the Church in its most precious possession and its most powerful activity. To cast doubt on the role of a single sacrament compromises the economy of salvation established by God when He sent His Son into our midst. The Savior has confided all the sacraments to His Church, to equip the Church for its mission of saving mankind by means that are visible and thus befit both the Church and men. We must seek an understanding of the sacraments from a Christological and ecclesiological point of view; we must come to a perception that the sacraments are the concrete expression of the apostolic life of the Church, the visible continuation of the God-man's saving activity among men. In the sacraments Christ's unceasing act of redemption is directed to all men through His Church, which manifests and conveys His redemptive will to the world.

Blessed are we if by the mercy of God we have found the true Church on earth, the promise and the beginning of the Church of eternity, which has received its everlasting life from the sacraments of Christ in the Kingdom of His love.

References

[1] Ephesians 187:34 (*PL*, 33,845).
[2] Serm. 74:2 (*PL*, 54,398).
[3] *AAS*, 35 (1943), 218.
[4] Cf. Pius XII, *Mystici corporis Christi, AAS,* 35 (1943), 218.

PAUL F. PALMER, S.J.

The Theology
of the "Res et Sacramentum"

The ecclesiological dimension of the sacraments has been emphasized in modern sacramental theology. By current examination of
the *res et sacramentum* (symbolic reality) modern theologians can
more specifically locate the sacraments in the Church. The following article considers the historical evolution of the notion of *res
et sacramentum* and applies this concept to the sacrament of
Penance.

Father Palmer is Professor of Dogmatic Theology at Fordham
University, New York. He is the author of *Sources of Christian
Theology* (2 Vols.).

Salvation Through the Community

Basic to Jewish-Christian tradition is the belief that man is
saved in and through the community. The ancient Hebrew "could
not make his unique answer to God as an isolated individual." [1] If he
was to live at all, he had to be one with the community, one with
the people of God. To be separated from the community was death.
To be restored to the community was life. Similarly, the early
Christian did not believe that he could have access to God apart
from the community. But for him the community was the new
people of God, the body of Christ which is the Church. "For in one
Spirit we were all baptized into one body" (1 Cor 12:13). Separation from this body was death. Reconciliation to the body was life.

This article was first published in the *Proceedings of the Fourteenth Annual
Convention of the Catholic Theological Society of America*. It is reproduced
here with permission.

For outside the body there is no salvation. Thus, in the early third century Origen has the sinner ask three questions, but they are really one: "How can I who have fallen be saved? . . . How can I have access to God? How can I return to the Church?" [2]

This idea of corporate salvation, of salvation in and through the Church, has always been foreign to Protestantism. More recently salvation has come to be regarded by many as the result of a personal encounter with God, an encounter which found its highest expression in the soul of Jesus, an encounter which is the exemplar and earnest of what can happen to all of us. We can all become Christs by sharing the experience of Jesus who became the Christ.

Although this individualism in religion is basically Protestant, something of its spirit has rubbed off on Catholics. Until recently, the impression was frequently given that "God is never faced with anything but an untold number of individuals, every one of them regulating on his own account the measure of his personal relationship with God." [3] True, Catholic theologians have always stressed the essential mediatorship of Christ and the secondary mediatorship of His Church, but all too frequently Christ and His Church have been regarded as catalytic agents, necessary to bring about the union of God and man, but somehow external to the unifying process.

Today, there is a growing awareness that salvation is not only mediated by Christ and His Church, but that the life of grace, which is produced and maintained by the sacraments is conferred in and through the Church. To quote Henri de Lubac, "grace does not set up a purely individual relationship between the soul and God or Christ; rather, each one receives grace in the measure in which he is joined socially to that unique organism in which there flows its own life-giving stream. . . . All the sacraments are essentially 'sacraments in the Church'; in her alone they produce their full effect, for in her alone, 'the society of the Spirit,' is there, normally speaking, a sharing in the gift of the Spirit." [4]

This social or ecclesiological aspect of the sacraments, according to which the Christian is united to God and to Christ through his union with the community, is regarded by de Lubac as the "constant teaching of the Church, though it must be confessed that in practice it is too little known." [5]

The purpose of this paper is to explore a long neglected aspect of sacramental theology in order to make better known this social stamp which all the sacraments bear. I refer to the theology of the

res et sacramentum, the symbolic reality which is both the immediate effect of the sacramental rite (*sacramentum tantum*) and the
sign, pledge, or disposition for the ultimate effect of the sacrament
which is sacramental grace (*res tantum*). For it is in the *res et
sacramentum* that a growing number of theologians today find a
special bond or relationship with the Church, the Mystical Body of
Christ.

I say "today," since it is only in comparatively recent years that
theologians have stressed the ecclesiological significance of the *res
et sacramentum*. And yet early speculation on the nature of the
res et sacramentum furnishes some basic ideas for a right understanding of the sense in which the Church is intimately involved in
the sacramental economy of grace. For this reason it may not be
amiss to trace quite briefly the history and development of the *res et
sacramentum* and its earliest applications.

History and Development
of the *Res et Sacramentum*

The expression *res et sacramentum* or, as it was originally phrased,
sacramentum et res, resulted from Berengar's denial of Christ's true
presence in the Eucharist. Augustine had distinguished between the
sacrament of Christ's body and the reality or effect of the sacrament
when received. According to Augustine, "a good man receives the
sacrament and the reality of the sacrament, but a bad man receives
only the sacrament and not the reality." [6] By reality or *res* Augustine
had in mind the ultimate effect of the Eucharist which is the grace
of union with Christ.[7] And this reality Berengar readily granted.
For him the Eucharist was the sign of Christ's body, and yet the
efficacious symbol of spiritual nourishment and union with Christ.
Berengar denied, however, that Christ's true body was present in
the Eucharist. For Berengar there were but two elements in the
sacrament, the external sign or symbol, and the ultimate effect, the
grace of spiritual nourishment and charity.[8]

Faced with this difficulty, it was necessary for the theologians of
the day to find a third element in the Eucharist which would preserve the symbolism of the Eucharist and yet safeguard the reality
of Christ's presence in the Eucharist. The search lasted for almost
a century. Tentative replies were given by Lanfranc of Can-
terbury, Guitmund of Aversa, and Durant of Troarn in the second

half of the eleventh century, but the definitive reply was slowly evolved by Hugh of St. Victor and by Peter Lombard in the twelfth century, and given official approval by Pope Innocent III in the beginning of the thirteenth century.[9] A third element had to be considered in the Eucharist. It was not enough to speak of the *sacramentum tantum* and the *res tantum*, as Berengar insisted; account had to be taken of an element which is both sacrament and reality, *sacramentum et res*. To quote Innocent III:

> A careful distinction must be made between three different elements in this sacrament, namely the visible form, the truth of the body, and the spiritual power. The form is of bread and wine, the truth is of the body and blood, the power is of unity and charity. The first is a sacrament and not a reality. The second is both a sacrament and a reality. The third is a reality and not a sacrament. But the first is a sacrament or sign of a double thing. The second is the sacrament of one thing and the reality of another. The third is the reality of a double sacrament.[10]

When Innocent speaks of the *sacramentum tantum* of the Eucharist he has in mind the permanent sacrament and not the words of consecration spoken over bread and wine. In the course of time, however, when application had to be made to the other sacraments which do not visibly remain, the expression *sacramentum tantum* was applied to the sacramental rite which has for its immediate effect the *res et sacramentum* and for its ultimate effect the *res tantum* or sacramental grace. The application of the *res et sacramentum* to the other sacraments, however, was not easy. It was easy enough to see the sacramental character of three sacraments, a reality which is prior to grace and in some sense dispositive for grace. But in what sense could this invisible reality be called a sacrament or sign?

William of Auxerre (d. 1231) crystallized the difficulty in speaking of the sacrament of baptism: "a sacrament is a visible form of invisible grace; but the character is not visible, since it is only in the soul, and hence it is not a sacrament, and so it is not baptism." [11] And yet some answer had to be found since Augustine time and again had referred to the character as a sacrament or sign which distinguishes the Christian from the unbeliever, which identifies the sheep which are members of Christ's flock, and the soldiers, who are enrolled in His service, even though they be deserters.[12] Peter of Potier (d. 1205) had given the rather despairing answer that the character is visible to God and to angels. A much better solution was given by William of Auxerre himself. The character is not a sensible sign but an intelligible sign—*signum non sensibile sed intelligibile*.[13] St. Thomas accepts and elaborates this distinction, when he states: "The character imprinted on the soul is a kind of sign in so far as it is imprinted by a visible sacrament: since we know that a certain one has received the baptismal character through his being cleansed by the sensible water." [14] In other words, the existence of the character can be proved by establishing the fact of a valid baptism. Thus, the character is an intelligible sign, in the sense that it can be known, even though it is not a sensible sign, in the sense that it can be seen.

Having established the propriety of referring to the character as a *res et sacramentum*, theologians began to discuss the nature of this third element in the sacraments which is both reality and sign. At first their discussion centered on the sacraments which imprint a character, baptism, confirmation, and orders. And it is principally from their discussion of the sacramental character, which is materially identified with the *res et sacramentum*, that a theology of the *res et sacramentum* develops.

Since Augustine had likened the permanent effect of baptism to a brand or mark burned on animals or tattooed on soldiers, it is understandable why William of Auvergne (d. 1245) should see in the character a sign of ownership, a sign of consecration, not unlike the consecration given to churches and sacred vessels, a consecration which implies an objective holiness which is distinct from grace or charity. Through the character the baptized becomes in a special way God's property. In view of the character, God considers the baptized as his own and fills him with His grace. Accordingly the character is at once a reality, since it establishes an objective bond between God and the soul, and at the same time a sign or earnest of God's grace since it is the ultimate disposition for grace.[15] What William of Auvergne failed to see or, at least, to express, although it is quite explicit in the teaching of Augustine, is that the character unites the baptized more directly with Christ, since the character is actually the character of Christ, the image of Christ, marking the baptized as one who belongs to Christ, identifying him as a member of His flock, and a soldier in His company.

William of Auvergne's teaching on the character as a disposition or prelude to grace was accepted by all the great scholastic doctors, including St. Thomas. In fact, it is this aspect of the *res et sacramentum* as a disposition for grace which explains the all but general acceptance of the theory of dispositive causality of the sacraments. St. Thomas, however, went further than William of Auvergne and his contemporaries in explaining the nature of the character. Without denying that the character is prior to grace and a disposition for grace,[16] Thomas added an altogether new dimension to the character by considering all three characters as orientated toward Christian worship. Admittedly the character configures or likens the soul to the whole Trinity, as the magistral definition of the day insisted, but in the mind of Thomas the character assimilated or likened the soul more directly to Christ, and more specifically to Christ in His role as Priest. Finally, this assimilation or likeness is not static but dynamic, since through the character the Christian is deputed to Christian worship, and through participation in the priesthood of Christ, he is given the power, active in confirmation and in orders, passive in baptism, to participate in Christian worship.[17]

From this rather brief . . . presentation of scholastic teaching on the theology of the sacramental character the following conclusions may be derived relative to the theology of the *res et sacramentum:* (1) The *res et sacramentum* is an effect which is prior to grace and yet dispositive to grace; (2) In the case of the sacraments which produce a character, the *res et sacramentum* establishes a bond or relationship with God, with the Holy Trinity, or more particularly with Christ; (3) This relationship is both a consecration and a dedication; a consecration insofar as the Christian becomes the property of God, the Trinity or Christ, and in this sense objectively holy; a dedication insofar as the Christian assumes new obligations to continue Christ's office as priest, obligations which will be fulfilled with the aid of the sacramental grace which is peculiar to each sacrament. Thus, early speculation on the nature of the character reveals both a Trinitarian and a Christological stamp. It does not, however, reveal what I have already referred to as an ecclesiological stamp. Except for the Eucharist, in which the *res et sacramentum* is both the real body of Christ and yet the sign of Christ's mystical body which is the Church, there is little stress on the social significance of the *res et sacramentum.*[18] This is particularly true of the sacraments which do not imprint a character. In these sacraments the *res et sacramentum* is quite personal, an adornment or embellishment of the soul, the *ornatus animae.* Thus, the *res et sacramentum* of penance is internal repentance, *poenitentia interior,* the effect of the external sacrament and the ultimate disposition for the forgiveness of sin; the *res et sacramentum* of extreme unction is the spiritual anointing which is symbolized by the external anointing, and which effects in turn the final remission of venial sins or the remains of sin, thus preparing the soul for immediate entrance into glory.

It would be ungracious to criticize the early scholastics for failing to define more clearly what they called the *ornatus animae* or embellishment of the soul which is the immediate effect of those sacraments which do not produce a character. If criticism is in order, and I am not so sure that it is, it would be more proper to criticize the failure of subsequent theologians to continue the development of the theology of the *res et sacramentum*, which was brought to a rather abrupt close at the time of the Protestant Reformation. And yet even they are to be excused. The climate of the times was not favorable for Catholic theologians to stress a sacramental effect which is prior to grace, a concept which is basic to the theology of the *res et sacramentum*. The theory of dispositive causality, which was universally accepted by all the great scholastic doctors, could easily be misconstrued as meaning that the sacraments did not produce grace *ex opere operato*, but some disposition which is prior to grace. Protestants at the time were insisting that this disposition for grace or, better, the remission of sins, was faith, and, if they were sufficiently informed, they could have appealed to William of Auxerre and St. Albert the Great who held that the *res et sacramentum* or *ornatus animae* implied an illumination of faith which disposes the recipient for the reception of grace.[19] Whether Cajetan, the greatest of the Dominican doctors at the time of the Reformation, sensed this fear of playing into the hands of the reformers, I am not prepared to say. However, Cajetan rejected the theory of dispositive causality in favor of a theory of perfective causality and even argued that St. Thomas in his later writings had done the same.[20]

In any event, from the time of Cajetan and due to his influence, theologians generally have held that the sacraments produce grace immediately, some interpreting the causality as physical, as most Dominicans, and some as moral, as most Jesuits. In such a climate it is understandable why the theology of the *res et sacramentum* failed to develop and why it ultimately languished until revived by Cardinal Billot. Writing in the early years of the present century, Billot complains: "Modern authors have very little indeed to say about the *res et sacramentum*. And yet you will scarcely find anything in the present matter which is of greater importance and which throws more essential light on the many obscurities which repeatedly occur." [21]

The chief obscurity in sacramental theology is the manner in which the sacraments cause grace, and Billot believed that renewed study of the *res et sacramentum* would throw essential light on that problem. Like the earlier scholastics, Billot regarded the *res et sacramentum* as a disposition for grace, but, unlike his predecessors, who had regarded the *ornatus animae* as an entity in the physical order, Billot insisted that the *res et sacramentum* was a title to grace in the juridical or intentional order. True, Billot admitted the ontological or physical reality of the character, but even in the case of those sacraments which imprint a character, it is the accompanying title to grace and not the character itself which sets up the exigency for grace.[22]

Another defect in Billot's system, at least from the point of view of this . . . [article], is that it too fails to stress the sociological or ecclesiological stamp of the sacraments. The sacraments produce a title to grace, but the title itself is not founded in any new relationship of the individual with the Mystical Body of Christ.

The Ecclesiological Stamp of the *Res et Sacramentum*

The first theologian, to my knowledge, to stress the ecclesiological character of all seven sacraments was Matthias Scheeben writing in the closing decades of the last century. However, it has only been in more recent years, with the translation of his great classic, *Die Mysterien des Christentums*, that theologians more generally have become aware of Scheeben's contribution to the theology of the *res et sacramentum*.

Returning to the original use of the term *res et sacramentum* as applied to the Eucharist, Scheeben concludes that "It is only through the body of Christ and our union with it in one mystical body that its fullness of grace is communicated to us, and we share in the divine life coursing in it." [23] And it is this idea of a "special union with the God-man as head of His mystical body," which dominates Scheeben's teaching on the significance of the *res et sacramentum*. In the sacraments which imprint a character, Scheeben, like William of Auvergne, sees a special consecration, an objective holiness, which, with a stroke of theological genius, he likens to the objective holiness or substantial sanctity of the humanity of Christ. For Scheeben the character has its archetype or exemplar in the grace of the hypostatic union, by which the humanity of Christ is united through the Word to the whole Trinity, thus setting up an exigency for habitual grace in His soul.[24] Similarly, it is through the character or the *res et sacramentum* of the other sacraments that we are united to Christ in and through His Mystical Body, thus setting up an exigency for the special sacramental graces which flow from the Head to the various members. Scheeben, like Billot, refers to the *res et sacramentum* as a title to grace, but the title is not an entity in the juridical or moral order alone. We are entitled to grace because we are united in a special manner to the God-man as Head of His Mystical Body. Speaking of the *res et sacramentum* of the sacraments other than the Eucharist, Scheeben concludes that the *res et sacramentum* "consists in a special union with the God-man as head of His mystical body, by which participation in the spirit, that is, in the divinity and the divine life of the God-man, is granted to us on the basis of a special supernatural title, and for a special supernatural end." [25]

It is not the purpose of this . . . [article] to determine the special bond or relationship with Christ and His Church which results from the various sacraments. In the case of the sacraments which imprint a character, the determination is not too difficult. In these sacraments the character itself guarantees the ontological reality of the bond. In each of these sacraments we can discern a special configuration to Christ as priest, prophet, and king, and a resultant title to the graces necessary to continue Christ's office in the Church.

But in the sacraments which do not produce a character, it is not only difficult to establish a new relationship to the Church, but it is even more difficult to describe the specific manner in which the Christian is likened or configured to Christ, a configuration which would further determine the sacramental grace of each sacrament. The sacrament of extreme unction is a case in point. . . . [Some have proposed] the thesis which states that "the immediate effect of the sacramental rite is a state of relationship to the Mystical Body of Christ; for example, the immediate effect of extreme unction is a relationship to Christ in His suffering and dying."

Now this concept of extreme unction as an incorporation to Christ in His suffering and death has been attractively presented by

Michael Schmaus in his *Katholische Dogmatik*. In fact, for Schmaus, extreme unction is basically the sacramental consecration of death.[26] To establish his point, Schmaus quotes liberally from the commendation of a departing soul, but fails to cite the liturgy of extreme unction itself, which has no reference to death but which asks instead for the recovery of perfect health, of soul, of mind and body. Actually, if we may judge from the liturgy, the sacrament which consecrates the Christian's death is not extreme unction, since it can be given only to those who are in danger of death from sickness, but viaticum, which can be given to all who are faced with death.[27]

A number of popular writers have gone beyond Schmaus in their understanding of the sacrament of unction of the sick. Not only is the anointing an anointing for death, but an anointing for glory. It configures the soul of the Christian not only to Christ in His suffering and dying but in His resurrection and glory.[28] Admittedly, this idea of unction as an anointing for glory is well founded in the teaching of the early scholastics who regarded the purpose of unction as the immediate preparation of the soul for the beatific vision. In fact, St. Albert the Great, who regards all the sacraments as a configuration to Christ either in His suffering or in His resurrection, concludes that "by extreme unction we are configured to Christ in His resurrection; it is a sacrament given to the Christian about to leave this world, as a prefiguration of the anointing that is the glory to come when the elect will be delivered from all mortality." [29]

. . . [I personally hold] that the purpose of extreme unction is not so much to prepare the Christian for death but to comfort and to strengthen him and to restore him to the Church.[30] Accordingly, if I were to determine the *res et sacramentum* of extreme unction I would establish a special bond with the Church as comforter and healer, insofar as the Church continues Christ's ministry of comforting and healing the sick. And if I were pressed to liken or configure the soul of the anointed Christian to Christ, I would suggest that he is likened not so much to Christ in His death and resurrection but rather to Christ in His agony, when He was comforted by a visitation of an angel. In other words I . . . relate the sacrament of unction more closely to the sacrament of confirmation or strengthening than to the sacrament of baptism, which symbolizes death and resurrection in Christ.

I mention all this only to point up the problem of determining the special bond of relationship with the Church and the special configuration to Christ which each of the sacraments suggests. Much will depend on determining the purpose of each individual sacrament, and even after this purpose has been determined, much will depend on the genius with which the individual theologian is gifted in explaining his position.

Application of the *Res et Sacramentum* to Penance

Fortunately, the sacrament of penance has received sufficient development in Sacred Scripture and in the early tradition of the Church to enable us to determine more precisely the *res et sacramentum* of this sacrament. More important, the sacrament of penance is today a test case in justifying recent teaching on the ecclesiological character of the sacraments.

The case was first presented some thirty-five years ago by Father Bartholomew Xiberta in a doctoral thesis which has since become famous.[31] From the time of the Reformation, and for reasons already explained, few theologians even mentioned the *res et sacramentum*, and the few who did merely stated without further elucidation the opinion of St. Thomas that the *res et sacramentum* of penance was *poenitentia interior*, an effect which is caused by the external acts of the penitent and by the act of the absolving priest.[32] Father Xiberta, however, attempted to prove from Sacred Scripture and the writings of the Fathers that the immediate effect of the priest's absolution is reconciliation with the Church.

The thesis itself was daring since it seemed to play into the hands of non-Catholic historians of penance who had argued that the early penitential discipline of the Church was introduced for the purpose of reconciling the sinner to the Church as an external society, leaving untouched the sinner's relationship with God. Reconciliation with the Church, they argued; hence not reconciliation with God. Xiberta's thesis was also novel, since at the time most theologians were persuaded that the bishop's reconciliation following the performance of the canonical penance was not the sacrament of penance but either the lifting of an excommunication in the external forum or the grant of an indulgence.[33]

Today, all Catholic historians are agreed that the final reconciliation of penitents by the bishop was actually sacramental. In fact, there is no certain evidence, apart from emergency cases, that sacramental absolution followed immediately upon confession, in the

Church of the first nine centuries. Again, as Father de la Taille, one of the few theologians of the day who looked kindly upon Xiberta's thesis, expressed it: Reconciliation with the Church, therefore reconciliation with God. For de la Taille saw that reconciliation with the Church is the pledge and sacramental sign of divine pardon, that reconciliation with the Church, as Xiberta concludes, is the *res et sacramentum* of the sacrament of penance.[34]

Space does not permit us to do justice to the arguments which Xiberta adduces to substantiate his thesis. They begin with the formulas which Christ used in promising and in conferring the apostolic ministry of forgiveness: "Whatsoever you shall loose on earth shall be loosed in heaven" (Mt 18:18) and "Whosesoever sins you shall forgive, they are forgiven them" (Jn 20:23). In both instances the action of the Church in loosing or forgiving is prior to God's action of forgiving the sinner. In other words, whom the Church reconciles to herself God reconciles to Himself. Obviously, God's confirmation of this action of the Church will depend on the penitence of the sinner. But, granted this condition, it appears quite clear that God's reconciliation of the sinner awaits the action of His ministers, who act, however, in the name of the Church. Father Xiberta marshals a number of passages from the early Fathers of the Church which stress the priority of ecclesiastical pardon in the drama of divine forgiveness. One passage which he does not cite, and which I had the good fortune to stumble upon, expresses quite eloquently the initiative of the Church in the final act of divine reconciliation.

The passage is from St. Ephrem the Syrian, a fourth-century doctor of the universal Church. Commenting on Christ's commission to forgive and to retain sins, Ephrem has Christ say: "Receive a power which will neither leave you nor fail, because your word is guaranteed. Your words I shall not gainsay. If you shall be angry, I too shall be angry; if you shall be reconciled [to the sinner] I too shall be reconciled. Behold I hang at your sides the keys of the kingdom. Open and close it with fairness until I shall come in glory." [35]

This idea of reconciliation with the Church as a pledge or earnest of reconciliation with God is confirmed, I believe, by the very terms which the early Church used to express the immediate effect of her ministry of forgiveness. The effect is described as *communio* or fellowship of the Church, as the fellowship of peace (*communio pacis*), as the peace of the Church (*pax Ecclesiae*) and finally as reconciliation with the Church. It is only when this peace or reconciliation with the Church has been established that there can be question of the forgiveness of sins. Thus, St. Cyprian in his exegesis of the power of the keys interprets the words "to loose" as meaning to restore "to peace and fellowship," with the result that "in the peace which has been given [sinners] receive the pledge of life," and "in the peace which has been received they receive the Holy Spirit." [36]

This same idea of peace with the Church as the pledge of the Spirit by whom sins are forgiven is basic to the teaching of St. Augustine: "The peace of the Church forgives sins and estrangement from the Church's peace retains sins." [37] And the reason is always the same: "The remission of sins, since it cannot be granted except in the Holy Spirit, is granted only in that Church which has the Holy Spirit." For "outside this body the Holy Spirit vivifies no one." Accordingly, "the charity of the Church which is poured out into our hearts forgives the sins of those who are members of the Church, but it retains the sins of those who are not her members." [38] Texts could be multiplied to show that for Augustine the forgiveness of sins, whether through baptism or penance, is had only through the Spirit who is poured out on those who are united to the Church. Even Father Galtier, who severely censures Xiberta's thesis, unwittingly, I believe, subscribes to Xiberta's basic premise, when he states:

> This effusion of charity or the Holy Spirit into the heart does not take place except where "peace" or "reconciliation" is received from the Church herself. This is the firmly founded (*firmissima*) teaching of St. Augustine and from it he deduces the conclusion that there can be no remission of sin except in and through the Church.[39]

Today's Xiberta's thesis is accepted by most Catholic scholars in the field of penance and sacramental theology, including such names as Poschmann, Karl Rahner, Amann, Schmaus, de Lubac, and Leeming. D'Alès and Galtier are notable exceptions.[40] Both critics question the general relevance of the *res et sacramentum*, since it is based on what they regard as the antiquated and discredited theory of dispositive causality. And they question more particularly the propriety of referring to reconciliation with the Church as the *res et sacramentum* of penance.

In the first part of this . . . [article] we attempted to show that the theology of the *res et sacramentum* has received a remarkable revival and that it is far from discredited. We shall attempt to show now the propriety of referring to reconciliation with the Church as the *res et sacramentum* of penance. To do this we shall explain first, the sense in which reconciliation with the Church is a permanent effect and a reality in the physical order, secondly, the sense in which such reconciliation can be called a sign or sacrament, and thirdly, the sense in which the sign is both a disposition for grace and a configuration of the penitent to Christ.

An Analysis of the *Res et Sacramentum* of Penance

To explain the permanent character of reconciliation with the Church it is necessary to distinguish between the act of reconciling and the state of reconciliation which results, between what might be called reconciliation *in fieri* and the reconciliation *in facto esse*. Reconciliation *in fieri* is the sacramental sign, and it is identified principally with the absolving action of the priest. Reconciliation *in facto esse* is the *res et sacramentum*, and it implies a bond of restored friendship with the Church, a relationship which remains so long as serious sin does not sever the bond or venial sin does not strain the relationship. Since this bond or relationship is the effect of the sacramental rite in which the Holy Spirit is operative, we should regard the bond itself as having the same ontological reality as the sacramental character. Incorporation into the Church and restoration to the Church are both the effect of the Spirit, not as yet indwelling, but as forging the bond or relationship with the Church in which the Spirit dwells and in which the charity of the Spirit is poured out on those who are her members.

Granted that reconciliation with the Church is a reality in the physical order, in what sense is it also a sacrament or sign? As already noted, William of Auxerre and St. Thomas defended the propriety of referring to the sacramental character as a sacrament on the grounds that the character could be known even though not seen. In other words the character is a *signum intelligibile* and not a *signum visibile*.[41] Similarly, reconciliation with the Church can be known by establishing the fact that the penitent has been absolved by a duly authorized minister of the Church, a fact which was more easily established in the early Church when reconciliation was public. Furthermore, since the reconciled penitent enjoys the privilege of approaching the Eucharist, the sacrament of Christian unity, we can say that in the penitent's reception of the Eucharist the bond of friendship with the Church is manifested visibly.

Granted that reconciliation with the Church is both a reality and a sign, in what sense is it a disposition for grace or a *signum dispositivum?* Father D'Alès, one of Xiberta's earliest and severest critics, insists that reconciliation with the Church in the internal forum can only mean an effective and vital union with the Mystical Body, a union which is itself the effect of grace and not the preparation or prelude to grace.[42] Father Galtier says the same but even more pointedly: "The sinner is not understood to be justified simply because he is reinserted into the Mystical Body of Christ. . . . On the contrary, he is understood to be restored to that body and privileged to partake once more of its benefits, because he has already been justified by absolution." [43]

Now this objection of D'Alès and Galtier has particular relevance to the sacrament of penance. All will admit that the sacramental character or the *res et sacramentum* of baptism, confirmation, and orders is prior to grace not only in nature, but, occasionally, even in time. Thus, one who receives the sacrament of baptism validly, but unworthily, is incorporated into the Church, but he does not receive the grace of justification. But unless we extend the principle of reviviscence to the sacrament of penance, and not all authors do, it is difficult to see how reconciliation with the Church is in any sense prior to grace. In fact, how can we speak of a bond of restored friendship with the Church unless the bond itself is the effect of the grace of charity? And yet the New Testament formulas for the forgiveness of sins and the passages which we have cited from Ephrem, Cyprian, and Augustine seem to suggest, if not to express quite definitely, that peace with the Church is in some sense prior to God's act of justifying the sinner. To quote Cyprian again, "In the peace which has been given [sinners] receive the pledge of life," and "in the peace which has been received, they receive the Holy Spirit." [44] And to add to the citations from Augustine, "The city of God by receiving [sinners] makes them innocent." [45]

Both Galtier and D'Alès would lead one to believe that the sinner is first reconciled to God and then restored to the Church. The teaching of Augustine is quite the other way round. To quote

Galtier's own appraisal of Augustine's teaching: "there can be no remission of sin except in and through the Church." [46] Accordingly, reconciliation with the Church must be prior at least in some sense to reconciliation with God. But how explain this priority?

Two explanations suggest themselves. The first is implicit in what we have already said of the action of the Spirit in reconciling the penitent with the Church, an action which is distinct from the operation of the indwelling Spirit through whom we are justified, but an action which prepares for justification. Thus, reconciliation with the Church is by nature prior to grace since it is the ultimate disposition for the grace of the indwelling Spirit.

A second explanation is prompted by St. Thomas's theory of reciprocal priority and posteriority in the conversion of the sinner. According to St. Thomas, interior penance or contrition is the ultimate disposition for the grace of forgiveness, but interior penance by which the sinner turns from sins and turns to God must be informed by charity. Thus, in the order of dispositive causality contrition is prior to grace, but in the order of efficient and formal causality contrition is the effect of grace.[47] Although we do not personally find this theory of St. Thomas congenial, it will appeal to most Thomists and may be applied to reconciliation with the Church as the *res et sacramentum* of penance. Accordingly, reconciliation with the Church is the ultimate disposition for the grace of charity, and yet it is the effect of the grace of charity. In the order of dispositive causality, reconciliation is prior to grace; in the order of efficient and formal causality, reconciliation is posterior to grace.

Granted, then, that there is some propriety in referring to reconciliation with the Church as a *signum dispositivum* or disposition for grace, we can now inquire into the manner in which such reconciliation is a *signum configurativum* or an assimilation of the penitent to Christ. Now it would seem that St. Thomas limits the notion of configuration and consecration to those sacraments which imprint a character, to those sacraments which are strictly consecratory and which demand a special power or potency, either active or passive, to confer or to receive the other sacraments, and thus to participate in Christian worship. Accordingly, St. Thomas does not associate *poenitentia interior* with any special consecration or configuration to Christ.[48] However, St. Albert the Great believed that all seven sacraments "configure us to Christ our head." According to Albert, penance configures the soul to the suffering Christ, whereas extreme unction configures the soul to Christ in His Resurrection.[49]

Although we have suggested a different type of configuration for the *res et sacramentum* of extreme unction, we feel that Albert the Great is correct in likening the penitent to Christ in His expiatory suffering. True, all the faithful have the obligation "to fill up what is wanting of the sufferings of Christ . . . for his body which is the Church" (Col 1:24). Since, however, the reconciled penitent differs from one who has never severed or strained the bond of charity which unites the members of Christ's Mystical Body, it is understandable why the reconciled penitent is deputed in a special way to atone for the injury which he has done to that Body. And it is precisely in submitting to the penances imposed by the Church through the ministry of her priests that we are, as the Council of Trent asserts, "made like to Christ Jesus who satisfied for our sins— *dum satisfaciendo patimur pro peccatis, Christo Jesu, qui pro peccatis nostris satisfecit . . . conformes efficimur.*" [50]

. . . Father Reginald Masterson, O.P., [has] presented a doctoral thesis which states that the sacramental grace of penance is *gratia satisfactoria*. To quote Father Masterson directly, "the modality proper to this sacrament gives the penitent a *gratia satisfactoria*, making of him a more perfect sharer in the satisfactory power of Christ's Passion." [51] Father Masterson arrived at this conclusion from an analysis of the acts of the penitent, "since it is the matter which determines the precise formality of grace as it flows through the sacramental instrument." [52]

Without denying that the matter of the sacrament plays a part in determining the nature of sacramental grace, we believe that the symbolism of the sacrament derives more from the sacramental form and from the *res et sacramentum* or symbolic reality which results. Accordingly we would regard the sacramental grace of penance basically as a grace of reconciliation,[53] a *gratia restaurata*, a special modality of sanctifying grace, implying the infusion of the special virtue of penance, by which the sinner is moved to make reparation for his sins. All this is symbolized quite adequately by reconciliation with the Church as the sign of reconciliation with God. However, if the virtue of penance is to become operative in works of satisfaction the sinner needs a special actual grace, a grace which Father Masterson happily refers to as *gratia satis-factoria*. But here again, I would suggest, at least by way of complement to his own arguments, that this grace is symbolized and pledged by the penitent's configuration to Christ in His expiatory suffering and death. For it is a known principle in theology and recurrent in the teaching of St. Thomas that no one is deputed to an office without receiving those special graces which are necessary to fulfill that office.

Conclusion

We introduced this . . . [article] on the theology of the *res et sacramentum* with a quotation from de Lubac which stresses the social or ecclesiological stamp of the grace of the sacraments. With that rare insight which distinguishes the theologian who is well versed in the Church's long tradition, de Lubac concludes that it is only through union with the community that the Christian is united to God and to Christ. De Lubac applies this master principle to baptism, penance, and the Eucharist. The parallel he draws between baptism and penance will serve as an excellent summary of this . . . [article].

> The first effect of baptism, for example, is none other than this incorporation in the visible Church. To be baptized is to enter the Church. And this is essentially a social event. . . . The efficacy of penance is explained like that of baptism, for in the case of penance, the relationship between sacramental forgiveness and the social reintegration of the sinner is just as clear. . . . The Church's primitive discipline portrayed this relationship in a more striking manner. The whole apparatus of public penance and pardon made it clear that the reconciliation of the sinner is in the first place a reconciliation with the Church, this latter constituting an efficacious sign of reconciliation with God. . . . It is precisely because there can be no return to the grace of God without a return to the communion of the Church that the intervention of a minister of that Church is normally required. "Only the whole Christ," said Isaac de Stella in the twelfth century, "the Head upon His Body, Christ with the Church, can remit sins." [54]

It is the privilege of genius, as exemplified in this passage from de Lubac, to leave to others the speculative justification of its profound insights. This more prosaic task we have attempted in the present . . . [article].

References

[1] J. A. T. Robinson, *The Body* (London, 1952), p. 15.

[2] *Hom. 4, in Ps 36* (*PG*, 12, 1353).

[3] E. Masure, *Semaine Sociale de Nice* (1934), p. 230; cited by H. de Lubac, *Catholicisme*, 4th ed. (Paris, 1947), p. 277.

[4] *Op. cit.*, pp. 57f.

[5] *Ibid.*, p. 57.

[6] *In Joan., tr.* 26, 11 (*PL*, 35, 1612).

[7] *Ibid.*, 26, 17 (*PL*, 35, 1814).

[8] Cf. B. Leeming, *Principles of Sacramental Theology* (Westminster, Md., 1956), pp. 252f.

[9] Cf. Leeming, *op. cit.*, pp. 254f.

[10] *Cum Martha circa*, 29 (Nov.), 1202 (*DB*, 415).

[11] Cited by Leeming, *op. cit.*, p. 245.

[12] *De Baptismo contra Donat.*, 1, 4, 5 (*PL*, 43, 112); *Contra Cresconium Donat.*, 1, 30, 35 (*PL*, 43, 464).

[13] Cf. Leeming, *op. cit.*, p. 245.

[14] *Summa Theol.*, III, q. 63, a. 1, ad 2.

[15] Cf. J. Galot, *La Nature du Charactère Sacramentel* (Mechlin, 1956), p. 226.

[16] *Sent.* IV, d. 4, q. 1, a. 1, ad. 5.

[17] Cf. *Summa Theol.*, III, q. 63, a. 3.

[18] The question is one of stress. St. Thomas in the *Sentences* (note 16) indicates that the Christian is entitled to grace in as much as he is numbered among the members of Christ. Accordingly, the Christological aspect of the sacramental character would seem to include the ecclesiological aspect.

[19] Cf. Galot, *op. cit.*, pp. 227f.

[20] Cf. H. Lennerz, *De Sacramentis Novae Legis in Genere*, 2nd ed. (Romae, 1939), nn. 412, 413, 417; B. Leeming, *op. cit.*, pp. 324ff.

[21] *De Ecclesiae Sacramentis*, 7th ed., I (Romae, 1931), 112.

[22] *Ibid.*, p. 143, continuation of note; and cf. pp. 159f. for Billot's insistence that the power associated with the character is juridical and not physical.

[23] *The Mysteries of Christianity*, trans. C. Vollert, S.J. (St. Louis, 1947), p. 575.

[24] *Op. cit.*, pp. 584f.

[25] *Ibid.*, p. 575.

[26] *Katholische Dogmatik*, IV, 1 (München, 1957), 614-35.

[27] Cf. C. Davis, "This Sacrament of the Sick," *The Clergy Review*, 43 (Dec. 1958), 734.

[28] Thus, C. Howell, S.J., in *Of Sacraments and Sacrifice* (Collegeville, Minn., 1952), p. 75; H. A. Reinhold, "Anointing for Glory," in *The American Parish and the Roman Liturgy* (New York, 1958).

[29] Cited without reference by J. Robilliard, O.P., in *Initiation Théologique* (Paris, 1954), pp. 4, 687.

[30] "The Purpose of Anointing the Sick: A Reappraisal," in *Theological Studies*, 19 (Sept. 1958), 309-44.

[31] *Clavis Ecclesiae* (Romae, 1922).

[32] *Summa Theol.*, III, q. 84, a. 1, ad 3.

[33] A. Pérez Goyena, S.J., appeals to Collet, Palmieri, Pesch, De San, Hurter and H. Mazella to prove against Xiberta that reconciliation granted by the

bishop in the early Church at the close of the public penance was not the sacrament of penance: *Razon y Fe*, 65 (1923), 379-81.

[34] *Gregorianum* (1923), 591ff.

[35] Cited by P. Palmer, S.J., in *Sacraments and Forgiveness*, Vol. 2 of *Sources of Christian Theology* (Westminster, Md., 1959), 82.

[36] *Epist.* 57, 1; 55; 13; 57; 4.

[37] *De Baptismo contra Donat.*, 3, 18, 23.

[38] *Sermo* 71, 20, 33; *Epist.* 185, 50; *In Joan.*, *tr.* 121, 4.

[39] *De Paenitentia, Tractatus Dogmatico-Historicus*, ed. nova (Romae, 1950), p. 132. For Galtier's adverse criticism of Xiberta's thesis cf. the same edition, p. 341.

[40] A. l'Alès, S.J., in "La Pénitence," *Rescherches de Science Religieuse*, 12 (1922), 372ff.; P. Galtier, S.J., *op. cit.*, p. 341.

[41] See above, p. 6.

[42] *Art. cit.*, p. 374.

[43] *Op. cit.*, p. 341.

[44] See above, p. 17.

[45] *Contra Cresconium Donat.*, 11, 12, 16.

[46] See above, p. 18.

[47] *Summa Theol.*, I-II, q. 113, a. 8, ad 2. Cf. *ibid.*, a. 6, and *Contra Gent.*, 4, 72.

[48] *Sent.* IV, d. 4, q. 1, a. 4, ad 2. Cf. Galot, *op. cit.*, p. 175.

[49] See above, p. 13.

[50] *Sess. 14, cap. 8* (*DB*, 904).

[51] "The Sacramental Grace of Penance," *Proceedings of the Thirteenth Annual Convention of the Catholic Theological Society of America* (St. Paul, Minn., 1958), p. 47.

[52] *Art. cit.*, pp. 36f.

[53] In discussing the *res et effectus* of penance, the Council of Trent mentions in the first place *reconciliatio cum Deo* (Sess. XIV, *DB*, 896). Accordingly, the grace of reconciliation should be stressed, it would seem, in discussing the sacramental grace of this sacrament.

[54] *Op. cit.*, p. 62.

JAMES EGAN, O.P.

A Contemporary Approach
to Sacramental Grace

Because the Catholic tends to see the sacraments primarily as instruments of grace, it is imperative that he have some understanding of sacramental grace. In this article, the author reviews recent
theological contributions concerning the nature of sacramental
grace and proposes a description of it. In the light of the description, he examines each of the seven sacraments and indicates the
areas which still remain problematic for the contemporary theologian.

Father Egan is Chancellor of the School of Sacred Theology at
St. Mary's College, Notre Dame, Indiana.

. . . [Four brief texts provide a framework for a discussion on
sacramental grace.]

For His workmanship we are created in Jesus Christ in good works,
Which God has made ready beforehand that we may walk in them
(Eph 2:10).
Therefore, you are now no longer strangers and foreigners, but
you are citizens with the saints and members of God's household: you
are built upon the foundations of the apostles and prophets with Christ
Jesus Himself as the chief corner stone. In Him the whole structure
is closely fitted together and grows into a temple holy in the Lord, in
Him you too are being built together into a dwelling place for God
in the Spirit (Eph 2:19-22).

This article was first printed in the *Proceedings of the Eighth Annual Convention of the Society of Catholic College Teachers of Sacred Doctrine*. It is
reprinted here with the permission of the Society.

> . . . bringing every mind into captivity to the obedience of Christ . . . (2 Cor 10:5).
> O God, who renewest the world by Thine ineffable sacraments . . . (Collect, Friday, Fourth Week of Lent).

. . . Note, first, the immediate personal concern of God the Father in the continuous great events of salvation history, to the extent that He, through Jesus Christ and in His Spirit is more deeply immersed in history than He ever was in Old Testament times.

Note, secondly, the realistic intimacy between Jesus Christ and the vast array of His members, so that it becomes difficult (though necessary) to distinguish between the Incarnate Christ and the Mystic Christ, between the Christic Pleroma and the Mystic Pleroma.

Note, thirdly, the indescribable variety that is implied in the Mystic Christ, made possible only by the powerful, yet delicate, virtuosity of the Holy Spirit.

Note, finally, the reality of the Mystic Christ, the Mystic Pleroma, is thoroughly sacramental, only sacramental. The action of the Father, through Jesus Christ, in the Holy Spirit, is channeled primarily through the sacraments, secondarily, in reference to the sacraments.

Let us now fill in some of the traits of this sketch that are necessary for an understanding of . . . [sacramental grace]. Theologians and teachers of Sacred Doctrine should have no hesitation in being completely realistic in their understanding of sacramental causality. In the complex that is sacramental causality, there are, undoubtedly, elements that are moral, or intentional, or dispositive; this is no reason for not insisting that sacramental causality, as such, is physical. It may also be called "mystical," provided this term is not used to mask a sort of theological agnosticism, but is taken to mean supernatural physical causality, in the context of sacramental causality.

Theologians are receiving considerable support for a strong interpretation of sacramental causality from the areas of Sacred Scripture and the liturgy.

Von Allman[1] in his article on *Baptism*, apropos of New Testament texts linking baptism and salvation, says:

> Such New Testament statements may lack dogmatic wisdom: this does not alter the fact that a great deal of exegetical acrobatics is needed to deny the close and very realistic links by which Scripture binds salvation and baptism together.

In regard to the liturgy, Father Vagaggini, O.S.B.,[2] says:

> Finally, the liturgy owes to the *opus operatum* its realist character. God's action in the sacraments not only reaches man on the level of knowledge and of will, but transforms him in his very being: baptism and holy orders do not bring about a mere moral renewal, they effect a change which must actually be called physical.

Lastly, there is the powerful statement of the late Pius XII:[3]

> . . . the central element of the Eucharistic Sacrifice is that in which Christ intervenes as "offering Himself". . . . In reality the action of the consecrating priest is the very action of Christ who acts through His minister.

While the immediate acting of Christ is required here because of the unique character of the action—His sacrifice—there is no reason to presume that the minister has greater autonomy in the celebration of any of the other sacraments.

Spurred by the hardy speculations of Dom Odo Casel, O.S.B., to a serious study of the presence of Christ's mysteries and actions in the sacraments, theologians, for the most part, have not accepted his positions. Although this is not the place for a complete study of what theologians are saying about this question, a brief consideration of positions to be found in material that is easily available to us would not be out of place; especially since Casel's own work is appearing in translation.

Father Vagaggini[4] has a strong criticism of the basic contention of Casel: the sacraments re*present*ate the redemptive acts of Christ with the same ontological reality they had when they were elicited by Christ on earth. Father Vagaggini distinguishes two elements in the acts of Christ: one is momentary: the acts themselves as they are performed at a given moment; the other is permanent: the interior disposition, the stable *habitus* from which these acts proceed throughout His earthly life. Even acts of intellect and will, since they are connected with bodily organs, are momentary: "time enters into the individuation of the act." Of the permanent element, Father Vagaggini says:

> This disposition was permanent and constant in Christ, without interruption or diminution, from His Incarnation to His Ascension, and it remains in the glorified Christ. Through the liturgical action, the faithful are put in contact with that disposition, which is always in act.

Is this disposition to be taken as the action of Christ in the sacrament? Not quite. There is another element in the solution of Father Vagaggini. Still speaking of the momentary aspect of the acts (which, after all, is the core of the problem), he says:

> For Christ's actions were not simply human, entitled as such to an efficacy limited in space and time, but theandric, human-divine actions. Their human element was an instrument, and the divine power was at work, using that instrument. . . . Thus Christ's actions, though limited in time and space insofar as they are human, reach to all times and all places insofar as they are theandric.

What is the precise meaning of "theandric" here? Is not a theandric action one in which the second Person of the Trinity is *acting* according to His divine nature (in unity with the Father and the Spirit) and according to His human nature? In such an action, the human nature is serving as an instrument; but is it an inert instrument now that it is in glory? There must be action on the part of the human nature for an act to be theandric; otherwise, is it any more than a Trinitarian action that produces an effect with a reference to the actions of Christ on earth? But what of the permanent aspect of those acts of Christ. As explained by Vagaggini there is an *habitual disposition*, which is not action, though it may be looked upon as the source of action. Perhaps, the solution does lie along this line, but let us first look at two other positions.

Judging from the only available presentation of the position of Father Schillebeeckx, O.P.,[5] we are forced to conclude that he solves the problem by eliminating it, or, at least, by a unique application of the traditional *communicatio idiomatum*. In line with the title of his essay: "The Sacraments: An Encounter with God" (Note: God), he states:

> Although this is true of every human activity of Christ, it is especially true of those human actions of Christ which are exclusively actions of God, although accomplished in a human manner, that is, His miracles and, more especially, redemption itself which finds its consummation in the sacrifice of the Cross.

Like Father Vagaggini, Father Schillebeeckx rejects any possibility of a re*present*ation of the acts of Christ which He elicited during His passion. Like Father Vagaggini he also appeals to an aspect of these acts that surpasses time. "Yet, the historical acts of Christ, who is personally God, are the *personal* acts of the second divine

Person, even though performed through His humanity." What can be the meaning of "even though"? It is clarified in the following:

> Therefore, Jesus' sacrifice on the Cross, as a personal action of God, is an eternally present actuality, which is imperishable. The sacrifice of the Cross, not in its historical form as a human act, but as *this* kind of human act which proceeds from the *Son of God*, who *personalizes* the *human* act of Jesus—this sacrifice of the Cross, in its inner nature a truly divine act of sacrifice (although performed in the humanity and therefore in time) is—as is everything which is divine—eternal, and not past. Redemption, therefore, if considered exclusively as an action of God (only God can redeem us) is, although achieved in this humanity, an eternally present divine act. The death on the Cross, then, itself possesses a "mystery" content, which transcends time.

This is somewhat breath-taking. Father Schillebeeckx wishes us to contemplate an historical action of Jesus Christ—His death on the Cross—as it is exclusively an action of the second Person of the Trinity. From this viewpoint, it is an action common to Father, Son, and Holy Spirit; this is the meaning, supposedly, of the statement, "Only God can redeem us." Yet from an exclusively divine point of view, this action is *not* an act of redemption. God, acting exclusively as God, can do numberless things for us sinners: He cannot *redeem* us. Redemption, as wrought by Christ, is not even a theandric action. The continuous effecting of the fruits of redemption in us, is, according to tradition, a theandric act. But in the account of Father Schillebeeckx it is an exclusively divine action, which may be denominated redemptive, by what appears to be only an extrinsic reference to the fact that it had been performed by Jesus Christ. The redemption is a personal act of the second Person, not "even though performed through His humanity," but only in so far as it was performed through His humanity. This action can be predicated of the Son of God (and not the Father or the Holy Spirit) only because it is an act of Him who subsists in human nature and acts through that nature.

In a recent issue of *The Thomist*,[6] Father Colman O'Neill has discussed . . . [the] problem [of sacramental grace] in a way that satisfies a solidly traditional position and, despite a certain ambiguity, opens the way to answering our contemporary question. The basis of the article is a principle of St. Thomas, which is equally applicable to the humanity of Christ and the sacraments of the Church.

> For just as an instrument acquires its instrumental power in two ways, namely, when it receives the form of instrument and when it is moved by the principal agent, so also the matter of a sacrament required a two-fold sanctification, by one of which it becomes the proper matter of the sacrament, while by the other it is applied to the effect (*S.T.*, III, a. 72, a. 3, ad 2um).

Father O'Neill makes a strong case for saying that the humanity of Christ is made a fit instrument of our redemption by the historical undergoing of the mysteries of His life, death, resurrection, ascension. It is this "formed" humanity in heaven which God uses as an instrument for the production of grace through the sacraments. This places the mysteries of Christ where they belong, in *Christus resurgens*, in the glorified Christ. The humanity of Christ has received the form of an instrument, the capacity to be a fitting instrument in the work of salvation (that is, of applying the fruits of redemption).

There remains the question of the actual exercise of this instrumental causality. Here Father O'Neill seems to back down. There is no true action of Christ in the sacraments other than the Eucharist.

> It will be understood, therefore, that when we speak about a presence of Christ *secundum actionem* (in sacraments other than the Eucharist) we are accepting for the sake of convenience a proposed terminology, and are quite prepared, and even inclined, to deny that there is any true presence of Christ at all.[7]

We are here at the heart of the ambiguity that affects not only Father O'Neill's discussion, but the whole discussion aroused by Casel. In support of the statement just quoted, Father O'Neill writes in a footnote: "Pius XII, *Mediator Dei*, indicating the teaching of the Doctors of the Church on the 'presence and operation' of Christ's mysteries, speaks of 'models of virtue,' 'sources of divine grace' by reason of the merits and intercession of the Redeemer. The mysteries live on 'in their effects in us.' There is no question here of the presence of the mysteries themselves." This is really not surprising, for the reference here (not made explicit) is to the section of the encyclical devoted to the *Cycle of Mysteries of the Liturgical Year*, in other words the entire historical life of Christ in its mysterious aspect.

To avoid confusion, a clear-cut distinction must be made between the presence of the mysteries of Christ's life in the sacramental complex and the immediacy of the action of Christ. *There is only one mystery* of the life, death, resurrection, ascension of Jesus Christ made *really* present within the sacramental system and that is His *passion and death*. No other mystery is sacramentally re-enacted as it is a mystery of the Incarnate Christ; many of them (may we say, all?) are re-enacted as mysteries of the members of the mystical Christ. This is quite distinct from the problem of the reality and immediacy of Christ's action in the Eucharistic sacrifice and all the other sacraments.

Father O'Neill implicitly admits that only the sacrifice of Christ is re-enacted sacramentally, since in his discussion of the Mass he seeks to explain the reality of Christ's sacrifice. While it is true that there is a special character to the Mass that requires the presence of an action of Christ, any reasonable explanation of such an action will be valid for all the sacraments. The re-enactment of the sacrifice of the Cross is sacramental and therefore the mode of causality required by it is not fundamentally distinct from that of the other sacraments. It is as necessary to realize that the risen Christ re-enacts the mystery of His death and resurrection in the newly baptised, as that He offers the Eucharistic Sacrifice.

Concerning the Eucharistic Sacrifice, Father O'Neill says:

> Now, not only does the sign of Christ's body really contain the body, but the priest, offering the Church's sign-sacrifice, contains the actual act of Chrit's offering. It is by one and the same instrumental power, imparted by God to the humanity of Christ in heaven, that Christ's native action and the native action of the priest are elevated and applied. The native action of Christ thus brought to the altar, at one and the same instant, transubstantiates and offers.[8]

Father O'Neill then cites various attempts at explaining the "native action of Christ." His own explanation is most suggestive. . . .

> A variation of this (namely, that Christ in heaven maintains the self-same act of offering which He elicited on earth) which has not been sufficiently noted makes a distinction between the inner worship of Christ and the *imperium* of the practical intellect which designated the killing of Christ, as a sacrificial externalization of His worship, that is, which designated what others were doing to His body as the sign of His charity. While the worship is maintained for ever in the beatific vision, the act of intellect is preserved until the end of the world in the discrete time of Christ's infused knowledge, always consisting in designation of a suitable sign of inner sacrifice.[9]

. . . [It should be remarked that] this appeal to the beatific knowledge and love of Christ does not seem to be in accord with the thought of St. Thomas. This act of knowledge and love was unchangeable; by it Christ was, from the instant of His conception, *in patria;* it was not in any sense a proximate principle of His merit. This is one of the strongest arguments for the existence of infused knowledge in Christ. It was this knowledge, in intimate union with, but in no sense entirely dependent upon, His experiential knowledge, that enabled Christ to act as a principal cause during His life on earth and to elicit, as man, those actions which were instrumentally elevated by the Father for miracles and the forgiveness of sin.

We get a precious insight into the content of this act of infused knowledge and meritorious love from the *Epistle to the Hebrews:* "Therefore in coming into the world, he says: 'Sacrifice and oblation thou wouldst not, but a body thou hast fitted to me: in holocausts and sin-offerings thou hast had no pleasure.' Then said I, 'Behold I come—(in the head of the book it is written of me)—to do Thy will, O God'" (10:5-7). This is the act that ruled all of Christ's actions while He was on earth; there is no reason to doubt that it is this same act, or some modality of it, that still rules all His actions in heaven until all be consummated. The psychology of this act has been studied by St. Thomas.[10] Since this act is not limited by time and space, there seems to be no difficulty in attributing to it all the actions of Christ's humanity that are instrumentally responsible for communication of grace through the sacraments. Moreover, it is likely that this act was elicited by Our Lord, either at the moment He entered the world, or at the moment He entered into his Passion. In other words, by this act, He freely determined to be the instrument of the Father in every offering of the Sacrifice of the Cross, in the upper room, on Calvary, in every assembly of the People of God. He likewise determined His action in every administration of the sacraments, which were destined to re-enact in His members the mysteries of His own life. The sweep of His vision would include the ultimate glorification of the sons of God at the last Day.

It may seem that we have wandered far from our subject. But if we do not have a definite position on the question of the presence of the mysteries of Christ in the sacramental reality of the

Church and the immediacy of His action, especially in the sacraments which are the separated instruments of Jesus Christ, we
can scarcely appreciate the reality of what the sacraments are
destined to accomplish in the people of God. For we must insist
on the historical continuity of God's dealing with men; and the
New Dispensation must be even more profoundly historical than
the Old. Everything that happened to the Old Israel in figures,
in shadows, happened to Jesus Christ in reality, happens to the
New Israel in sacraments, just as really, but in symbolic actions
and words that cause the reality they signify, a continuation within
the people of God of the culmination of the Old Covenant that
was realized in Christ, our Israel, our Pasch.

A possible source of confusion is the use we make of the expressions, "habitual grace," "sanctifying grace," "the grace of the virtues and gifts." The conceptual note proper to these expressions
is generic; hence, as such, it is never found in reality any more
than animal is. The generic notion of grace is of a reality communicated to intellectual creatures that is a participation in the
divine nature whereby they are ordered, for the glory of God,
to an intimate life of union with God, immediately known and
loved. All grace (including actual grace, in some sense) must have
this generic mark. But grace never exists in the pure state of its
generic perfection. Even the fulness of the grace of Christ is a
mode of grace suited to His special place in the designs of God.
Certainly, if He had been destined to come into the world under
different circumstances, there would have been a different modality
to His grace. In fact, then, all grace as existent in diverse subjects
is grace modified. God tailors grace not only to angels and men,
but also to individual angels and men. While we have no way of
knowing the marvelous diversity of grace in the angels, we do
know that all of it is nonsacramental. In men the diversity of grace
is totally sacramental. The Son of God took unto Himself a human
nature so that He might perform divine acts (that is, acts attributed
to a divine Person) in a human mode; He established for us the
sacraments so that we might perform human acts in a divine mode.
The world of sacramental reality is a distinct mode of being. As
Dom Vonier put it very accurately:

> The sacramental world is a new world created by God entirely
> different from the world of nature or even from the world of spirits.
> . . . Sacraments are a unique creation with entirely new laws. . . .

There is nothing like the sacraments in heaven or on earth and it would be a great disparagement of their character to look upon them as mere veils of more substantial spiritual realities. They are not veiling anything, but they are complete realities in themselves, existing in their own right. . . . Sacraments have a mode of existence of their own, a psychology of their own. If they are not being in the sense in which man is a being, or an angel is a being, they are beings nevertheless, resembling God's nature very closely.[11]

The question of "before and after" intrudes itself twice in connection with this sacramental world. There is the "before" of this life, the "after" of eternal life. While the ultimate culmination of all sacramental activity will be realized in the hereafter, it is important to note that the sacraments as such concentrate on effects that can be brought about in this life. The sacraments cannot operate beyond the grave, except by what they effect here below. Since God loves variety, He would not create without variety,[12] there must be infinitely greater variety in the supernatural order than there is in the natural order. The creation of this variety must take place in this life and the sacraments are the means used by God to do it. Sacramental grace, understood as a mode of habitual grace, is the root cause of the variety willed by God. Since sacramental grace is the deepest reality caused by the sacraments and the most hidden, we must use the sacrament itself, with its fullest meaning (*sacramentum tantum*), and the sacramental reality, the symbolic reality (*res et sacramentum*), to lead us to a grasp of sacramental grace (*res tantum*). Fortunately, it is almost impossible to catch up with the wealth of insight that is coming to us from studies in Sacred Scripture, Liturgy, patristics, and the reflections of contemporary theologians.

This brings us to the second "before and after." By a priority of nature (and, on occasion, of time), the sacramental reality is produced before sacramental grace. Are we not too inclined to think, however, that the effect principally intended in every sacrament is grace? Yet, this is not true in three sacraments, the Eucharist, Order, and Marriage. In these three, the sacramental reality, the sacrifice of Christ and His presence as victim and as the unity of His Mystical Body, the power of the priesthood, the bond of marriage have a pre-eminence and grace is consequential and ordered to the sacramental reality. I am strongly inclined to believe that the same relationship is true of the sacramental reality of confirmation in relation to its grace. In fact, if the previous point is valid, namely, that the sacraments, as sacraments, are deeply involved in the Christian life in this world, I would be inclined to say that this is true of every sacrament. The specific determination of sacramental effects for this life depends primarily on the sacramental reality, and grace, precisely as sacramental grace, is given for accomplishing, in a very personal way, these specific determinations. This in no way disturbs the ultimate finality of all grace to the life of the elect in heaven.

How is all this brought about? May I be permitted to express this vital communication of the richness of God's grace to men in the familiar terminology of scholasticism. The initiative lies with the Father, who orders all things to His ultimate glory. He sends His Son as man to accomplish all His design. In Jesus Christ is the fullness of divinity in all reality. There is the Pleroma of the second Person of the Trinity, the personal being of the Word; there is the Pleroma of grace and knowledge. The Father wills that all His intentions be fulfilled in the redemptive action of Jesus Christ and that the humanity of this same Jesus be the living instrument for the communication of His rich and varied heritage. At the will of the Father, Jesus, in turn, wishes to communicate His Pleroma to men, who are to be identified with Him as His Body, the people of His Father, the temple of His Spirit. For this purpose He devises seven precise, yet flexible, instruments through which He will create another Pleroma.

Perhaps all this may be expressed in a more ancient image. The Father dwells in light inaccessible. He sends His Son, who, as man, is the Light of the world, the blinding white light, which enlightens every man that comes into this world. This light passes through the prism of the sacraments and bathes the faithful in myriad colors and shades of color, for the manifestation of the glory of God's light and to prepare them all to shine out like the sun in the Kingdom of the Father.

To get some idea of the vast work that must be accomplished by the Father through Jesus Christ and His sacraments in the Spirit, let us recall the texts cited at the beginning of this paper. (1) "For His workmanship we are." Individually and with loving attention, each child, each member, each citizen, each stone, must be carefully fashioned. (2) But not just for its own sake. "In Him the whole structure is closely fitted together." The whole family, the mystic body, the people of God, the temple has to be built up, for as common goods, these are diviner goods, giving greater glory to God. (3) So far the work has been directed to the inner growth of the Church. It, however, must look outwards, to the world, to all those who imperfectly, or not at all, are children, members, citizens, stones. The Church has a vast mission to proclaim the good news to all men, to witness to the designs of God on all men, to bring "every mind into captivity to the obedience of Christ."

All this is done "by thine ineffable sacraments." And it is done by the powerful combination of sacramental reality and sacramental grace. As we consider, briefly, the sacraments, we shall utilize what we know about both these realities. But first, a description of sacramental grace.

> Sacramental grace is a mode of the grace of the virtues and gifts, which (1) directly orders it to the specific effects of the Christian life signified by the sacramental rite and the sacramental reality and at the same time tends to heal the wounds of sin that would hinder these effects; (2) gives a special title to actual graces needed for these effects in existential circumstances; (3) brings about a concomitant modification of the infused virtues that are specially connected with the attainment of the same effects.
>
> The immediate result is a life of virtue for the people of God that will be the praise of the glory of God's grace in this life. The final result will be the glorious company of the elect in heaven where the Christic Pleroma will subject Himself and His mystic Pleroma to the Father so that God may be all in all.[13]

Baptism

The first sacrament is almost inexhaustible in meaning and hence in power. It contains radically and virtually all the effects of salvation, including the complete renovation of human nature. It plants in the body the seed of immortality, which it will bring to fruition in the resurrection.[14] Through it, each human person has re-enacted within himself two mysteries of the life of Christ, the Incarnation and the Passion-Resurrection, but in inverse order. In the Incarnation, a human nature becomes the natural Son of God, destined to attain glory through the Passion. In Baptism, each human person becomes an adopted son of God by undergoing the Passion-Resurrection of his Savior.

In baptism, there is the first of two major missions of the Holy

Spirit. As the Spirit formed the human nature of Jesus and filled it with grace at the instant of the Incarnation, so He forms children of God in baptism. This is an intimate, almost maternal, mission of the vivifying Spirit. By it, the full power of the Passion of Christ is applied, as in no other sacrament. All sin and all punishment is entirely removed. The person is made totally pleasing to God; the shaping and perfecting of the individual is begun, a profound configuration to Christ is impressed on each of the baptised, on which is built the real relation to Christ and to all the other members of Christ that is the reality of the mystic Christ. The sacramental reality is the power of the royal priesthood, which each one will exercise primarily by offering spiritual sacrifices and sharing in the one eucharistic sacrifice.[15]

In a word, baptism starts the two great works mentioned in our texts—the shaping of the individual stones, the building up of the whole temple.

A point stressed by St. Thomas is a source of obvious concern to some contemporaries: it is the note of passivity he attributes to the baptismal character. Perhaps, we would appreciate the profound truth of this point better if we realized that for St. Thomas all our external senses are passive powers, and that passivity is primordial in our internal senses, our intellects, our appetites, both sensitive and intellective. Think for a moment of the contribution made to our whole life by the passivity of the sense. Without this complete receptivity, we would be completely isolated from reality, or run the risk of receiving it in a distorted manner.

Similarly, the predominant sacramental effect of baptism is vital receptivity. The *new creature* is new, because the basic attitude of the old creature is obliterated: "You shall be like gods, knowing good and evil."

Confirmation

I think we are all aware of a considerable uneasiness about confirmation. Just what is its role and when should it be administered? Frankly, the only logical conclusion I can draw from many recent studies of the sources is that we should return to the primitive practice of giving the three sacraments of initiation togther, even to an infant. However, I am convinced that the insight of the western Church has firm foundations.

The character and grace of confirmation are precious in their own right; they do not perfect baptism in what might be called a merely linear fashion, but mark a distinct sharing in the mysteries of Christ that no other sacrament can provide.

At confirmation, the second mission of the Holy Spirit takes place; this is no hidden quiet coming. This is as public as possible, for it is concerned with the Church facing the world. This mission to the confirmed is ordered to the same end as that to Christ at His baptism—the beginning of his proclamation of the good news, of his witnessing to the "mystery" hidden in the designs of the Father from eternity.

Confirmation is the Pentecost of the individual; by it he is made an official witness of Jesus Christ and his Church. By the character (which, as I suggested previously, may well be the principal as well as the primary effect) each child of God is set up as an instrument of the Spirit of Christ for the immense task "of bringing every mind into captivity to the obedience of Christ." This is predominantly a kingly character rather than priestly; it is also in a sense a prophetic character. It should be given by the bishop and is most effectively used under the mandate of the bishop. Personally I should like to see it given to young adolescents, preferably after a retreat modeled on the first two weeks of the spiritual exercises of St. Ignatius.

The special sacramental effect of Confirmation is vividly presented in Jeremia

> "Ah, Lord God!" I said, "I know not how to speak; I am too young." But the Lord answered me. "Say not, 'I am too young.' To whomever I send you, you shall go. Whatever I command you, you shall speak. Have no fear before them, because I am with you to deliver you, says the Lord." Then the Lord extended his hand and touched my mouth, saying, "See, I place my words in your mouth! This day I set you over nations and over kingdoms, to root up and to tear down, to destroy and to demolish, to build and to plant" (1:6-9).

Note that the liturgy uses the last verse as the offertory antiphon of the Mass of a Sovereign Pontiff.

Eucharist—Sacramental Sacrifice

Confining ourselves to the sacramental grace of the Eucharist, let us point out first the necessity of combating any purely private attitude toward the reception of the Eucharist. There is no question but that the Eucharist is the most effecive sacrament for shaping to perfection the individual members of the Mystic Christ. But this power is released most abundantly where there is participation in the total Eucharist. Its full mystery is meaningless without the key element—the re-enactment by our High Priest, Jesus Christ, of the sacrifice of Calvary. The sacrifice of Christ is the culmination of all the sacrifices of the Old Law. On Calvary the aspect of holocaust and expiatory sacrifice is predominant, but this is also a communion-sacrifice and this aspect is accomplished sacramentally at the altar. Of the communion-sacrifices of the Old Law, Father de Vaux, O.P., says:

> its characteristic feature lies in the fact that the victim is shared between God, the priest, and the person offering the sacrifice, who eats it as a holy thing; and it is to be noted that the part returned to the offerer, he eats together with his family and with any guests he may invite.[16]

Whenever Christ is lifted up in sacrifice, He draws all to Himself; since He is lifted up as man, He draws to Himself as man. This is why the sacramental reality of the Eucharist is the *unity* of the Mystical Body. The special effect of the sacramental grace of the Eucharist is precisely the unity looked at from the side of the members. To put it negatively, but in terms that should be enlightening, the sacramental grace of the Eucharist continuously works to remove the danger of schism from the body of Christ. It attacks deeply the relic of original sin that would repel men from working as a part of the whole—the one people of God. Positively stated, the sacramental grace of the Eucharist is the grace of the Mystical Body, the grace by which above all and with visible manifestation "the whole structure is closely fitted together and grows into a temple holy to God." So important is this aspect of sacramental communion, that all who attend Mass and do not, for some reason, receive Communion, should be urged to make a spiritual communion with the intention of uniting themselves to the communion-sacrifice of Christ and His Church. If the obstacle is the consciousness of mortal sin, what more propitious moment to try and arouse perfect contrition than that in which one is forbidden to share with the community in the victim Christ.

Penance

Much interesting work is being done on the rite of Penance within the Church by our contemporaries. But it is concerned more with the setting than the sacrament itself, for the role of the Church, as Church, is about the same in penance as it is, for example, in the complete rite of baptism.

There are certain determined situations in which, by a jurisdictional act, the Church must first reconcile the excommunicated sinner to herself (even though he may already be reconciled to God), before he can submit himself to the sacrament of penance.

Certainly, a mortal sinner has done inestimable damage to God and Christ, to himself, to the whole Church. The Church, in mercy and in charity, must be concerned about such a member, anxious for his restoration. But there seems to be no place for an act of reconciliation on the part of the Church distinct from, and prior to, reconciliation to the Head and to God.

The attempt to apply the same notion of the sacrament of penance to one confessing venial sins only, or sins of the past, seems to be an unjustifiable stretching of the notion of reconciliation. The very concept of venial sin implies that it does not disrupt the bonds of friendship. Certainly, the venial sins of priest and people are obstacles to full union with Christ and each other in the presence of the Father, but the public confession at Mass is sufficient to remove any tension they might cause.

According to the present understanding of the Church, anyone who commits a mortal sin must receive the sacrament of penance. The reason for this is that the mortal sinner has rejected the salvation communicated to him by Jesus Christ through baptism. The guilt of a mortal sin and the eternal punishment due to it can be removed only by a personal application of the merits and satisfactions of the Passion of Jesus Christ. This is done in the sacrament of Penance. A sinner submits himself to the judgment of God and receives the word of forgiveness through the sacramental action of the priest. Emphasis on this aspect of penance would, I believe, help our non-Catholic brethren to a more sympathetic attitude toward it.

But emphasis on the sacramental grace of penance will bring us even closer to them. For they are terribly aware of the fact that they always stand under the judgment of God as sinners, whereas we tend to dismiss sin once it has been absolved. This is to block the sacramental grace of penance, which tends to penetrate the whole life of the Christian with sorrow for sin and the desire to satisfy for it.

Our sorrow and desire for satisfaction must not be confined to our own contributions in the way of mortal sin to the awful burden of sin resting on the world: they must also embrace our negligence which betrays itself in venial sins and our lack of generosity in responding to the appeals for penance that would stem the tide of the world's sin.

It occurred to me recently that this is the meaning of pre-Lent, if we note the Scripture readings assigned for these weeks. According to scripture scholars, the sacred author was concerned to show the rising tide of evil that followed the original fall and merited the deluge. What a story could be written of the evil today (crowned by the incineration of six million children of the Old Israel and the ashes of Hiroshima and Nagasaki) with the continued threat of a deluge of nuclear destruction. We, the people of God, *need* the sacramental grace of penance. . . .

The Sacrament of (The Last?) Anointing

There is something akin to a tug of war going on with this sacrament: anointing of the sick or anointing of the dying? It is, fortunately, somewhat one-sided, because those who would like to draw unction toward the sick are unwilling to sacrifice its power in the face of death.

An adequate discussion of this problem requires an investigation of the entire healing mission of Christ and His Church. This is not possible here; however, we may note some of its elements. There is the power of the entire sacramental system to communicate spiritual health so fully as to reduce considerably the intrusion of physical and mental disease. There is the charismatic ministry of healing, which still accounts for many miraculous cures throughout the Church. There is the power of exorcism, which if used in conjunction with modern mental healing techniques could be of great benefit to many troubled members of the Church.

That out of the vast complex of its healing ministry, the Church recognized one rite (promulgated by St. James) as sacramental, seems to me possible only because she was conscious of the fact that Christ had prepared one sacrament for His children at the great crisis of the Christian life. St. Thomas sums up the thought of the Middle Ages and the Council of Trent consecrated that thought in the phrase *"consummativum totius vitae christianae."* [17] Faced with the approach of death (because of an illness which doctors judge to be critical) the Christian may have two desires, expressed in a very apt phrase: "to be lifted up to heaven, or out of his sick bed." [18] Above all, though, he must prepare for death in such a way that he is truly sharing in the death of Christ Himself, paying the last farthing, it could well be, of the debt of sin. Is it surprising, then, that for this critical time, Christ would provide a final application, a final anointing, of His own Passion and Death, which, in a properly disposed Christian, could eradicate all the remains of sin, all the punishment due to sin, so that the soul would enter heaven immediately.

Many authors concentrate on the prayers to be recited after the anointings. It is to be hoped that the Church will do something about those prayers. At least, another prayer should be added to the ritual, to be used at the discretion of the minister, begging God in His mercy to release from misery a child of His, suffering from an incurable disease. This would free relatives and friends from foolish guilt feelings.

If, however, God raises the sick man up from his bed, he will arise strengthened in body and immeasurably invigorated in spirit. There should be no greater spur to a vigorous life of virtue than a brush with death, experienced with the aid of a "last" anointing that turns out to be not the last.

Orders and Matrimony

In the last two sacraments, the sacramental reality undoubtedly takes precedence in importance over the sacramental grace. In orders, it is the power of the hierarchical priesthood; in matrimony, the sacred bond, which is the permanent sacramental image of the union of Christ and His Church. Hence, the meaning of sacramental grace in these sacraments is wholly determined by the sacramental reality.

In speaking of orders, the emphasis should be placed on the bishops. They, as direct successors of the apostles, receive the fullness of the priesthood of Christ when they are consecrated; they alone can transmit it to others, who become bishops, priests, and deacons. The possession of hierarchical power, even though it be only instrumental to Christ, places these men in positions of superiority in the Church. But this is a completely unique superiority, for they must be at the service of all. This is the only kind of primacy that belongs to the Church of Christ. Obviously, for the worthy fulfilling of their offices they need a special mode of grace which will eradicate as much as possible the will to power, which was so badly distorted by original sin, and which will arouse in them a supernatural generosity in serving the faithful.

Something strikingly similar takes place in marriage. The attainment of the full perfection of Christian marriage, radically enshrined in the bond, can be reached only by the mutual service of husband for wife, of wife for husband, of father and mother for children.

The symbolic reality of marriage is the bond, which, as we know, symbolizes the union of Christ with His Church. It is a great good prepared by God for His children. It is a permanent, *common good*, which, invisible in itself, should be made as visible as possible in the lives of those bound by it. It is a common good on both the natural and supernatural levels. It is a good destined by God primarily for the offspring, but capable, in a subordinate way, of perfecting the spouses.

The sacramental grace of marriage is ordered to the fulfillment of Christ's will in admittedly difficult circumstances. It is a modification produced by the sacramental rite in the grace of the two being wed, which orders that grace and all appropriate virtues to the special effects of the Christian life demanded by the bond and remedies the defects of nature that are especially difficult to control in the marriage situation.[19]

In concluding this . . . [article], may I express the hope that the thoughts offered here may enable us all to repeat with awe the words of the liturgy: "O God, who renewest the world by Thine *ineffable* sacraments. . . ."

References

[1] J. J. Von Allmen, ed., *A Companion to the Bible* (New York: Oxford University Press, Inc., 1958), p. 34.

[2] *Theological Dimensions of the Liturgy* (Collegeville: The Liturgical Press), p. 57.

[3] *Christ, the Center of the Liturgy* (Clyde, Mo.: Benedictines), pp. 17-18.

[4] *Op. cit.*, pp. 6off.

[5] "The Sacraments: An Encounter with God," in *Christianity Divided* (New York: Sheed & Ward), esp. pp. 259-60.

[6] "The Mysteries of Christ and the Sacraments," *The Thomist*, XXV, 1 (1962), 34.

[7] *Ibid.*, p. 37 with n. 99. Vd. n. 191, in English translation of *Mediator Dei* in *Four Great Encyclicals of Pius XII* (New York: Paulist Press), p. 149.

[8] *Ibid.*, p. 46.

[9] *Ibid.*, p. 48 (it seems that Father O'Neill is making his own a suggestion of Father Barden, O.P., *What Happens at Mass*, Dublin, 1960).

[10] *S.T.*, III, q. 9, a. 3; q. 11, esp. a. 1, ad 3 um; q. 13, a. 2; q. 43, a. 2.

[11] *The Collected Works of Dom Vonier, O.S.B.*, II, p. 245.

[12] *S.T.*, I, q. 47.

[13] For a fuller development of this notion of sacramental grace, cf. R. R. Masterson, O.P., "Sacramental Grace: Modes of Sanctifying Grace," *The Thomist*, XVIII (1955), 3; J. M. Egan, O.P., "The Sacramental Grace of Matrimony," *Proceedings of the Eleventh Annual Convention of the Catholic Theological Society of America*, 1956.

[14] *S.T.*, III, q. 69, a. 3.

[15] Charles Schleck, C.S.C., "The Sacramental Character of Baptism and Worship," *National Liturgical Week* (Notre Dame, Ind., 1959).

[16] *Ancient Israel* (New York: McGraw-Hill Book Company, Inc.), pp. 417-18.

[17] *Summa Contra Gentiles*, IV, 73.

[18] Vd. J. S. Selner, S.S., *The Sunday Visitor* (Feb. 18, 1962).

[19] Egan, *art.* cit.

EDWARD KILMARTIN, S.J.

Patristic Views
of Sacramental Sanctification

The writings of the Fathers of the Church during the first centuries of Christianity manifested a continual development in their
understanding of the sacraments. In the following article, an
examination of the patristic writings on baptism shows how sacramental sanctification is essentially that of the Scriptures. Yet
at different periods early writers emphasized certain aspects without denying other considerations which their predecessors had
noted. The modern theologian is in the favorable position of
being able to synthesize these patristic reflections while he
continues the work of the theologian in attempting to come to a
fuller understanding of the sacraments.

Father Kilmartin is Professor of Sacramental Theology at Weston
College, Weston, Massachusetts.

Introduction

Several times in his Epistles, St. Paul speaks of Christ as the
mysterion of God.[1] In the very pregnant passage of 1 Timothy 3:16,
which apparently is a precipitate of a primitive liturgical hymn,
Christ is described as . . . the mystery of godliness

> Which was manifested in the flesh,
> Appeared to angels,
> Was preached to Gentiles,

This paper appeared first in the *Proceedings of the Eighth Annual Convention of the Society of Catholic College Teachers of Sacred Doctrine.* It is
reprinted here with the permission of the Society.

> Believed in the world,
> Taken up in glory.

Nevertheless this term was not restricted to Christ. The plan of redemption foreordained from all eternity by divine love and manifested in the fullness of time through the salvific work of Christ is called a *mysterion*.[2] Christ in us, the hope of our glory, is called a *mysterion*.[3] In Ephesians 3:3 the election of the Gentiles is called a *mysterion*.

From these observations we can conclude that for St. Paul *mysterion* refers to the whole redemptive plan of God which culminates in the union of Christ with redeemed mankind—in the perfection of the pneumatic Body of Christ. The sanctification of men will, therefore, be effected by a participation in this concrete *mysterion*. Though he does not use the word *mysterion* to explain the nature of the sacramental rites,[4] Paul certainly understands that the participation in the *mysterion* of salvation takes place above all in the sacraments of baptism and the Eucharist. The Pauline doctrine of the sacramental economy of salvation is summarized succinctly in the statement of St. Leo the Great: ". . . *quod itaque Redemptoris nostri conspicuum fuit, in sacramentis transivit*."[5] After His Ascension, in the words of St. Leo, the sacraments serve to render visible Christ and His redemptive work and lead the participant in the mystery celebration to a share in the life, death, and glory of the Lord.

The full import of this Pauline teaching about participation in the redemptive work of Christ through the sacraments, so clear in St. Leo's writings, was not always uppermost in the minds of Christians of the early Church. In fact it was slow to come to the surface in the patristic period. Some aspects of it are found in the writings of the second century. Origen, in the third century, shows a profound grasp of it. But it is not until the fourth century that it reaches its most perfect expression. However, while the nature of the sanctification effected by a participation in the redemptive *mysterion* was only gradually deepened, we may say without hesitation that from the beginning patristic writings relate this participation to the visible acts of the Church. From the Apostolic Fathers onward, we find an acute awareness of the essential *re-presentative* function of the Church. These writings witness to the task and power of the Church to *re-present* the redemptive work of Christ for the benefit of all men. This *re-presentative* function was considered to be operative for the individual first in the rite of baptism. While this visible rite aggregated the neophyte to the visible Church, the effect was understood to be more than juridical. It was spiritual —a participation in the *mysterion* of salvation.[6]

Moreover, though patristic writings stressed that the new life began with the rite of initiation and was nourished by the Eucharist, they did not limit sacramental sanctification to a participation in the Church's sacraments properly so called. They accentuated also the sanctifying power of the inspired word spoken in the Church and the other cultic acts of the Community. All these various actions were seen as being an epiphany of the sanctifying work of Christ, as efficacious for man's salvation; a means of effecting a salutary encounter with the glorified Lord. Hence Christian existence was above all characterized as sacramental: an existence continually determined by an encounter with the redemptive work within the bounds of history. Christian existence was above all related to the liturgical acts of the Church. In and by an encounter with the *mysterion* of Christ's redemptive work, through the mediation of the visible Church, man was sanctified. This life he received was a life flowing forth from the Community in its Liturgical celebrations.

By baptism the Christian became a participant in the new life in such wise that, while the mystery celebration passed, the mystery, the life, remained. Thus the author of the so-called *Second Epistle of St. Clement to the Corinthians* could address his fellow Christians as "we the living." [7] So close is this fellowship that, according to the revelation given to St. Patrick, Christ actually draws us into His dialogue with the Father: "He who laid down His life for you, He it is who speaks in you." [8] But however awesome, this life received in baptism was not conceived as something static. The Fathers of the Church look upon it as something that must grow. In its expansion, stress is placed on the function of the liturgical acts of the Church. For in the process of sanctification, while patristic writers unanimously insist upon personal effort, it is a personal effort which always draws its supernatural strength and inspiration from the liturgy.[9] Here in the midst of the brethren, Christ, the High Priest was understood as *re-presenting* anew the redemptive work by word and gesture in order that the Christian might be sanctified by taking part in the "redemptive drama" [10] as actor, by word and gesture cooperating in the mighty work of redeeming the world.

From what has been said it should be clear that to speak of patristic views of sacramental sanctification is to deal with a very extensive subject. There is the basic question of the actual understanding of sacramental sanctification at any particular period in the early Church. Again while sacramental sanctification refers radically to sanctification resulting from a participation in the redemptive work of Christ effected through the *re-presentative* power of the Church, one must distinguish degrees of sacramental participation effected by the various acts of the Church: the word spoken in her midst, the liturgical celebrations surrounding the sacraments, the seven sacraments. To a certain degree this distinction was made by the Fathers. We find an awareness from the beginning of the different effects of baptism and the Eucharist. Some writers such as St. Ambrose make a distinction between the nucleus of the baptismal rite—the dipping in water—and the lesser rites surrounding it. St. Ambrose calls Baptism the "*Magnum Mysterium*"; [11] the other rites, though efficacious mysteries, [12] are not placed on the same level with the bath. In this connection St. Leo the Great is of interest since he attributes significant value to the annual celebration of the mysteries of Christ's life. He does not conceive baptism, for example, operating independently of the liturgical mystery, precisely because these mysteries renew the corresponding mysteries of Christ's life from which the sacraments draw their efficacy. Nevertheless it is clear that St. Leo would distinguish degrees of efficacy between the scriptural reading of the feast, and the Eucharist (or baptism) which was associated with the complete liturgical celebration.

While the Fathers of the Church recognized the efficacy of the word and the cultic acts of the Church, within the scope of this sacramental action they were unanimous in according to the sacraments properly so called a unique place. They recognized sacraments "in particular" which served as means of an especially fruitful encounter with the Lord. Certainly they did not know of a treatise *De sacramentis in genere*, nor of the customary enumeration of the seven efficacious signs of grace which we have at hand today—an elaboration which would lead Western theologians to distinguish (too sharply at times) between a sacramental grace peculiar to each sacrament in contrast to a common effect, sanctifying grace, produced by all.[13] Nevertheless the Fathers recognized that the different sacraments had different effects. They were considered to mirror different life-giving traits of Christ and therefore of the Church,

His Body. We can say that the understanding of the individual sacraments at any time in the early Church concerned primarily the meaning of the sacraments for furthering the life of the Church. Through the sacraments man was understood to have received the new life or growth in that life.

Faced with the unanimous agreement of the patristic writers on the efficacious nature of the sacraments with respect to the new life and growth in that life, we should not immediately jump to the conclusion that the full meaning of that life, and so the full meaning of the sanctification effected by the sacraments, was equally recognized in each period of the patristic era. Actually it would seem that the New Testament understanding of sacramental sanctification, which reached its most advanced expression in the *Pauline Epistles*, was only gradually grasped. This can be shown especially in the matter of the baptismal teaching of the early Church, in conjunction with which the Fathers usually exposed their theology of grace.

This brings us to the main topic of this . . . [article]. Since it would be impossible to treat of all the aspects of sacramental sanctification found in patristic literature, the present discussion will be confined to the baptismal rite. Proceeding chronologically, we will trace the development of the understanding of important aspects of the sanctification effected by this rite. This study will help us to penetrate how the Fathers understood the function of the other sacraments in the economy of salvation. In particular we will draw some conclusions with regard to the sanctifying effects of confirmation.

Apostolic Fathers and Apologists

An analysis of the writings of the Apostolic Fathers and Apologists on the subject of baptismal sanctification reveals the following common doctrine.[14] (1) Baptism inserts the neophyte into the history of salvation by incorporating him into the Church. (2) Baptism bestows on the neophyte an existential change which effects his whole being. It gives him a new life. (3) This new life involves purification from sin and evil spirits, an illumination of the intellect and a divine presence. (4) All this is brought about by the redemptive work of Christ which is operative in this ecclesial rite.

If we prescind from St. Ignatius of Antioch, scarcely any hint of the effect of configuration to Christ, the presence of Christ in the Christian, or the divinization of the newly baptized is mentioned. In the written documents of this period, the new life is seen in the perspective of a moral engagement. Holiness is linked to the observance of the commandments. The new life involves especially purification from sin and the consequent obligation of guarding this purity. But this new life is not conceived as something static; it must grow in perfection by obedience to the law of God. While mention is made of the gift of the Spirit and His help in leading the new life, this aspect is not stressed, nor is the sanctification brought about by this divine presence developed. Perhaps we could say that the *Letter of Pseudo-Barnabas* is indicative of the concept of baptismal sanctification current at this period. In this document baptismal grace is pictured as fruit of a tree which gives eternal life.[15] While Barnabas sees baptism as efficacious through the Cross of Christ,[16] and while he speaks of Christ as the source of life,[17] seeming to indicate a presence of Christ in the Christian,[18] he does not develop the baptismal theology of Paul.[19] The concept of baptismal sanctification is not that of being crucified with Christ upon the Cross but rather of taking fruit from the tree of life.

This viewpoint is characteristic of this period. Even St. Ignatius of Antioch does not seem to have the Pauline outlook of Baptism being a death and resurrection with Christ. To be sure his thought is filled with the *en Christou* theology of St. Paul. For him the essence of the new life consists in an intimate union between Christ and the Christian.[20] But he understands baptism to effect the beginning of a union of Christ with the Christian, the perfection of which comes about by undergoing death and resurrection with Christ through martyrdom,[21] or for the ordinary Christian through the Eucharist.[22]

Consequently even in St. Ignatius' writings we do not find the Pauline notion of baptism being a participation in the death and resurrection of Christ. For Paul, dying and rising with Christ is accomplished in the rite of initiation.[23] The rest of the Christian's life will be a development of this crucial event. For St. Ignatius, the death and resurrection with Christ is the point of arrival. Whence suffering is of great importance, especially to suffer as a martyr. The real imitation of Christ's sufferings effects the perfect union with Christ.[24]

St. Irenaeus

We have seen that up to the middle of the second century extant writings of Christendom emphasize the purification effected by baptism. When we turn to St. Irenaeus, a new viewpoint prevails. His theology is dominated by the theory of *recapitulation*, that is, the taking up of all things into Christ.[25] According to St. Irenaeus, God rehabilitates the original divine plan which was interrupted by the Fall of Adam and gathers up His entire work from the beginning to renew it in Christ, the Second Adam. In this perspective the pardon of sins which takes place in baptism is of secondary importance. He does not stress it. Remission of sins is a stage in the process of restoring the divine likeness in men, but the important thing is the gift of the Spirit which gives man a resemblance to God, whereby man is made spiritual and perfect.[26] Baptism is a sort of climax of the *recapitulation* of creation in Christ. Yet this state effected in baptism, the new life wherein man resembles the Father,[27] is not static. Rather the possession of the Spirit is the first stage in the process of making man the image and likeness of God.[28] The Spirit is the means of acquiring perfection,[29] the point of departure in the process of divinization. Thus baptism introduces man into the history of salvation, a dynamic state leading to man's final end, the vision of God.[30]

From his writings it is clear that St. Irenaeus stresses union of man with the Holy Spirit; a union resulting in union with the Father and Son. He differs from St. Paul who teaches that by baptism man is inserted into Christ, configured to Christ's death and resurrection as a point of departure for complete sanctification. For St. Irenaeus, Christ is inserted into man by the Holy Spirit.[31] Nevertheless it would seem that the union between the baptized person and Christ, the Incarnate Word, is of the same order as that advocated by St. Paul.[32] In the words of one author, P. Gächter, this union should be called a *unio hypostatica accidentalis*.[33]

During the second century, therefore, the purification from sin and the gift of the Spirit are mentioned frequently in relation to baptismal sanctification. St. Ignatius and St. Irenaeus speak of a presence of the Incarnate Word in the soul of the baptized but do not draw on the Pauline doctrine of configuration to the death and resurrection of Christ. The *Passover Homily* of Melito of Sardis, discovered and published by C. Bonner in 1940,[34] likewise strengthens the conviction that the Pauline motif remained at best in the background of the thought of second century Christians. Melito calls the redemptive acts of Christ a *mysterion* "in the sense of actions having a supernatural effect beyond their historical setting." [35] According to him, in baptism the Passover sacrifice of Christ is applied to the believer effecting the seal of the Lord,[36] an antitype of the blood of the Paschal lamb.[37] The Passover sacrifice of Christ is further said to effect the baptismal gifts of liberty, light, life, and a participation in the new priesthood.[38] Yet no mention is made of the teaching of Romans 6. This leads us to the conclusion that the Pauline motif of Romans 6 was not considered to be of paramount importance to him. For the Passover Feast of the Church of Asia Minor in the time of Melito, as witnessed by his homily and other sources,[39] was celebrated as a remembrance of the redemption wrought by the Cross. It was a feast of deliverance of which the Exodus was a type fulfilled in Christ, the true Paschal lamb. Baptism, celebrated and explained in this context, takes the same meaning. The seal of the Spirit, given through the blood of Christ, is a means of deliverance. Melito relates baptism to the New Passover which is a remembrance of the death of Christ (and not precisely of the resurrection) and, therefore, to the death of Christ whence it draws its efficacy. But although he stresses, as did the Church of his environment, the relationship of baptism to the death of Christ, he does not indicate how the death of Christ effects the liberation. The concept of Christ's death and resurrection effecting, through baptism, a configuration of the neophyte to the crucified and risen Saviour escapes him.[40]

Third-Century Writers of the West

At the beginning of the third century, Tertullian offers a summary of second century teaching about Baptismal sanctification in his *De baptismo*. This is the only anti-Nicene treatise written about any of the sacraments.[41] According to this document, Baptism is the basis of Christian existence: "We little fish, like our Fish (*Icthus*), Jesus Christ, are born in water, and it is only by abiding in water that we are safe." [42] There is some confusion about the time of the bestowal of the Spirit in the rite of initiation. In the *Adversus Marcionem*[43] he says that the Spirit is given in water baptism itself, but in the *De baptismo* and in the *De resurrectione*, the Spirit bestowal is linked to the imposition of hands.[44] The imposition of hands is understood as a type of the descent of the Spirit on Christ at the Jordan.[45] While he does mention the priestly anointing[46] and the gift of the Spirit as being involved in the complete rite of initiation, Tertullian emphasizes the forgiveness of sins.[47] It is true that he mentions the fact that the neophyte is baptized in "the Lord's Passion," [48] and he does say that the Passion and Resurrection give efficacy to the rite.[49] Nevertheless the effect of configuration to Christ remains in the background.

St. Hippolytus of Rome also repeats the common doctrine of the second century. Indicating an acquaintance with St. Irenaeus' doctrine of *recapitulation*, he teaches that baptism effects a deification of man.[50] In the *Apostolic Tradition* of Hippolytus a second bestowal of the Spirit is linked to the imposition of hands.[51] This bestowal gives the grace to serve God.

St. Cyprian refers especially to the gift of the Spirit in baptism,[52] which provides the power to do good works.[53] With the reception of baptism man is given a spiritual form.[54] He puts on Christ, says St. Cyprian.[55] Yet despite this and several allusions to Romans 6, St. Cyprian does not develop the notion of baptism being a communion in the death and resurrection of Christ.[56] In connection with the rite of initiation we should note that St. Cyprian clearly distinguishes baptism from confirmation.[57] The Spirit, given by the imposition of hands, makes the Christian perfect.[58]

As with St. Cyprian, the anonymous author of the *De rebaptismate* makes no reference to the Pauline doctrine of Romans 6. But again he does distinguish baptism from confirmation. The imposition of hands gives the Holy Spirit.[59]

Third-Century Writers of the East

Clement of Alexandria summarizes much of the traditional understanding of baptismal sanctification: "Being baptized, we are illuminated: illuminated we become sons; being made sons, we are made perfect; being made perfect, we are immortal." [60] In his estimation baptism is the boundary line between life and death: "We then alone, who first have touched the confines of life, are made perfect; and we already live who are separated from death." [61] Moreover, he refers to the Pauline notion of the union between Christ and the Christian effected by baptism, quoting Galatians 3:26-28.[62] However he does not develop the consequences in accord with Pauline teaching. His theological synthesis, dominated by the idea of the Logos, led him down another path.[63]

Of far greater importance for the development of the understanding of baptismal sanctification is Origen, successor to Clement in directing the school for catechumens at Alexandria. Origen is quite conservative in his baptismal teaching apart from his speculation about baptism of fire to be administered before entrance into Paradise.[64] His teaching on baptism is uninfluenced by his speculations so often found in other matters. He faithfully records the tradition of his community.[65]

What is of interest for us is Origen's doctrine about the relationship of baptism to the history of salvation. He places in relief the fact that baptism accomplishes the salvation history process in us. It is a participation in the *Magnum Mysterium*—the triple manifestation of the Word in the Incarnation, the Church and the Scriptures. The place occupied by the tract *De sacramentis in genere* in modern theology is, in the Platonic theology of Origen, occupied by the *Sacramentum Genericum, Concretum.*[66] Thus the individual sacraments participate in a genus already concrete. By baptism, the communicated *mysterion* inserts man into the history of salvation; it reproduces the history of salvation in the individual. Working from this viewpoint, Origen insists on the effect of incorporation into the death and resurrection of Christ. Defining baptismal grace he says that it is a mystery which involves dying and rising with Christ: to be truly baptized is to be baptized in Christ's death.[67] He sees the perfect symbolism in the Holy Triduum of Christ,[68] and says that having been incorporated into the death and resurrection of Christ, "the Lord Himself will begin to guide you and show you the way of salvation." This important text shows, as Neunheuser points out,[69] how much Origen is inspired by St. Paul; how baptism inserts men into the history of salvation; how it reproduces this history in man.

Following upon this insight, Origen will insist on the presence of Christ in the soul of the baptized.[70] To this union with Christ (moral or ontological?) is joined the Holy Spirit who comes upon the baptized so that he possesses the gift of the Spirit and becomes pneumatic. This gift of the Spirit results in a true ontological sanctification: ". . . the grace of the Holy Spirit is at hand, that those beings who are not holy by their essence may be made holy by participating in this grace."[71] Nevertheless, despite the recognition of the possession of sanctity, Origen affirms the necessity of the progressive acquisition of perfection. The conformity to Christ dead and risen begins the process of transformation into the likeness of the Logos, the immediate image of the Father. But it must grow by the power of the Spirit. Perfection, however, will not be attained in this life. Only after death, in the bodily resurrection, will it be disclosed that the first conformity to the dead and risen Christ was a point of departure for the perfect conformity to the glorious humanity of Christ, and hence conformity to the Word of God and so to God.[72] In other words, as G. W. H. Lampe puts it, "The entire course of the Christian's progress in the spiritual life is an unfolding of what he already possesses and what in a sense he has already attained by virtue of being baptized." [73] The intimate relationship between baptism and the life of the Christian is described in Origen's *In Exodum homiliae* 10.4.[74] "In this remarkable passage," to quote Lampe again, "Origen explains that baptism is a proleptic summing up of the spiritual life which in its turn, is the working out in practice of that which baptism symbolizes; in and through the sacrament the believer is united to Christ, but the Logos comes to the soul as a child and as it were grows within it." [75]

For Origen, the truth of baptism, the mystery content of the symbol, is the mystical death,[76] a sacerdotal unction in view of the Cross;[77] just as the baptism of Christ in the Jordan was the image of that baptism more real which He awaited impatiently. For the Christian, Jordan and Calvary are inseparable. Whoever is baptized in water engages himself to realize the Cross.[78] Whence the deep mysticism of the Cross and the Crucified in Origen's writings.[79] The Christian is to live out of the mystery of baptism, out of the mystical death with Christ.

Fourth-Century Catecheses

The teaching of Origen on baptismal sanctification, unsurpassed in his own century, is found constantly in the great catecheses of the fourth century at Jerusalem, Antioch, and Milan.

The *Mystagogical Catecheses* of St. Cyril of Jerusalem[80] were addressed to the newly baptized after they had participated in the sacred mysteries. It was deemed more proper to receive the instruction on the full meaning of the Christian initiation after it had been experienced.[81] Already in the *Protocatechesis* St. Cyril had summarized most of the effects of baptism:[82] forgiveness of sins, adoption, the gift of the Spirit which sanctifies and deifies.[83] But now in the second *Mystagogical Catechesis* he emphasizes the effect of conformity to Christ crucified and risen: "Let no one then suppose that baptism is merely the grace of remission of sins, or further, that of adoption; as John's baptism bestowed only the remission of sins. Nay we know full well, that as it purges our sins, and conveys to us the gift of the Holy Ghost, so also it is the counterpart of Christ's sufferings. For, for this cause Paul, just now read, cried out aloud and says, *Know ye not that as many of us as were baptized into Christ Jesus, were baptized into His death? Therefore we are buried with Him by baptism into death.* These words he spake to them who had settled with themselves that baptism ministers to us the remission of sins, and adoption, but not that further it has communion also in representation with Christ's true sufferings." [84]

Just as with Origen, St. Cyril sees a perfect image of baptism in the Holy Triduum of Christ.[85] In baptism the neophyte dies and is buried and rises new born. That this death and resurrection is not physical, St. Cyril states clearly. It happens in figure; it is an imitation.[86] However the actual historically real death of Christ and the order of grace are so related to one another, that St. Cyril can say: "Christ was actually crucified, and actually buried, and truly rose again; and all these things have been vouchsafed to us, that we, by imitation communicating in His suffering, might gain salvation in reality." [87]

Baptism is thus depicted as the antitype of the sufferings of Christ. For St. Cyril the Platonist, however, there is no imitation, participation, or fellowship without the prototype being present. The natural, historical death of Christ and His resurrection is the prototype and the sacrament of baptism is the image. Thus in the sacrament, the neophyte is given a share in the historical death and resurrection of Christ. Yet this should not be understood as if the once-and-for-all physical reality of the death and resurrection of Christ is made present. St. Cyril does not say this. Nevertheless the image qualifies the faithful to experience the actual redemptive act and to share in the life it gives.[88] Baptism mediates a genuine share in the sufferings of Christ.[89] It accomplishes this in the symbolical rite. But this symbol is not a pure sign. It is filled with the reality of the new life. Its being is something intermediate between a pure sign and the pure reality.

What St. Cyril says of baptism in water holds also for the chrisma-tion which completes the rite of initiation.[90] Just as baptism is an antitype of the sufferings and resurrection of Christ, the chrismation is the antitype of the Spirit "wherewith Christ was anointed" at the Jordan.[91] In both cases there is question of a likeness in relation to the salvific work of Christ—a likeness of such a nature that it medi-ates the reality of the prototype. The result of the chrismation is to bring about the formation of the perfect Christian. Thus St. Cyril says: "Having been *baptized into Christ*, and *put on Christ*, ye have been made conformable to the Son of God; for God having *pre-destined us to the adoption of sons*, made us *share the fashion of Christ's glorious body*. Being therefore made *partakers of Christ*, ye are properly called Christs, and of you God said, *Touch not My Christs*, or anointed. Now ye were made Christs, by receiving the emblem of the Holy Ghost; and all things were in figure wrought in you, because ye are figures of Christ." [92]

By the rite of initiation the new Christian has been incorporated into the history of salvation. He has been incorporated not only into the death and resurrection of Christ but also into the mystery of Christ's public life. Furthermore he has been given the grace to live that life: "For as Christ after His baptism, and the descent of the Holy Ghost, went forth and vanquished the adversary, so like-wise, having, after Holy Baptism and the Mystical Chrism, put on the whole armour of the Holy Ghost, do ye stand against the power of the enemy and vanquish it, saying, *I can do all things through Christ which strengtheneth me*." [93]

The common faith of the Church of Antioch concerning bap-tismal sanctification is eloquently witnessed by the catecheses of St. John Chrysostom and Theodore of Mopsuestia.[94] The catecheses of St. John Chrysostom were discovered in 1955 by A. Wenger and edited by him in 1957. The catecheses of Theodore of Mopsuestia were found and published by A. Mingana in 1932.

In harmony with the teaching of St. Cyril of Jerusalem, St. Basil,[95] St. Gregory Nazianzus,[96] St. Cyril of Alexandria,[97] St. Gregory of Nyssa,[98] St. John Chrysostom makes use in his other writings of the concept of baptism being an insertion into the death of Christ.[99] He also takes up this theme in his *Baptismal Catecheses*.[100] Along with the traditional effects attributed to baptism,[101] Chrysostom stresses that the baptized has put on Christ, that Christ is present in the soul of the baptized.[102] He does not explain the ontological consequences of this presence of Christ, of the baptized being incorporated into Christ, but as Wenger points out[103] they are indicated in the *Commentary on the Epistle to the Galatians*: "Since you have the Son in you, configured to Him, you have been introduced into one and the same family and led to a like resemblance." [104]

The idea of putting on Christ is mentioned often.[105] Since the Christ present in us is the crucified Christ, it follows that the life He gives is marked as a life of crucifixion. This life will be expanded only in a crucified flesh.[106] And as it begins in the sacred liturgy of the Church, Chrysostom exhorts the newly baptized that they daily renew themselves both morning and evening in the midst of the brethren at Church.[107]

As with St. Cyril of Jerusalem, Chrysostom sees the rite of initiation as the beginning of a spiritual combat[108] in which the baptized, a soldier of Christ,[109] will be assisted by Christ who will provide the necessary weapons.[110] It is a spiritual combat set in the context of the Exodus from Egypt;[111] a spiritual battle in which one must not be concerned for himself alone. The neophyte has been introduced into the history of salvation of the People of God, initiated and being brought to consummation by divine love.[112] In consequence of God's purpose and in imitation of God's love, the baptized must be especially solicitous for all the members of the Church.[113]

In the *Catechetical Homilies* of Theodore of Mopsuestia we again meet the classical patristic approach of the East. Baptism is a type which affords us a participation in the redemptive work of Christ, especially His death and resurrection,[114] which happened in Christ once-and-for-all and which in us will reach full perfection in the resurrection.[115] While Theodore stresses that baptism is a type, this does not mean that it is an empty sign.[116] By this type we already participate in the future reality.[117]

Theodore speaks of a sealing before baptism which signifies that the Christian is a soldier of Christ.[118] The sealing after baptism mediates the Spirit which from now on continually remains with the person.[119] This latter sealing is compared to the anointing of Christ by the Holy Spirit at the Jordan after His baptism.[120]

In the West St. Ambrose provides us with a witness to the understanding of baptismal sanctification in the Church of Milan. His *De mysteriis* and *De sacramentis* are both mystagogical catecheses. It would seem that the *De mysteriis* is a literary work intended for publication, while the *De sacramentis* contains the notes written down by a scribe during the actual instructions.

Differing only in minor detail with the other catecheses we have seen, St. Ambrose stresses that Christ is actually present in the baptismal mystery.[121] The implications of Christ's presence are brought out in the *De sacramentis*, where he expresses the Pauline teaching of the configuration to the death and resurrection of Christ.[122] The neophyte dies to sin and rises to the new life in the rite of initiation. He accomplishes a Pascha, that is, a transition from sin to sanctification.[123] This sanctification, signified and effected by baptism, involves the indwelling of the Holy Spirit[124] who effects the new birth,[125] imprinting in the neophyte the divine image[126] by the formation of Christ within the soul.[127] Whence St. Ambrose is able to say: "Not we, who were, live, but Christ lives in us." [128]

A post-baptismal sealing is mentioned by St. Ambrose in both the *De mysteriis* and the *De sacramentis*. It gives perfection, the seven virtues of the Spirit.[129]

Conclusion

During the fourth century the Pauline teaching about baptismal sanctification being a configuration to the death and resurrection of Christ and the consequent indwelling of Christ was brought into prominence. It was the dominant motif. And the doctrine was not reserved for the elite. It was preached to all as the catecheses used at Jerusalem, Antioch, and Milan indicate. Both the learned and the simple understood the baptismal grace to be the gift of Christ Himself and His redemptive work mediated through the Spirit. Thus the crucial *New Testament* concept of filial adoption was developed to its fullness: (1) configuration to Christ; (2) a life of love in the Spirit.

But this conformity to Christ effected by baptism was never looked on as something static—a gift merely to be preserved. Rather it introduced the Christian into the history of salvation. It was a sanctification which bore a dynamic character for the People of God who remain under the sign of the *pas encore*. The Christian initiation implied, therefore, action for the future—not an action of a purely negative nature (the avoidance of sin or the protection of the baptismal gift of the Spirit), but action related to growth.

The Christian who received the new life was inaugurated on the way of perpetual progress. But this progress did not take the form of a *processus in infinitum*. It was a *processus in Christum*—in the Christ who was already present in the soul. Thus the passage from death to life was not reckoned as something purely eschatological. For it had actually happened in baptism. On the other hand it was not something completed in all its actuality with the rite of initiation. More properly it was understood to be taking place constantly while men remained in their mortal bodies. The function of the other sacraments, in this context, would be to expand this resemblance to Christ; to realize in the Christian a further aspect of the personal life of Christ. This outlook can be verified in the case of the sacrament of confirmation.

We have seen that the Fathers of the Church, where they distinguish confirmation from baptism, relate it to a special bestowal of the Spirit. Some Fathers, such as St. Cyprian and St. Ambrose, speak of confirmation as giving a perfection. But what is the nature of this bestowal of the Spirit? What is the nature of this perfection? To say, as St. Ambrose, that the new gift involves the seven virtues of the Spirit does not exhaust the meaning of confirmation for the Fathers. More accurately, as with baptism, the meaning of confirmation is found in its relation to salvation history—its relation to Christ and His redemptive work. We have already seen indications of this in the writings of Tertullian, St. Cyril of Jerusalem, and Theodore of Mopsuestia who link confirmation to the mystery of Christ's baptism at the Jordan. They understood that the second bestowal of the Spirit in the rite of initiation configures the Christian to the Christ of the public life.

In this context the idea of the Christian becoming a soldier of Christ, linked to the whole rite of initiation by St. John Chrysostom and Theodore of Mopsuestia, and explicitly related to confirmation by St. Cyril of Jerusalem, takes on its full significance. As soldier of Christ, consecrated as Christ was at the Jordan, the Christian is configured to Christ the worker in the Kingdom of the Father. The sanctification effected by confirmation, this new configuration to Christ, qualifies the Christian in a special way not only to struggle against the enemies of the Church, but also to work for the increase of the Kingdom. This was the meaning of Christ's unction at the Jordan according to the New Testament[130] and such is the meaning of confirmation in the Fathers. This interpretation is confirmed by a study of the relation which patristic writings make between Pentecost and confirmation.[131]

The classical patristic view of sacramental sanctification is really that of the Scriptures. It differs from the so-called traditional presentation found in the late Western Church which tends to view the work of Christ as completed on Calvary, while the fruits of that achievement are applied in the Mass and the other sacraments of the Church. For the Fathers, as for the Scriptures, the economy of salvation is presented as a process of redemption still in progress. The event of initiation is not described as something sufficient in itself, extratemporal, but as an episode in a long history of salvation, in an immense drama, which began with creation and ends with the parousia.[132]

In this framework, the function of the rite of initiation is not so much to bestow on us the fruit of the Cross, as to crucify us with Christ. And having been incorporated into Christ, the Christian, sharing the same Spirit, shares also the same drive of the Spirit which urges the Christ within him to save the world about him. The sacraments, therefore, are the means by which the Christian, configured more perfectly to Christ, is implicated more profoundly in the *processus in Christum:* the salvation history which, while completed in Christ, must be realized in the individual and, indeed, in the whole Church. In this perspective sacramental grace is precisely a special participation in the life of Christ, an elevation of the whole being, whereby the Christian, according to his grade, is enabled to share actively in the very redemptive work of Christ as another Christ.

References

[1] 1 Corinthians 2:1—variant reading; cf. Colossians 2:3, 4:3.

[2] 1 Corinthians 2:7-10; Ephesians 3:2.

[3] Colossians 1:27.

[4] Ephesians 5:32 does not speak of matrimony as a *mysterion* in so far as a sacramental rite.

[5] *Sermo,* 74.2 (PL, 54.398).

[6] The importance of the *re-presentative* function of the Church in the eyes of the Fathers is well known. Through union with the Community the Christian was understood to have obtained fellowship with God and Christ. This doctrine is treated by H. de Lubac in *Catholicisme,* 4th ed. (Paris, 1947), who considers it the "constant teaching of the Church" (*ibid.,* p. 57). Thus sacramental sanctification is conferred in and by the Church. Such is the relation-

ship between the sacraments and the Church that, to quote de Lubac, "All the sacraments are essentially 'sacraments in the Church'; in her alone they produce the full effect, for in her alone, 'the society of the Spirit', is there, normally speaking, a sharing in the gift of the Spirit" (*ibid.*, pp. 57-58).

[7] *Epistula II ad Corinthios* 3.1; ed. K. Bihlmeyer, *Die Apostolischen Väter* I, 2nd ed. (Tübingen, 1956), p. 72.

[8] *Confessio*, 24; cf. O. St. John Gogarty, *I Follow St. Patrick* (New York, 1938), p. 299.

[9] Generally the Fathers of the Church do not discuss the mediation of divine life outside the sacraments. Cf. M. Schmaus, *Katholische Dogmatik*, IV, 1 (München, 1957), p. 65.

[10] Clement and Alexandria, *Protrepticus*, 110.2 (*Die griechischen christlichen Schriftsteller* 1.78. Hereafter: *GCS*).

[11] *De mysteriis*, 19 (*Corpus scriptorum ecclesiasticorum latinorum*, 73.96. Hereafter: *CSEL*).

[12] For example, the rite called "the mystery of the opening" [*De mysteriis*, 3 (*CSEL*, 73.90)] and the washing of the feet, thought to remove hereditary sin [*De mysteriis*, 32 (*CSEL*, 73.102); *De sacramentis*, III.5 (*CSEL*, 73.40)].

[13] There is a growing tendency to look on all grace in this economy of salvation as sacramental. For an explanation of this viewpoint, cf. J.-H. Nicolas, "La grâce sacramentelle," *Revue Thomiste*, 61 (1961), 523-38.

[14] For an analysis of the teaching of the Apostolic Fathers (*Didache, The Epistle of St. Clement of Rome to the Corinthians, The Letters of St. Ignatius of Antioch, The Letter of the Pseudo-Barnabas*, The homily called *The Second Epistle of St. Clement, The Shephard of Hermas*) and the *Apologists* (St. Justin, Tatian, Theophilus of Antioch), cf. A. Benoit, *Le baptême chrétien au second siècle. La théologie des Pères* (Paris, 1953), pp. 1-185.

[15] *Epistula Barnabae*, 11.10 (Bihlmeyer, *op. cit.*, p. 24).

[16] *Ibid.*, 11.1.8 (Bihlmeyer, pp. 23-24).

[17] *Ibid.*, 11.2-3 (Bihlmeyer, pp. 23-24).

[18] *Ibid.*, 6.14-15 (Bihlmeyer, p. 17). Concerning this text, cf. P. Prigent, *L'Epître de Barnabé I-XVI et ses sources* (Paris, 1961), pp. 89-90.

[19] Romans 6.

[20] *Epistula ad Magnesios*, 12; *Epistula ad Ephesios*, 9.2; 15.3 (Bihlmeyer, *op. cit.*, 92.85.87). St. Ignatius does not stress the presence of the Holy Spirit nor the ontological sanctification resulting from this presence.

[21] *Epistula ad Ephesios*, 1.2; *Epistula ad Trallianos*, 5.2; *Epistula ad Romanos*, 4.2; 5.2; 6 (Bihlmeyer, pp. 82, 94, 98, 99, 99-100).

[22] Cf. A. Benoit, *op. cit.*, p. 81.

[23] Romans 6.

[24] Cf. A. Benoit, *op. cit.*, pp. 80-81, where he summarizes the endeavor of Th. Preiss ("La Mystique de l'imitation du Christ et de l'unité chez Ignace d'Antioch," *Revue d'Histoire et de Philosophie Religieuses*, 18 (1938), 197-241) to distinguish between the Pauline conception of sanctification (one of participation) and that of St. Ignatius (one of imitation).

[25] J. Quasten, *Patrology*, I (Westminster, 1950), 295-97, with biliography.

[26] *Adversus haereses*, 5.6.1; ed. W. W. Harvey, *Sancti Irenaei episcopi Lugdunensis libros quinque adversus haereses*, II (Cantabrigiae, 1857), 333. Cf. E. Peterson, L'Immagine di Dio in S. Ireneo," *Scuola cattolica*, 19 (1941), 3-11.

[27] *Adversus haereses*, 5.16.1-2; Harvey, 367-68.

[28] *Adversus haereses*, 5.8.1; Harvey, 339.

[29] *Adversus haereses*, 5.8.1-2; Harvey, 339-41.

[30] *Adversus haereses*, 4.20.1-10; Harvey, 214-21.

[31] A. Benoit, *op. cit.*, 220.

[32] *Adversus haereses* 3.19.1; 5.1.3; 5.2.1-3; 5.14.2; 5.6.2. Harvey, 102-103; 316-317; 317-324; 361-362; 335-336. Cf. M. Schmaus, *op. cit.*, III, 2 (München, 1956), 60.

[33] P. Gächter, "*Unsere Einheit mit Christus nach dem hl. Irenäus*," *Zeitschrift für katholische Theologie*, 58 (1934), 503-34. It is worthy of note that St. Irenaeus is vitally cognizant of the ecclesial aspect of the rite of initiation. Baptism is said to effect the union of Christians among themselves: "For our bodies have received unity among themselves by means of the laver which leads to incorruption. . . ." *Adversus haereses*, 3.17.2; Harvey, 93.

[34] *The Homily on the Passion by Melito Bishop of Sardis;* Studies and Documents, 12 (London, 1940). For the latest edition of the Greek text, cf. B. Lohse, *Die Passa-Homilie des Bishofs Meliton von Sardis;* Textus Minores, 24 (Leiden, 1958).

[35] J. Quasten, *op. cit.*, I, 243.

[36] C. Bonner, *op. cit.*, 11.4-9; B. Lohse, *op. cit.*, 25.

[37] C. Bonner, *ibid.*, 3.4-14; B. Lohse, *ibid.*, 13-14.

[38] C. Bonner, *ibid.*, 11.15-20; B. Lohse, *ibid.*, 26.

[39] E. J. Kilmartin, "Liturgical Influence on John 6," *Catholic Biblical Quarterly*, 22 (1960), 185.

[40] That the Pauline motif is absent from the second-century orthodox writings is the main burden of Benoit's book already mentioned. B. Neunheuser, *Taufe und Firmung* (Handbuch der Dogmengeschichte IV; Freiburg im Br., 1956), 40, concurs on this point.

[41] The only other anti-Nicene document devoted to a sacrament is St. Cyprian's *Epistula*, 63 (CSEL, 3.701-17) which deals with the Eucharist.

[42] *De baptismo*, 1 (CSEL, 20.201).

[43] *Adversus Marcionem*, 1.28 (CSEL, 47.329-30).

[44] *De baptismo*, 6-8 (CSEL, 20.206-208); *De resurrectione*, 8 (CSEL, 47.37).

[45] *De baptismo*, 8 (CSEL, 20.207).

[46] *De baptismo*, 7 (CSEL, 20.206-207).

[47] B. Neunheuser, *op. cit.*, 40.

[48] *De baptismo*, 19 (CSEL, 20.217).

[49] *De baptismo*, 11.13.19 (CSEL, 20.210.212-13.217).

[50] *Philosophumena*, 10.34 (GCS, 3.293); *Sermo in sancta Theophania*, 10 (GCS, 1.2.262-263).

[51] B. Botte, *Hippolyte de Rome. La Tradition Apostolique* (Sources Chrétien, 11; Paris, 1946), 52.

[52] *Epistula*, 74.5 (CSEL, 3.2.803).

[53] *Ad Donatum*, 3-4 (CSEL, 3.1.5-6).

[54] *Epistula*, 74.5 (CSEL, 3.2.803).

[55] *Ibid.*

[56] B. Neunheuser, *op. cit.*, 46.

[57] *Epistula*, 74.7; 73.9 (CSEL, 3.2.804.784-85).

[58] *Epistula*, 73.9 (CSEL, 3.2.784-85).

[59] *De rebaptismate*, 4-6 (CSEL, 3.3.73-76).

[60] *Paedagogus*, 1.6.26.1 (GCS, 1.105).

[61] *Paedagogus*, 1.6.27.1 (GCS, 1.106).

[62] *Paedagogus*, 1.6.31.1 (GCS, 1.108).

[63] For Clement's teaching on the progressive intellectual assimilation to God, cf. A. de la Barre, "Clément d'Alexandrie," *Dictionnaire de théologie catholique*, 3.171ff.

[64] *In Lucam homiliae*, 24 (GCS, 9.158).

[65] J. Danielou, *Origen* (New York, 1955), p. 52.

[66] H. Urs von Balthasar, *Parole et mystère chez Origène* (Paris, 1957), p. 99.

[67] *In Romanos commentarii*, 5.8 (PG, 14.1040).

[68] *In Exodum homiliae*, 5.2 (GCS, 6.186).

[69] B. Neunheuser, *op. cit.*, 32.

[70] *In Romanos commentarii*, 8.2 (PG, 14.1164); 5.9 (PG, 14.1043); *In Lucam homiliae*, 22.1 (GCS, 9.144).

[71] *De principiis*, 1.3.8 (GCS, 5.61). Cf. W. Burghardt, *The Image of God in Man According to Cyril of Alexandria* (Woodstock, 1957), p. 79.

[72] Cf. W. Burghardt, "The Image of God in Man: Alexandrian Orientations," *Proceedings of the Sixteenth Annual Convention of the Catholic Theological Society of America* (1961), pp. 150-52.

[73] G. W. H. Lampe, *The Seal of the Spirit* (London, 1951), p. 163.

[74] GCS, 6.250.

[75] G. W. H. Lampe, *op. cit.*, 169.

[76] *In Romanos commentarii*, 5.8 (PG, 14.1040).

[77] *In Leviticum homiliae*, 9.9 (GCS, 6.436).

[78] Urs von Balthasar, *op. cit.*, 104.

[79] J. Quasten, *op. cit.*, II, 100.

[80] F. L. Cross, *St. Cyril of Jerusalem's Lectures on the Christian Sacraments. The Protocatechesis and the Five Mystagogical Catecheses* (Texts for Students, 51; London, 1951). On the authenticity of this work, cf. F. L. Cross, *ibid.*, xxxvi-xxxix; also, J. Quasten, *op. cit.*, III, 363-66.

[81] *Mystagogical Catechesis*, 1.1.

[82] *Protocatechesis*, 16.

[83] *Catechesis*, 4.16 (PG, 33.476).

[84] *Mystagogical Catechesis*, 2.6 (Cf. F. L. Cross, *op. cit.*, 61-62).

[85] *Mystagogical Catechesis*, 2.4.

[86] *Mystagogical Catechesis*, 2.5.

[87] *Mystagogical Catechesis*, 2.5 (Cf. F. L. Cross, *op. cit.*, 61).

[88] *Mystagogical Catechesis*, 2.7.

[89] *Mystagogical Catechesis*, 2.6-7.

[90] *Mystagogical Catechesis*, 3.

[91] *Mystagogical Catechesis*, 3.2.

[92] *Mystagogical Catechesis*, 3.1 (Cf. F. L. Cross, *op. cit.*, 63-64).

[93] *Mystagogical Catechesis*, 3.4 (Cf. F. L. Cross, *op. cit.*, 65-66).

[94] A. Wenger, *Huit catéchèses baptismales inédites* (Sources Chrétien, 50; Paris, 1957).—A. Mingana, *Commentary of Theodore of Mopsuestia on the Lord's Prayer and on the Sacraments of Baptism and the Eucharist* (Woodbrooke Studies, 6; Cambridge, 1933). French translation and reproduction of the Syriac text by R. Tonneau and R. Devreesse, *Les Homélies catéchétiques de Théodore de Mopsueste* (Studi e Testi, 145; Vatican City, 1949).

[95] *De Spiritu Sancto*, 15.35 (PG, 32.129).

[96] *Oratio*, 40.9 (PG, 36.369).

[97] *In Lucam commentarius*, 2.22 (PG, 72.497).

[98] *Oratio catechetica magna*, 32-36 (PG, 45.84-92).

[99] *In epistula ad Romanos homiliae*, 10.4 (PG, 60.480); *In Joannem homiliae*, 25.2 (PG, 59.151).

[100] *Catechesis*, 7.22 (Wenger, 240).

[101] *Catechesis*, 3.5-6 (Wenger, 153-54).

[102] *Catechesis*, 4.4; 4.17-18; 5.18 (Wenger, 184.191-92.209).

[103] A. Wenger, *op. cit.*, 184, n.2.

[104] *In epistula ad Galatas commentarius*, 3.27 (PG, 61.656).

[105] *Catechesis*, 4.16; 5.18 (Wenger, 191.209).
[106] *Catechesis*, 4.28 (Wenger, 196-97).
[107] *Catechesis*, 8.16-17 (Wenger, 256-57).
[108] *Catechesis*, 3.8 (Wenger, 155).
[109] *Catechesis*, 1.18; 4.6; 5.27 (Wenger, 118.185.213).
[110] *Catechesis*, 3.8-11 (Wenger, 155-58).
[111] *Catechesis*, 3.23 (Wenger, 164ff).
[112] *Catechesis*, 1.8; 2.4 (Wenger, 110.229).
[113] *Catechesis*, 2.30; 6.18-19; 5.14 (Wenger, 150.224.207).
[114] *Homily*, 14.5; 6.13; 10.19; 13.14 (Tonneau, 413.155.273.393).
[115] *Homily*, 14.2-6; 14.24 (Tonneau, 405-13.453).
[116] *Homily*, 14.6 (Tonneau, 413).
[117] *Homily*, 14.27; 14.7 (Tonneau 457-59.417).
[118] *Homily*, 13.17-18 (Tonneau, 397-99).
[119] *Homily*, 14.27 (Tonneau, 457).
[120] *Ibid.*
[121] *De mysteriis*, 26-27 (CSEL, 73.99-100); cf. *De mysteriis*, 7 (CSEL, 73.91); *Apologia prophetae David*, 12.58 (CSEL, 32.2.340: "*Faciem ad faciem te mihi, Christe, demonstrasti; in tuis te invenio sacramentis.*"
[122] *De sacramentis*, 2.20.23; 3.2 (CSEL, 73.34-35.37-38).
[123] *De sacramentis*, 1.12 (CSEL, 73.20).
[124] *De Spiritu Sancto*, 1.6 (PL, 16.752); *De sacramentis* 6.6-7 (CSEL, 73.74).
[125] *De mysteriis*, 59 (CSEL, 73.116).
[126] *De Spiritu Sancto*, 1.6 (PL, 16.752).
[127] *De sacramentis*, 6.6-7 (CSEL, 73.74).
[128] *Epistula*, 44.16 (PL, 16.1190).
[129] *De mysteriis*, 42 (CSEL, 73.106); *De sacramentis*, 3.8 (CSEL, 73.42).
[130] Luke 4:18-19.
[131] J. Lecuyer, "La Confirmation chez les Pères," *Maison-Dieu*, 54 (1958), 47-51.
[132] J. Lecuyer, "Théologie de l'initiation chrétienne d'après les Pères," *Maison-Dieu*, 58 (1959), 5-26.

CHARLES SCHLECK, C.S.C.

The Sacramental Character of Baptism and Worship

The sacraments are actions in which Christ continues the worship of God while He sanctifies His members. Baptism and its character play an important role in the economy of Christian worship because, by baptism, a man is incorporated into Christ and shares in the Christian priesthood. In this article, the concept of the priesthood of the laity is examined; the author accepts the distinction between the spiritual and sacramental priesthood and attempts to suggest deeper insights into a very complex and basic mystery.

Father Schleck teaches theology at The University of Notre Dame, Notre Dame, Indiana.

Whenever the negative manifestations of any institution begin to increase (and this very often occurs when an historical epoch is coming to an end) there arise tensions, crises, experiments, and questionings, a kind of groping for new ways and lights by which the deeper shades and shadows within an ancient truth might be the more richly grasped. Our own age is just such an era of transition in many ways; and this searching and probing finds its expression and realization even in the Church herself. The struggle for rebirth (since the Church is often presented to us under the figure of a phoenix) is very evident in our time and its course is at once full of

This article first appeared in *Participation in The Mass*, the Proceedings of The Twentieth North American Liturgical Week. It is reprinted with permission of The Liturgical Conference.

mistakes as well as of happy triumphs, of humiliations as well as of great promise.

This struggle is not something that is necessarily opposed to wisdom. For it is a clear principle of wisdom that all progress is truly such if it knows how to add new conquests to old, to join new benefits to those which have been acquired in the past, if it realizes that wisdom is an accumulation of knowledge, that capital is acquired or made out of experience. Nor is it opposed to tradition, for if this means anything, it means a "receiving of a heritage and the handing on of it, but in such a way that vital additions are made to it, original contributions which, although they do not at all change its essence, nevertheless enable that essence to meet the constantly emerging situations and needs of its day." [1]

In our own day we are seeing just such a renovation regarding the precise role of the laity in the Church, and perhaps in a special way, in their relationship to its worship. And because this renovation has been directed largely to the laity itself, it has often been presented by what we might call intermediate, or better, mediating images which attempt to bring down abstract truths to life. The reason for this is, I think, somewhat obvious. For the more a supernatural truth is presented in purely intellectual terms, the greater the risk there is of its becoming desiccated, even, we might say, of its becoming unuseful and inapplicable to the piety of the faithful and the building up of the City of God in love. Mere knowledge is rarely a stimulus to love. And so if we would receive a truth into our very being, into the marrow so to speak of our body and soul, the best way is to use some natural basis or to discover some affinity, some sort of echo of it in our own acquaintance. Thus, for example, if beauty were presented to the mind alone instead of being incarnated in the difference of sex, it is probable that its ardent devotees would be few. Or if, for example, divine love were presented to us merely in abstract philosophical terms rather than by means of symbols, such as the Sacred Heart or the Eucharistic Heart, acting as a kind of "mediating image," we would hardly reach the majority of people. Such imagery, common to the learned and the ignorant alike, is often the only means by which simple souls can grasp the faith or an object of faith in a way that is capable of influencing their lives. But in such an attempt—to bring down abstract and revealed truths to life—we must be most cautious. For the mediating image, unless it has been given to us in revelation or through the magisterium of the Church or through time-worn and well-accepted tradition, could be somewhat misleading.

For this reason it is above all necessary for those who are charged with the duty of protecting and of explaining or unfolding the riches of revealed truth to go beyond or behind the mediating image involved and find the exact rational content of the institution or aspect of the mystery before our gaze. And this they must do without creating a divorce between knowledge and affective love, or between doctrine and life. Thus, if it is a mark of a true intellectual to discover the principal outlines of his field and then consecrate himself to them, then the theologian cannot without betraying himself and his discipline neglect what is perhaps the most urgent part of his illuminating mission. For one of the principal functions of theology is to explore and coordinate by rational analysis the content of Scriptural revelation made under the guidance of tradition, the living voice of the Church.

The approach which we will take in the consideration of the problem at hand—the relation of the sacramental character of baptism to worship, or more exactly to the Sacrifice of the Mass—will not be the positive approach, which would include a detailed study or analysis of the Scriptural, historical, and magisterial sources. Rather, it is our intention to set down certain conclusions that can be gathered from recent papal pronouncements in this regard, and from there by a rational analysis attempt to embody in human language the response of faith to this teaching, by attempting to make clearer (to the human mind) the depth of the mystery that is contained in it. It is precisely there that the theologian in general and myself in particular will encounter our greatest challenge.[2] The presentation that will be set forth here is not at all meant to be the only or the unique solution possible; nor is it even being proposed as the best that has been arrived at thus far. I am merely proposing it as an attempt to make some contribution to, or at least inaugurate or stimulate, further thought and reflection on the problem before us. What we will attempt to do is to present a kind of X-ray image of the fundament of the lay priesthood or of the character of baptism by which this is essentially and fundamentally constituted, and its relation to the Sacrifice of the Mass. And while we admit that an X-ray image cannot be as attractive as the smiling face of the reality, so to speak, still it does reveal the structure of such to a decided advantage at times; indeed, for some purposes it is the only picture which can actually be of service.

In recent years there has been a flood of literature on the subject of the priesthood of the laity, some of which has deepened our understanding of this mystery and some of which has obscured it. It was for this reason that our late Holy Father, Pius XII, spoke on the subject on several occasions indicating both his interest in the research and investigation that was going on, as well as his concern over some of the explanations that had been advanced,[3] because some authors had not only exceeded the bounds of caution and prudence, but even of truth. While it must be admitted that no final and philosophical analysis of the lay priesthood has as yet been given by the magisterium of the Church, still it seems that we do have a working fundament at our disposal, enabling us to carry out a bit of research along these lines with a certain amount of directed vision. It seems that we might say that the following are the guiding norms which the speculative theologian must keep in mind in his attempt to arrive at some understanding, analogical of course, of this mysterious reality which lies at the very foundations of the Church, the Mystical Body of Christ:

1. The priesthood of the laity, profound and mysterious as it is, differs not merely in degree, but in essence from the priesthood properly so called. This latter resides in the power of taking the place of the High Priest, Christ, and enacting the sacrifice of Christ Himself. Consequently, because the faithful do not possess the priesthood properly so called, they do not possess in any way sacerdotal right or true power to offer sacrifice, which is the chief duty of the priest.[4]

2. On the other hand, the faithful do have some kind of priesthood called "common" which may not be minimized. This priesthood is founded on the sacramental character of baptism by means of which they are incorporated into the Mystical Body of Christ.[5]

These seem to be the guiding lines from which all rational analysis must flow in order for us to arrive at some understanding of this most mysterious and intriguing reality possessed by all the baptised, who as we are told, "exercise an active liturgical participation by virtue of their baptismal character, because of which in the Holy Sacrifice of the Mass they offer in their own way and along with the priest, the divine victim to God the Father." [6] All the words of this last statement coming to us from the now well-known instruction of the Sacred Congregation of Rites must be kept in mind as we attempt to grasp or understand the relationship between the sacramental character of baptism and worship.

The Lay Priesthood, Spiritual and Sacramental

There is an old scholastic adage which reads . . . "he who distinguishes well, does well," and I believe that this is also very true in the present problem. For to understand the sacramental priesthood of the laity we must distinguish it from their spiritual priesthood. For it seems that much of the difficulty involved in the question comes from a failure to understand the import of these two aspects of the one lay priesthood. In fact we can say that the exposé of the solution to be given lies merely in an analysis of these two facets of the one reality.

The Spiritual-Real Priesthood of the Laity

If we consider the various texts in the New Testament which speak of the royal priesthood or spiritual priesthood of the faithful [7] we find that in them there is always reference made to the priesthood of holiness. And this is the common or general consensus of biblical scholars in their view of these texts. Thus for the faithful to be a holy priesthood—to make spiritual offerings—is for them to build a sanctuary wherein God dwells and is honored.[8] The very acts of this priesthood, such as they are indicated in the sacred writings, clearly indicate that there is question here of a priesthood which has as its *immediate and proximate* fundament that effect of Christ's sacrifice which we call sanctifying grace. They are sacrifices of praise, the confession of faith, and the various spiritual and corporal works of mercy—charity, generosity, alms-giving, teaching, the handing on of saving truths—all of which are definitely not of a liturgical or ritual nature, at least directly in the strict sense of that word. By saying this, we do *not* mean or intend to say that the linking up of the royal or spiritual priesthood with the Eucharist was something that did not at all exist in New Testament times. What we mean to say is that the other idea—that of the spiritual priesthood referring to the priesthood of holiness—is the *predominant* idea and the one that is directly intended by the inspired writer. The sacrifice and cultus to which the priesthood of the faithful is expressly attributed or referred is chiefly that of a good life, the exercise of the theological virtues, of mortification—especially that which consists in martyrdom—family prayer, celibacy or virginity, insofar as these are connected or linked up with the virtue of religion and are consequently acts of worship. Thus the moral life, or more widely the whole spiritual life, is able to rank as worship. Nor was this notion something that was abandoned rather quickly with the passage of the years. In fact it is one of the striking features of the study of theology such as we find it in the *Summa* of the Angelic Doctor. For the entire Second Part treats of man's return to God from whom he has come forth in his creation, a return which is realized in and through man's spiritual or virtuous activity. There is, then, very definitely more than a coincidence of matter and content between man's spiritual activity analyzed so thoroughly in this part of the *Summa* and the concept of sacrifice described by St. Augustine and St. Thomas.[9] For the latter, we know, the whole life of the Christian can have the value of worship and even of sacrifice insofar as it grows under the influence of the virtue of religion. Moreover, even today it is with reference to this "spiritual priesthood" and its corresponding "liturgy" that we find authors speaking of the liturgy as a cosmic work—the offering to God of all that is his; space, time, and all inanimate matter.[10]

Thus we can say that it appears that there is a direct connection between the thought of Peter and that which had been so often expressed in the Old Testament. For just as there was something priestly about Israel such that this quality was attached to the people as such, making them a praising and worshipping people set aside as a kind of living witness or sign or sacrament to the peoples about them, so too, in the New Covenant, what God wanted of His *plebs sancta* was the man himself, a spiritual, rational, holy worship that he might render to Him as a son, as one sharing and participating in his own intimate life.[11] The "title" by means of which the people would be able to exercise this priesthood was the seal or the consecration which we call sanctifying grace, as St. Thomas has so clearly pointed out.[12] Thus in the order of "sacrifice" we are considering it is by means of grace that the order or relationship required for one to have access to and acceptance before God is realized.

From this it follows that the spiritual priesthood of the laity, established or found as it is on the reality which we call sanctifying grace, is not necessarily and probably not even wisely called meta-phorical. The faithful are said to be priests truly and properly, but *in the order of reality under consideration*, that is, in the order of sanctifying grace. Consequently, we can speak of the spiritual priest-hood of the faithful, by means of which they offer spiritual sacri-fices acceptable to God, or by means of which they unite themselves or adhere to God in holy fellowship, as a real and true priesthood; it is one which they exercise not as an instrument of Christ (which is true of the so-called sacramental priesthood) but rather, as an adopted son of God, exercising divine-like actions after the manner of a secondary principal cause, since it is precisely in virtue of this reality that they are said to offer reasonable service or worship unto God.[13] If we take the term or expression "spiritual or royal priest-hood" in the biblical, and Augustinian sense (that is, every work done with the aim of uniting oneself with God in holy fellowship or every work that is referred as its end to that good which can make us truly blessed)[14] we can say that all in the state of grace have a priesthood that is true and real *in its own order*—that of grace. For this has also been considered in Catholic tradition as a state in which the economy of God's gifts reaches its end and is realized, that is, attains its truth, within man himself. If, however, we take the words "real and true" as referring *only* to that sacrifice and priesthood which has reference to a worship that is exterior and public, then the laity, by reason of their title of holiness or in virtue of the sanctifying grace which they possess, can be called priests only in a wide or broad and perhaps even equivocal sense, because grace and the sacramental character confer two specifically distinct modes of participation in the priesthood of Christ,[15] modes which although ordered to one another, do not at all seem to be *analogically* related to one another. Supposing, then, we were unable to speak of any other sacrifice as such other than that which is a ritual, liturgical sacrifice, then the term "spiritual priesthood" under-stood as we have described it would be a misnomer. But since we know that the notion of "sacrifice" in Christian tradition has re-ferred to and does even now refer to a wider field of exercise and endeavor and activity than the strictly liturgical or ritual, the notion of priesthood can also have a wider application than that which is possessed only by those who offer up a strictly liturgical or ritual sacrifice or cult.[16]

The Sacramental Priesthood of the Laity

In addition to this aspect of the lay priesthood there is another, one which from our point of view is perhaps more important; and that is the sacramental priesthood of the laity. The fact of its existence is beyond questioning, since it has been the object of repeated pronouncements on the part of the magisterium itself in the last few years. Moreover, even the very title or fundament of this priesthood has been more than adequately determined. Thus Pius wrote in the encyclical *Mediator Dei:*

> Nor is it to be wondered at that the faithful should be raised to this dignity. By the waters of *Baptism* as by common right Christians are made members of the Mystical Body of Christ the Priest, and by the *character* which is imprinted on their souls they are appointed to give worship to God. Thus they participate according to their condition in the priesthood of Christ.[17]

While it is true that the late Sovereign Pontiff repeatedly underscored the fact that the faithful possess no sacerdotal rights or power to perform or enact or produce a visible liturgical or ritual sacrifice (for this is the unique privilege of the priest celebrant taking the place of Christ and through whom he intervenes as *seipsum offerens*) nevertheless they do have a priesthood by means of which they enjoy an active participation in worship. And it is precisely because they do possess this active participation in worship that they are said to offer the divine Victim, or that the oblation of the Victim is said to be made by the priests in company with the people;[18] this has been declared by the Church herself and is also signified by the rites themselves.[19]

The fact of the faithful's active participation in worship founded on the baptismal character is beyond contesting, but the nature or the mode of their active participation remains to be explained. While there are extrinsic or remote explanations offered to show exactly in what way the laity may be said to offer sacrifice by their sacramental participation or sharing in the priesthood of Christ, such as joining their prayers with those of the priest, or offering to the ministers at the altar the bread or wine to be changed into the Body and Blood of Christ, or giving the stipend for the Mass, still there is a much more profound reason why they are said to offer the

Sacrifice of the Mass. It is this we shall attempt to explain in the following paragraphs.[20]

We might indicate at the outset that the Sacrifice of the Mass is at one and the same time the sacrifice of Christ and the sacrifice of the Church, the Mystical Body of Christ, or His spouse and bride. Thus, by divine dispensation, the Mass is at one and the same time the *sacramental* sacrifice of Christ *and* the *sacramental* sacrifice of the Church.

It is, we might say, the sacrifice of a Mystical Person in which we find Christ as Head and the Church, the bride of Christ and a moral person distinct from Him, forming as it were one mystical person giving worship to the Father. By the divine decree, then, the Sacrifice of the Mass necessarily and of its very nature has always and everywhere the character of a public and social act inasmuch as he who offers it acts in the name of Christ and of the faithful (in a certain sense) whose head the divine Redeemer is. This is true whether the faithful are present or not, since the sacrifice is said to be offered by the Church as we have seen, considered not so much as a gathering of individuals, but rather as a moral person, the immaculate bride of Christ whose actions are always and everywhere efficacious.[21]

In the unbloody immolation occurring at the words of the Consecration, when Christ is made present on the altar in the state of victim, the priest acts as the representative of Christ and not of the faithful. But after the Consecration is performed the offering or oblation of the Victim placed on the altar can be accomplished not only by the priest-celebrant, but also by the Church, by other priests, and by each of the faithful. The faithful, then, are said to share in the oblation so understood, in the sense that their interior homage (the exercise of their spiritual priesthood) is *officially* joined to that of the priest and Christ Himself and presented to God through the ritual act of oblation. This exercise of their spiritual priesthood, however, is truly liturgical because of their baptismal character, which incorporates them into the Church, the bride of Christ, and because of the fact that these actions take place in reference to an act which is recognized as being liturgical. Thus, when those marked or sealed with the baptismal character worthily participate in the Sacrifice of the Mass, their act of the practical intellect together with the bodily actions which put their intention into effect constitute an external act of the virtue of religion imperated by charity.[22] The Mass as we know adds nothing to the merit of Calvary. What it does add, precisely as the Sacrifice of the Church, offered by men, is the *actual signification* of the charity of those who participate. This was present in the sacrifice of Calvary *only virtually*, that is, as something that was included in the charity of Christ. Now in the Mass it is derived from Head to members in such a way that it is *formally* theirs. It is by reason of their baptismal character that the faithful can be said to "offer" the Mass, because only they, only those marked with this seal can *officially* designate the double Consecration as the sacrificial *sign* of their charity. In fact, this is made even clearer from a consideration of the sacramental form of this sacrifice, which is, as we know, that of a meal. Participation in this sacrifice is confined to those who may receive food from the table, that is, the baptized, since they alone possess the power to receive. Thus, in the Mass also we see verified the theological assertion of St. Thomas that the *formal* effect of the character of baptism is not grace but cult, that is, the making of a valid sacramental sign.

From these notions we can see that when the Church offers up the sacrifice of Christ she offers up the sacrifice of herself, the sacrifice of the *totus Christus*, under a *single sacramental sign*.[23] The hierarchical priesthood, therefore, in celebrating Christ's sacrifice does so ritually or liturgically only in making it the Church's sacrifice—which does not mean that it necessarily involves the presence of the faithful as a congregation, nor even the presence of a server. Yet by the very fact that the Church has constantly insisted on the presence of a server, the exercise of the ministerial priesthood or the priesthood of orders is shown at least to involve *some* reference to the people's sacrifice or the liturgical service of the ecclesial community. It is for this reason that the Christian priesthood which celebrates Christ's worship cannot be thought of without there being implied at least some reference to the sacrifice of the faithful, that is, to all that they do in order to unite themselves together to God in a fellowship that is one and holy.[24]

It is for this reason that a theology of the liturgy must learn from an ecclesiology which considers or regards the Church as bride, since it is this quality or aspect which we see shared in by a diocese or parish or religious community when such an entity is said to worship. In this worship, that of the ecclesial community, all the faithful can be said to be celebrants, or better and less ambiguous, to offer, even though the hierarchical priest still is the normal minister speaking and acting for them, or technically speaking *in persona Ecclesiae,* just as he acts *in persona Christi* at the moment of Consecration. It is for this reason that we find the Angelic Doctor carefully distinguishing in the Sacrifice of the Mass between the properly sacramental work done in the person of Christ (which is the work of the specially ordained minister) and the sacrifice of praise, and so forth, done in the person of the Church. It is into this latter element of worship that the faithful are said to enter, not only by reason of their holiness of life, but also, and in an *official* capacity and one that is specifically earthly and ecclesial, by reason of their baptismal character which in a certain sense incorporates them visibly into this visible society. It goes without saying, of course, that perfect "active" participation on the part of the laity is achieved when they sacramentally participate or share in the Victim offered by the reception of the Eucharist as the Instruction referred to above very clearly points out.

The Role of the Character in this Active Participation

Thus far we have seen that the sacramental participation of the faithful in the Sacrifice of the Mass, such as that can be attributed to them, rests upon their possessing the sacramental character of baptism. We might proceed just a little further now and try to understand why the baptismal character is required for this exercise and how its exercise differs from that of the character of orders in this regard. The probable reasons, I think, for which the reality which we call the sacramental character is given are two: (1) because of the very nature of the Church, here on earth, since this as we know contains both visible and invisible elements; and (2) because of the very nature of man, especially considering it after the Fall. To grasp this we have only to recall some of the simple and yet profound reasons why sacraments are said to be necessary for men.

Theology teaches us that the very condition of man's nature is such that he is led to a knowledge of things spiritual and intelligible by sensible and corporal things. This natural need or dependence of man was intensified by the Fall, since in committing sin he had subjected himself to corporal things. So constituted, therefore, it was only right that man be offered spiritual things and express himself in regard to them in some visible manner. While it is true that the temple (the soul), the sacrifice, and the priesthood of the New Dispensation are spiritual, God has nevertheless provided a *sacramentum* to forward their realization. Instead of leaving the spiritual reality which is man's return to God to chance, He has appointed a very definite sensible and visible program to bring about its ultimate realization, one to which we must have recourse, at least in the ordinary sequence of events. There is, therefore, a *visible* economy of salvation, comprising not merely the one Mediator, Christ, but also the Church, as the great sacrament or sign of what He did for us. If man's inward spiritual sacrifice or the sacrifices of his spiritual priesthood are to be accepted, then they must pass (at least *in voto*, or in desire) through the *sacramentum* established by God. Thus we have the following situation: corresponding to the spiritual sacrifice of ourselves, through a life completely ordered to God, there exists a priesthood of holiness, which is called spiritual; similarly, corresponding to the liturgical or sacramental worship (Christ's sacrifice including that of our own, existing under a sacramental-liturgical form in the sacrament of the Eucharist), there exists a sacramental or liturgical priesthood for which one must be sacramentally deputed in accordance with the precise manner or mode in which he can be said to enter into it. For it is only if he possesses the character that man can be said to share *officially* and *sacramentally* in those acts which form the cult and worship of the Church, and in particular, that action which we call the Sacrifice of the Mass. The character is required, then, because of the nature of the Church and that of man himself, especially considering this after the Fall.

Coming to the second point, the function or role of the characters of baptism and of orders in the Sacrifice of the Mass, we find that it is not at all the same. This might be shown from the following reflections. While it is commonly said by theologians that the priesthood of the ministers is an "active" power and that of the faithful a "passive" power, still, it is perhaps much more accurate to speak of the latter's power as being active also under certain considerations. But the sense of the word "active" as applied to the laity's part in the Sacrifice of the Mass has to be well understood. For the word does not have the same meaning when applied to the activity of the hierarchical minister and to that of the laity. This, I think, can already be more than adequately deduced from the fact that the idea of joint celebration in the *causative sense* was clearly rejected by the late Supreme Pontiff as erroneous, even when appeal is made to the social character of the sacrifice.[25]

The hierarchical priesthood and the character upon which it is founded are said to be "active" in this sense, that those who belong to this priesthood celebrate and give in order to perfect others, whereas the priesthood of the laity and the character upon which it is founded, are said to be "active" in this sense, that those who belong to this priesthood share and receive in order to perfect themselves by receiving.[26] Moreover, the priestly character is effective independently of the moral dispositions of the celebrant, because the celebrant produces or effects the sacrifice in its immolatory aspect as the physical instrumental cause of Christ's activity. The laity, on the other hand, offer or designate the Body and Blood of Christ as a *sign* of their own worship. It is because of this that the Church literally fills up what is lacking in the sufferings of Christ, because the charity of her members is now explicitly signified by the identical sacrifice sacramentally renewed, which on Calvary signified the charity of the Church only as virtually included in Christ's. The Mass is in no sense of the word dependent on the faithful so far as the sacramental rite is concerned; for that is perfected at the moment of Consecration, which is the act of the celebrant alone. Consequently, the sacramental "power" or activity of the faithful is posterior to this by a posteriority of nature, enabling them to make the sacrament-sacrifice the sign of their own charity. Hence it seems that we can say that the character of baptism intervenes only or simply as a physical entity, in this sense, as something *implied* or *presupposed* on the part of the faithful by the sign. It gives *validity* to their *intention* of participating or associating themselves with the sacrifice of Christ and the Church, as well as to their intention of receiving the sacraments, but in a different way. In the Mass, for example, unlike confirmation, penance, and some of the other sacraments, there is no question of the character exercising an instrumental material causality. Rather, it acts as a permanent quality incorporating one into Christ sacramentally, making one *qualified* to use the sacrifice, in this case the Mass, as the expression of his own charity. Consequently, it seems that in regard to the sacramental priesthood of the laity, as in the case of their spiritual priesthood, there is no question of whether it is metaphorical or real. This would be to confuse the issue, since we are speaking of two completely different exercises of cultual power. Rather, the laity have a real and true sacramental priesthood, but again *in and of its own order,* one that differs not only in degree but in essence from that priesthood properly so called, or the hierarchical or ministerial priesthood of those in orders. It is real, therefore, in its own order, which seems to be one of association, one of consent, properly understood of course, something like that of Mary's role at the foot of the cross. For they alone, that is, those marked by the sacramental character, are able, by reason of their *official* incorporation into the Mystical Body, *officially* or *sacramentally* to designate the sacramental Body and Blood of Christ as the sacrificial *sign* of their charity, as we have mentioned above.

The Relationship Between the Spiritual and Sacramental Priesthood of the Laity

From this analysis of the two titles which the laity have to priesthood, that of the sacramental character of baptism and that of sanctifying grace, we might attempt to see the relationship which they have with one another. This it seems is most important so that we have a proper and correct understanding of the relative importance which each of these should have in the Christian consciousness and conscience.

The sacramental priesthood of the laity, that which they have by reason of their sacramental character of baptism—which is the ability they enjoy to participate officially in the official and public worship of the Church—is ordered to the spiritual priesthood in such a way that it is *subordinate* to it. For the character, precisely because it draws the Christian into Christ's offering of Himself as Victim, constitutes and establishes a call to self-immolation, because it demands a union of will with the obedient and suffering Christ. This self-immolation, however, is something which is efficaciously brought about by the priesthood of holiness or the spiritual priesthood, as Pius XII so clearly pointed out. Thus he wrote:

> But the *chief* element of divine worship must be interior. For we must always live in Christ and give ourselves to Him completely, so that in Him, with Him, and through Him, the Heavenly Father may be duly glorified. This recommendation the Liturgy itself is

careful to repeat, as often as it prescribes an exterior act of worship. Thus we are urged when there is question of fasting, for example, to give interior effect to our outward observance. Otherwise religion clearly amounts to mere formalism, without meaning and without content.[27]

From this it is clear that the more important of the two titles which the laity have to share in the priesthood of Christ is that which constitutes their spiritual priesthood, or the priesthood of a good life, sanctifying grace. And it seems that today it would be good for us to insist somewhat more often on this, so that the more important aspect of our worship and union with God will not be lost sight of in our new-found possession of the riches which are contained in the sacramental character of baptism. What must be avoided at all costs is to consider these two titles as radically independent or coordinate titles. This would not be consonant with the teaching that the whole Christian rite is *subordinate* to the union of the soul with God, which is brought about by grace formally and not by the character. Here again it seems that there is something that can be learned from a consideration of the priesthood of Christ Himself, from which every form of priesthood is derived. The external priestly acts of Christ, culminating in His immolation on the cross were acceptable to God because of the charity and obedience out of which they were performed. In a similar manner, the Christian draws near to God or is united to Him through grace and the practice of virtue, even though this is made possible in the normal order through his being marked with the sacramental character of baptism, by means of which he is assimilated to Christ the Priest and enabled to associate himself with the rite of the Christian religion.[28]

Thus, the character is ordered to this—that one may be sealed with the grace which deputes him to eternal glory, precisely because cult or worship itself is ordered toward and is an expression of the interior union of the faithful with God. The reason for this is rather obvious, it seems. If consecration to God demands as its natural consequence the infusion of a principle of supernatural life, then we can say that in the normal order of events the spiritual priesthood of the laity (that of a holy life) is something demanded by the cultual or liturgical priesthood of the laity (that emanating from the character of baptism); and we can also say that the exercise of the liturgical or sacramental priesthood makes possible the

exercise of the priesthood of a good Christian life by enabling this
latter to express itself visibly. While the sacramental character effects an official union between Christ and the soul, of itself it does
not and cannot effect what we might call a personal union between
these. That always remains the function of grace. For the sacramental characters, although truly spiritual bonds linking the soul
with Christ in various ways, are not to be numbered among the elements which give life-giving union with the Head. We might say
that the characters erect the Church as an organization, whereas
grace vivifies it, making it a kind of organism. Thus the characters
order the members, whereas grace gives them life.[29] Our spiritual
priesthood, then, through which we offer ourselves as spiritual victims to God, is joined with our baptismal priesthood through which
we offer the sacrifice of Christ liturgically. There is a sort of osmosis, or presence of each in the other, or almost circumincession, so to
speak. For as members of the liturgical gathering we offer ourselves with Christ, achieving the act of our inward spiritual priesthood in that of our baptismal priesthood; then we are called upon
to give the Mass all of its reality in our life, thus achieving the act
of our baptismal priesthood in that of our spiritual priesthood, which
is coextensive with our grace existence.

From all this it seems that we can very definitely conclude that
as far as the lay priesthood is concerned we can find in it two titles,
two ways of realizing the attribute whereby we are enabled to stand
before God to acquire His grace and fellowship by the offering of
an acceptable sacrifice. Just as we can speak of one Church, rather
than two, made up of two aspects, one spiritual and invisible, the
other external and visible, so too we can speak of there being one
priesthood of the laity reflecting this structure of the Church—at
once sanctified community and hierarchically organized congregation. These two aspects of the lay priesthood, it seems, are not, however, to be analogically compared with one another or with the
sacramental hierarchical priesthood. Rather, all three titles to priesthood, each in its own way makes a person priest in a way that is
true and real; that is, they are something, some reality by which
the economy of God's gifts reaches its goal. Thus each in its own
order, so to speak, or under its peculiar consideration can be said
to be a real and true priesthood. However, we must not forget,
only one of them, the hierarchical or ministerial priesthood of orders
can be said to be true and real if we limit these words so that they

signify the sacrificial office or function in an exterior and public worship. In this case the lay priesthood would be such not properly, as has been clearly pointed out by Pius,[30] but only improperly and probably equivocally, since under both of its aspects it is of another order than that of the ministerial priesthood.

Conclusion

We might attempt to sum up what we have seen in this paper under the following concluding points:

1. We have seen that the faithful are said to possess a priesthood in virtue of two titles. They possess a spiritual priesthood in virtue of sanctifying grace, which enables them to offer spiritual sacrifices to God, the sacrifices which we call, for the most part, virtuous actions. They also possess a sacramental priesthood in virtue of their baptismal character, which enables them to participate in properly sacramental worship, not by celebrating as hierarchical ministers, but by consenting thereto, by associating themselves with the Mass, by officially designating the double Consecration as the sacrificial sign of their charity. A character is required for this sacramental priesthood. For as St. Thomas in his treatment of the supernatural order frequently repeats: . . . "the order of the agents must correspond with the order of ends." Since the Mass, however, is a sacramental, or sign, or symbolic sacrifice (and by this I do not mean to say that it is not a real and true sacrifice) those who are able to offer it up must be sacramentally prepared or signed or sealed. That is the work of the various characters, depending upon the manner in which one can be said to participate or enter into the sacrificial offering.

2. Because the Mass, formally considered, is not just the sacrifice of the Head but also of the members, or because the Mass in a sense is not one but two sacrifices, that of Christ and that of the Church which have become one under a single sacramental sign, we can say that the hierarchical priesthood celebrates Christ's sacrifice liturgically only in making it the Church's sacrifice. Thus the act proper to the ministerial priesthood is at least shown to have a necessary reference, by divine determination, of course, to the people's sacrifice or the liturgical service of the ecclesial community, even though its validity does not at all require their consent or ratification, or even presence.

In a sense, therefore, *broadly speaking*, we can say that the Christian priesthood, or the sacramental priesthood celebrating Christ's worship, cannot be defined without reference to the sacrifice of the faithful. . . . The liturgical sacrifice, the Eucharistic sacrifice, pertains to the whole Church; and while only hierarchically constituted priests are able to carry out or to produce or create, if you will, the sacramental celebration, still the whole *plebs sancta* unites and cooperates in that celebration, by consenting to it and by associating itself with it. Their crowning act in this worship is their uniting themselves sacramentally and really with the Victim so as to form one body with him. It is here that the object of the sacrifice is realized visibly in the most marvelous and striking manner possible—*ut sancta societate Deo adhaereamus.*

3. The two aspects of the one lay priesthood are rather closely linked together, the outward sacramental priesthood (which the faithful possess in virtue of their baptismal character) being ordered to the inward spiritual priesthood (which they possess in virtue of sanctifying grace), since that sacrifice which God desires . . . is that of a humble and contrite heart. This is evident from the fact that the present dispensation will pass away, that the Church Militant or the Church of earth will give way to the Church Triumphant or the Church of heaven, because the law or economy of fulfilled grace is one of perfect inwardness. While in this life we live under a dual regime, one of inwardness—that of a priesthood of inner holiness, and one of outwardness—that of a priesthood of celebration of a sacramental worship: all this will cease when signs give way to reality. There is, therefore, this strange fact: since all priesthood is relative to sacrifice, and if when the present economy is fulfilled there will no longer be sacrifice, but only its effects or consequences—fellowship with God—we are forced to conclude that the priesthood of holiness, although real and higher than the sacramental priesthood, is less strictly and properly priestly than the latter, which is referred to Christ as a means to sacrifice strictly and properly so called.[31]

In God's designs our spiritual priesthood, by means of which we offer ourselves as spiritual victims, is joined with our baptismal priesthood, through which we offer the sacrifice of Christ and of the Church liturgically, in such a way that there is a sort of osmosis or interpenetration of the two in the normal life of the Christian.

4. If we accept the expressions "sacrifice" and "priesthood" in

the *strict* sense of these words, then, because they refer to that quality by which one is enabled to produce a liturgical and public sacrifice, the priesthood of the laity is a priesthood only improperly and, it seems, equivocally, and not analogically (whether of proper proportionality or of metaphor) since their priesthood under both of its aspects is of another order than that of the ministerial priesthood. This seems to be the import of the following section from the *Magnificate Dominum* of the late Pius XII: "But whatever is the full meaning of this honorable title and claim, it must be firmly held that the priesthood common to all the faithful, high and reserved as it is, differs not only in degree but in essence also from the priesthood properly so called which lies in the power of offering the sacrifice of Christ Himself since he bears the person of Christ the supreme High Priest." [32]

By way of conclusion, it might be well to remark that the ideas given in this . . . [article] are by no means complete or exhaustive. The theology of the lay priesthood, like that of the theology of the laity itself, is something that is very complex and basically a mystery. Like every other mystery, therefore, it can be increasingly made clearer and richer by constant investigation, as a diamond is made to yield its full beauty when it is held up and turned this way and that under a bright light. But this investigation, if it is to realize its highest and most fruitful results, ought not be done in a spirit of mere scientific endeavor. Rather it must be the result of a truly contemplative theology, of a gaze that rests lovingly and long on an object or reality that is part of the *magnalia Dei*, the great things of God, because it sees something of God there. For what our modern world needs is not only science, not only that understanding which scientific theology can communicate, but rather the vision which lies behind theology.

References

[1] On the nature and notion of tradition, cf. Gerald Vann, O.P., *The Water and the Fire* (London: Collins, 1953), esp. Chap. 10, "The Discovery of the Community"; also Joseph Pieper, "The Concept of Tradition," *The Review of Politics*, 20 (1958), 465ff. And also Jos. Sellmair, *The Priest in the World* (Westminster, Md.: Newman Press, 1954), p. 163.

[2] As Fr. Sellmair has pointed out, theology ought to be a kind of immersion of oneself into the heritage of revelation through a philosophical analysis that is carried on with all the confidence of a man of science, yet also in and with the spirit of the Church. In a sense we can say that theology and the

theologian pledge everything as though it were a question of life and death. As the science of faith, then, theology does imply daring and danger, and it is to be regretted that at times the fears which theological research inspire bring a kind of flight from the commitment that one makes of himself when he undertakes the study and the teaching of this discipline. *Op. cit.*, p. 60.

³ Cf. *Mediator Dei, AAS*, 39 (1947), 553ff; also *Magnificate Dominum, AAS*, 46 (1954), 667ff; and also the Address to the International Congress on Pastoral Liturgy, *AAS*, 48 (1956), 716-17. He speaks of that theory which holds that the faithful possess true sacerdotal power as being *erroneous:* "There are some who have not ceased claiming a certain true power to offer sacrifice on the part of all, even laymen who piously assist at the Sacrifice of the Mass. Opposing them we must distinguish truth from error and do away with all confusion . . . The people since they in no way bear the person of our Divine Redeemer and are not Mediators between themselves and God cannot in any way share in sacerdotal rights." *Magnificate Dominum, loc. cit.* This distinction had already been indicated in the first of the encyclicals dealing with this point, *Mediator Dei, loc. cit.*, 553-54.

⁴ *Magnificate Dominum, AAS*, 46 (1954), 669; *Mediator Dei, AAS*, 39 (1947), 553-54.

⁵ *Magnificate Dominum, loc. cit.*, 669.

⁶ Cf. the Instruction of the Sacred Congregation of Rites of Sept. 3, 1958: "*Laici autem participationem actuosam praestant et quidem vi characteris baptismalis, quo fit, ut in sacrosancto quoque Misse Sacrificio, pro modo suo divinam victimam Deo Patri cum sacerdote offerant.*" *AAS*, 50 (1958), 656. In this the Instruction is merely reechoing the teaching of Pius in the *Mediator Dei:* "By the waters of baptism as by common right, Christians are made members of the Mystical Body of Christ the Priest, and by the 'character' which is imprinted on their souls, they are appointed to give worship to God. Thus they participate according to their condition in the priesthood of Christ." *AAS*, 39 (1947), 555-56.

⁷ Peter 2:4-5; 9-10; Apocalypse 1:5-6; 20:6; 22:3-5. To these also might be added certain other passages: Ephesians 2:18-22; Philippians 3:3; Romans 6-13; 12:1; and Hebrews 13-15-16.

⁸ Y. Congar, O.P., *Lay People in the Church*, trans. Donald Attwater (Westminster, Md.: Newman Press, 1957), p. 122. This position is referred to by Father Kevin McNamara, writing in the *Irish Theological Quarterly*, as by far the stronger position: "that the faithful are priests (in these texts) because they have access to God through sanctifying grace and the practice of virtue, is by far the stronger position." "Aspects of the Layman's Role in the Mystical Body," *Irish Theological Quarterly* (April 1958), p. 128. Pius XII in the encyclical *Mediator Dei* seems to incline toward this position also when he writes: "In order that the oblation by which the faithful offer the divine Victim in this Sacrifice to the heavenly Father may have its full effect it is necessary that the people add something else, namely, the offering of themselves as a victim. This offering in fact is not confined merely to liturgical sacrifice. For the Prince of Apostles wishes us, as living stones built upon Christ the corner stone, to be able as a holy priesthood to offer up spiritual sacrifices acceptable to God by Christ Jesus." *AAS* (1947), 557.

⁹ *De Civitate Dei*, X, ch. 5-6, PL 41, 281-84. Cf. also St. Thomas, *Summa*, II-II, q. 85, aa. 2-3; III, q. 22, a. 2; q. 48, a. 3; and *In Boetium de Trinitate*, q. 3, a. 2.

¹⁰ We find this sense used today by many authors; e.g., Paul Claudel, *L'Of-*

frande du temps, and Gerald Vann, *The Water and the Fire* (London: Collins, 1953), esp. pp. 102ff.

[11] Y. Congar, O.P., *op. cit.*, p. 117.

[12] *S.T.*, III, q. 63, a. 3.

[13] Congar, *op. cit.*, pp. 179-80.

[14] *De Civitate Dei, loc. cit.* (cf. note 9). Holding to this idea of sacrifice being a total Godward movement that excludes the wretchedness of being separated from God, Augustine shows in these passages that this total sacrifice is the realization of the adherence to God of the *tota redempta civitas vel societas, hoc est congregatio, societasque sanctorum.* It is only this community of *holy* people alone that forms the *universale sacrificium* which is offered to God through the High Priest, Christ, who at the time of his Passion offered Himself for us that we might be the body of which He is the Head. It is at this point that Augustine associates with the theme of sacrifice in general, and with that of Christ's communal body, and with that of the cross, the sacrifice of the altar, which is the sacrament or sign or symbol of our oneness in Him: *S.T.*, III, q. 63, a. 6, ad 1.

[15] It was part of the originality of Thomas to distinguish rather sharply and clearly the two modes of participation in the priesthood of Christ, one given by the characters, the other by grace. Cf. "The Instrumentality of the Sacramental Character," by Colman O'Neil, O.P., *Irish Theological Quarterly* (July 1958), pp. 263-64.

[16] Cf. Kevin McNamara, *art. cit.:* "We must hasten to add that the New Testament texts cited as well as certain texts from the Old (cf. e.g., Psalms 50:19; Mi 6:6-8) describe certain virtuous actions and ascetical practices as sacrifices; and certainly Christian tradition recognizes a wider concept of sacrifice (and consequently of priesthood) than the strictly liturgical or ritual. Moreover, as we know, the celebrated definition of sacrifice of Augustine certainly extends far beyond the notion of mere liturgical sacrifice or ritual sacrifice, if you will."

[17] *Mediator Dei, loc. cit.,* 553-54, where it is stated that they possess no sacerdotal rights. Cf. also the Instruction of the SRC, *loc. cit.,* 717. In the *Magnificate Dominum*, the Supreme Pontiff writes: "The particular and chief duty of the priest has ever been to offer sacrifice; where there is no true power to offer sacrifice, there is no true priesthood. This is also true of the priest of the New Law. His chief power and duty is to offer the unique and divine sacrifice of the most high Eternal Priest. . . . He wished it to be constantly repeated . . . the apostles therefore and not all the faithful were ordained and appointed priests by Christ, and to them He gave the power to offer sacrifice. . . . Thus the priest-celebrant, putting on the person of Christ, alone offers sacrifice and not the people nor clerics, nor even priests who reverently assist." *AAS* (1954), 667-68.

[18] In a passage immediately subsequent to the preceding we read: "All, however, can and should take an active part in the sacrifice . . . The Christian people through participating in the Eucharistic sacrifice *do not thereby possess a priestly power.*" Cf. also *Mediator Dei, AAS,* 39 (1947), 553.

[19] E.g., the Orate Fratres, and the Canon of the Mass.

[20] This already can be considered to be "active" participation in the Sacrifice of the Mass. Cf. the Instruction of the SRC, *AAS,* 50 (1958), 637-38.

[21] Thus Congar speaks of two aspects of Christian worship: That coming from above and that coming from below. In the worship coming from below the priest acts as the representative of the community. But this ec-

clesial worship is not that of a particular Christian or even that of a particular group of faithful. Rather it is that of the Church considered as a *moral person*, the universal society of the faithful, one, holy, constituted as a real subject of rights and duties. She is the Bride of Christ, in a sense, more than His Body. *Op. cit.*, p. 199. Cf. also St. Thomas in IV Sent. Dist. 49, q. 4, a. 3, ad 4.

[22] Colman O'Neil, O.P., "The Role of the Recipient and Sacramental Signification," *The Thomist*, 21 (1958), 515.

[23] *Mediator Dei, AAS*, 39 (1947), 556: "Now the sacrifice of the New Law *signifies* that supreme worship by which the principal offerer himself who is Christ and in union with Him and through Him, all the members of the Mystical Body pay God the honor and reverence that are due to Him."

[24] Y. Congar, *op. cit.*, p. 167.

[25] Cf. Jos. Sellmair, *The Priest and the World*, p. 31.

[26] Instruction of the SRC: "They (the faithful) accept all that is offered to them—the graces of the sacrifice of the altar, of the sacraments and sacramentals—not as mere passive recipients of the graces flowing over them, but cooperating in these graces with all their will and strength, and above all participating in the liturgical offices or at least following them with fervor." *AAS*, 50 (1958), 714.

[27] *Mediator Dei, AAS*, 39 (1947), 531.

[28] Father Kevin McNamara writes: "In a similar vein Father Rea writes in his work on the lay priesthood: 'Out of the tendency to submerge the personality of the Christian at prayer in the social unity of the Church, there has grown a further tendency to consider the fruits of prayer as bestowed primarily upon the Mystical Body and only secondarily upon the members. . . . Although it is true that this priesthood is exercised only socially in union with the other members of the Mystical Body, it is exercised principally for the obtaining of grace which is realized immediately in each participant of the common priesthood and thence mediately in the whole Body. Social in its exercise, the common priesthood begets fruits that are primarily personal and secondarily, but necessarily, social in nature.'" *Art. cit.*, p. 138. Cf. J. Rea, *The Common Priesthood of the Members of the Mystical Body* (Westminster, Md.: Newman Press, 1947), pp. 228-29.

[29] Cf. John Dittoe, O.P., "Sacramental Incorporaion into Christ," *The Thomist*, 9 (1946), 487.

[30] *Magnificate Dominum, AAS*, 46 (1954), 669.

[31] Y. Congar, *op. cit.*, p. 159.

[32] *Magnificate Dominum, loc. cit.*, 669.

BONIFAAS LUYKX, O.PRAEM.

Confirmation in Relation
to the Eucharist

The sacrament of confirmation was understood as one of the three sacraments of initiation. By reviewing the historical development of the Church's doctrine and practice of confirmation, the following article attempts to restore this sacrament to its rightful place as the second link in an "organic continuity of three elements of the Christian initiation rite." In this examination the author insists that the reception of the Eucharist should naturally follow upon the reception of confirmation, and he suggests that the most fitting moment for the three sacraments of initiation is the Easter Vigil. Finally, confirmation is seen as the sacrament of the priesthood of the laity; the action of all Christian priesthood must center in the Eucharist.

Father Luykx teaches liturgy at the University of Lovanium, Leopoldville, Congo. He is a consultor on the liturgy at the Second Vatican Council.

State of the Question

Since this subject has not yet been studied very much, we have the advantage and the disadvantage of meeting here a rather virginal soil, which has not yet been ploughed much by the theologians and which is able, perhaps, to prepare some surprises for us. Nevertheless, this study is of great importance for the understanding

This article first appeared in *Participation in The Mass*, the Proceedings of the Twentieth North American Liturgical Week. It is reprinted here with permission of the Liturgical Conference.

187

and living of two important sacraments, and thus it is worth while studying this subject.

Our work will be first of all to examine the facts and the sources, and afterward to reflect upon these facts and texts, without any preconceived scholarly categories or schemes. This method seems to be the only right and fitting one for this subject. If the liturgy is really "the most important organ of the ordinary magisterium of the Church" (Pius XI in *Quas primas*, 1925), this applies certainly and above all to the liturgy itself as an object of research.[1] Moreover, the sacramental action of the Church is much more than "a means of grace," it is the Lord Himself and the Church worshipping together: through the sacramental signs and their whole ritual "dressing" the Church shows concretely and applies practically the real salvific contents of Christ's action in us and its organic place in the whole of the concrete Christian life.

Now, how is confirmation performed by the Church, and especially by the early Church, because at that time the real contents of that particular savifiic act of Christ was "sacramentally translated," that is, converted into rites, and this in the context of the whole Christian life?

The Facts

It is beyond our intention to go very deeply into the biblical background of confirmation. We would only refer to the conclusions on the Gospel of St. John by O. Cullmann (*Les Sacrements dans l'évangile johannique*, Paris, 1951), H. van den Busseke, and others, that there are clear references to a double "christening rite" in St. John. The general statement of John 3:5-8 on baptism in water and in the messianic Spirit is explained in a double description: John 5:1-19 (healing of the impotent man at the pool of Bethsaida) refers to the baptism in water; John 9:1-39 (healing of the man born blind) refers to the *photismos* by the baptism in the Spirit. Therefore, the early Church called the fully initiated *photizomenoi, illuminati*.

The first outlines can be recognized in the Acts of the Apostles. "Confirmation" was from the very beginning a different rite, separate from "baptism" (Acts 8:14-17: "Now when the apostles in Jerusalem heard that Samaria had received the word of God, they sent to them Peter and John. On their arrival they prayed for them, that they might receive the Holy Spirit; for as yet He had not come upon any of them, but they had only been baptized in the name of the Lord Jesus. Then they laid their hands on them and they received the Holy Spirit.")

This people were only baptized in the name of the Lord Jesus, and hence the apostles had to lay their hands upon them in order to give them the Holy Spirit, that is, the fullness of the messianic goods.[2]

The initiation of candidates into the new People of God in order to share in the messianic goods as being the true contents of Christendom, happened through a double stage, with both their own salvific contents and "sacramental causality":

—the imperfect stage by immersion or washing is related to the Lord Jesus,

—the real and full "taking up" of the candidates by imposition of the hands is related to the Holy Spirit.

The first stage (baptism) was, to a certain extent, felt as a preparatory rite, meant for cleansing, parallel with the baptism of John and of the Qumran people and so forth, without any visible effect, as for instance, the *charismata*. Whereas the imposition of hands (confirmation) was meant as the real "admission" of the candidates, in order to make them share in the messianic goods of the *Ekklesia*, the new People of God, upon whom the Spirit had been poured out as the sign and active fullness of the messianic goods.

Gradually these fundamental elements of Christian intiation rite were "organized," that is, given their organic expression in the whole of the concrete sacramental life of the Church. This maturation process must have reached a certain degree of perfection about 170, so that Hippolytus of Rome could give a detailed description in his Church Order ('*Apostolikè parádosis*, Apostolic Tradition) from the beginning of the third century.[3]

This description starts with the questioning of the sponsors, who were responsible for the request for "admission" of these (adult) candidates. After that follow the regulations for the catechumenate, which lasts three years (c. xvii; Di. 28), with regular prayers (c. xviii) and imposition of hands (c. xix) by the instructor (a layman). During that time the catechumens do not yet belong to the community; only after their full reception as Christians are they allowed to join with it in common prayer, the kiss of peace, and the Eucharist. Then, after a time of trial, consisting especially in the works of charity (c. xx) starts the immediate (liturgical) preparation: the

Church, as worshipping community, now takes the candidates over from the sponsors and the instructors (c. xx, 2; Di. 31). This liturgical preparation consists in "hearing the Gospel" (Gospel is not the written book or a sermon, but the liturgical Word Service) and in exorcisms and the imposition of hands, especially during the *Triduum Sacrum*.

The performance of the sacramental initiation rite itself is built up like a great drama. The holy oils are consecrated. The catechumens renounce for the last time the devil and his works, and they are anointed with the oil of catechumens. A priest immerses them three times in the baptismal water after a threefold profession of their faith. After the priest has anointed them with the oil of thanksgiving (later on they will at this point put on the white dress of the newly baptised), they go to the bishop, who lays his hand upon them and anoints their heads to complete the anointing of the body by the priest, as the final *consignatio* (confirmation). He gives them the kiss of peace to take them into the Church; and henceforth, says Hippolytus, they will be able to join the community in the common worship, as full members of the community (*photizomenoi* in the East).

This Church Order of Hippolytus may be considered as the pattern and model of the Christian initiation. Here we see how this has now fully developed into a mature institution, which is at the same time the expression of how the early Church looked upon the organic function of the initiation rite in the whole of Christian life and upon its constitutive elements. Furthermore, this institution is presented as being an "apostolic tradition," handed down to us by the apostles themselves; hence, Hippolytus' decisive influence upon the formation of the liturgy in the East and West, so that we might see him as the Father of the Christian initiation liturgy. This faithfulness to the primitive tradition explains why the early liturgy and the Fathers (save for a very few outsiders) are strikingly unanimous.

The constitutive elements of this initiation rite are in fact still the same as the three original nuclei of the Acts of the Apostles:

—baptism in water,

—baptism in the Holy Spirit by the imposition of hands and anointing,

—common Eucharistic worship as the final result of the whole Christian initiation.

But one element had become clearer in the religious experience of the primitive Church: the Christian initiation is finally a sharing in Christ's own "passage" from death to life; hence it should, normally only be performed during the Easter Vigil. So it became the Paschal event par excellence for the Church as well as for the new candidates. So that we can ascertain that "the normal moment, not only of baptism but also of confirmation and first Holy Communion was, in the Roman rite, up to the Carolingian era, the Easter Vigil." The same applies to all the other churches of East and West (save a very few exceptions, as for instance, Gaul).

To conclude this description of the facts we might quote the same author: "It would be an error, not only in theological method but also in liturgical structure, to withdraw the sacramental rite of confirmation from the whole of the Easter Vigil. Sacramentally seen, the place of confirmation is between baptism and the Paschal Eucharist, in the dynamism of the three initiation sacraments. And this trilogy is of such great importance in the Catholic tradition of the sacraments that we must undoubtedly wish that it (this trilogy) should be practised as the usual performance in the Easter Vigil by the bishop . . ." (ibid., pp. 137-38).

At least the theologian should take this organic continuity as the fundamental fact and hence as the basic frame for his study of the subject that has been assigned to us now. For the Church does not only give us the sacraments; she first receives them from her Lord to build up the People of God according to an organic structure, as the early Church has "incarnated" in the whole of the *oeconomia sacramentalis*.

Explanation of the Facts

Unity of the Christian Initiation

It is of great importance that the Fathers are practically unanimous in their description and catechetics of the Christian initiation. To quote only some text samples, we read in Tertullian (d. c. 200): "The body is washed to cleanse the soul . . . The hands are laid upon the body to enlighten the soul with the Holy Spirit . . . The body of the Christian is fed with the Body and Blood of Christ in order to feed (literally 'to fatten') the soul." This organic continuity also applies to the little children; St. Augustine (d. 430) refers to the general practice when he says: "Pope Innocent himself has said it: without baptism (in the water and the Holy Spirit) and without participation in the Body of Christ, the children have no life (of grace)." Gennadius of Marseille (d. 493) describes the general practice for Gaul: "If there are little children among the catechumens, who do not yet understand the teaching, their sponsors shall answer for them. One shall lay the hands upon them and one shall make them partake of the Eucharistic celebration." The reason lies precisely in the uninterruptible organic continuity of the three elements of the Christian initiation rite.

Even after the Roman town liturgy was introduced by the Carolingians in the countries beyond the Alps, in a more compulsory and artificial way, like a foreign and bookish import, even then this organic continuity was preserved, notwithstanding the serious difficulties this practice presented in these cold countries. So in the beginning the mothers were allowed to give the little babies the breast during that very long Easter Vigil celebration; and in spite of that they received their first Holy Communion right after confirmation (in the species of wine). But afterwards a more severe interpretation of the canons became prevalent: the babies had to stay sober all that long time and when a mother or a nurse had fed the little bawler to keep him still (and what would a good mother not do to stop him crying?) the mother must fast 40 days, because at any price the newly baptized and confirmed should receive Holy Communion. During Easter Week all of them, babies included, were obliged to come every day to Mass and to receive Holy Communion (the babies only under the species of wine), and their parents should make the offerings.

This practice was absolutely general in the Church of East and West and never met any opposition. It is still so in the Eastern Churches, where most of the early Christian traditions have been preserved.

But afterwards a new element came into the situation. The Church became too big when the *pagani* (countrymen) got converted, so that the *paroikia* extended outside the primitive nucleus of the *civitas* and the bishop could not cover his whole parish. He was not able to preside over the Easter celebration with the Christian initiation in the country churches. Consequently he had to choose between two possible solutions; either leave the whole celebration in the country to his helpers, the priests, so that the organic structure of the Christian initiation would be saved; or reserve the final completion of this initiation to the bishop as supreme leader of the community, but distort the organic structure of the Christian initiation.

The first solution is certainly the best, and has been adopted by the Eastern Churches, which have always lived in a stronger awareness of the early Church tradition; Spain and southern Italy followed this custom as well, up to the present time (except for first Holy Communion right after confirmation).

However, for the West it was impossible to follow this solution, for purely historical reasons. In virtue of the feudal system the bishops were obliged to keep up the mode of life of a *grand seigneur*, who was not allowed to leave his privileges up to officials of a lower rank. Hence he felt obliged to reserve jealously for himself the right of administering confirmation, with this very important consequence: where the bishop could not confer this sacrament at the right moment, that is, during the Easter Vigil, it had to be delayed, the Christian initiation had to be interrupted, and hence the whole sacramental structure was twisted.

As long as, also in the West, a living contact with the early Church tradition was kept up, this situation was felt to be an unhappy and almost unlawful solution, merely inflicted by the unfavorable situations. So we read in an Ordo of the . . . eleventh century: "Then [after baptism in water, during the Easter Vigil] the infant should be dressed and, if the Bishop be present, the infant must forthwith be confirmed and be given the Holy Communion. The greatest care must be taken that confirmation be not neglected because only on the confirmed is the name of Christian rightly bestowed. If the Bishop is not present let the infant receive from a priest the body and blood of the Lord before he be nursed or receive any other food." [4]

So the Western Church has gradually lost a capital feature of the sacramental discipline, allowing confirmation to break away from its organic ties with baptism and the Eucharist. Hence premises are placed for the further dissolution of the whole sacramental initiation system, as we shall see further on. This makes it difficult for a Western theologian to look with unprejudiced eyes upon the problem of the relations among baptism, confirmation, and the Eucharist, and particularly upon the problem we have to deal with here. In order to make the way clear, it will be necessary to go, once more, back to the early Church and the Fathers.

Baptism and the Eucharist

Theologically and sacramentally seen, there is no doubt any more that baptism and confirmation belong together as two specific acts of one "twin sacrament";[5] or rather, as two continuous moments of one organic action. They are so strongly "tuned" and structured to each other that the biblical and early ecclesiastical documents comprised both under one name: *baptismos*, that is, in water (our baptism) and in the Holy Spirit (our confirmation), while the latter completes and achieves what the first has begun.

There is a double biblical reason. First, in Christ's own baptism, which is the salvific background of the Christian initiation, both are likewise two continuous "moments" of one organic action;[6] He was filled with the Holy Ghost when He came out of the Jordan after His baptism (Lk 3:21-22). And next, Christ Himself presented the Christian initiation as a rebirth from water and Spirit in one continuous operation (Jn 3:5-8).

Though the Fathers and the early Church knew very well that there is a double nucleus in this one *baptismos*, each having its own "sacramental effect" (baptism in water washes away sin and "tunes" to the other sacraments, imposition of hands with "anointing" confers the messianic Spirit), nevertheless they saw both as one continuous salvific operation and gave both a single name. This is the clear and unanimous statement of Tertullian, Irenaeus, Cyprian, Ambrose, Pacianus of Barcelona, and practically all of the Fathers, from the Church Order of Hippolytus on. Only when they explain the different elements of the Christian initiation do they clearly speak of two different nuclei as the two constitutive elements, our baptism and confirmation, with the Eucharistic celebration as the final conclusion.

There was only one dissonant voice among the Fathers, St. Jerome. In his presbyterian position against the bishops he claimed that confirmation was a purely honorific ceremony, merely performed to stress the authority of the bishops and to feed their pride. This of course, is the negation of the sacrament itself. But . . . during the whole of the Middle Ages there was a tendency to belittle confirmation in the Western Church. So, for example, Bonaventure's position came very close to that of Jerome: confirmation was only an institution of the Church and not of Christ. This statement was quite understandable, for since the splitting up and partition of the twin sacrament, baptism in water became the exclusive heir of that long and solemn preparation during Lent which was really meant for the three initiation sacraments *together* (see, for example, the Mass texts on Wednesday after the fourth Sunday of Lent; also the salt of wisdom as an anticipation of confirmation, and so on).

This situation has shunted the later theology on to a wrong track, though she tried to explain it as a normal feature; hence she ascribed to the only baptism in water almost the whole content of the primitive baptism in water *and* in Spirit, since the latter was dropped from the Christian initiation but the general title "baptism," meant for both, from now on was taken only for the baptism in water. On the other hand, since confirmation was no longer a part of the whole Christian initiation rite, it got a completely different perspective: it was rather brought into relation with the so-called adult Christian life, apart from worship and its center, the Eucharist.

These two changes of perspective have deeply influenced the Western theological approach to confirmation: we feel it in St. Thomas and even in some ecclesiastical documents (which mostly follow the terminology of the current theology without any intention, generally speaking, of sanctioning this). So, for example, when St. Thomas or *Mediator Dei* quote the Fathers in favor of baptism as being the sacrament of the general priesthood of the faithful (and hence as the initiation to the Eucharist), it is clear that their sources mean "baptism in water *and in the Spirit*." Consequently it is a wrong method to detach their texts from the whole theological and above all liturgical tradition of East and West and from their biblical background. The same applies to some historical works [for example, the book of Chirat, *L'Assemblée chrétienne à l'age apostolique* (Paris, 1958), pp. 156ff.], which sometimes have not even suspected that *baptismos* means the whole Christian initiation and not our baptism; and so they even conclude that confirmation did not exist in the early Church. This mistake explains the uncertain position of confirmation in St. Thomas and in Western theology and ecclesiastical teaching, since it is built, not upon the proper and organic structure of the whole Christian initiation rite, but upon a "state of emergency and exception" (as we described above), which the Eastern Churches have never accepted; as if a physician would study a dislocated foot as a normal feature.[7]

This explains also why there could come about an almost complete "black-out" of confirmation in the fifteenth and eighteenth centuries: the sacrament was in many countries not administered any more, under the pretext that baptism already contained all the graces of the christening, and the rest was done by the Eucharist itself; so confirmation was quite superfluous. This, of course, points out that the feeling for the organic structure of the *oeconomia sacramentalis* was lost, not in the least because of this loosening of the organic bindings of the whole Christian initiation system.

This does not imply that there is no relation at all between our baptism and the Eucharist. Since the latter is the center of all sacramental life, baptism as well is directed to the Eucharist and consequently gives some ordination and ability toward active participation in it. This ordination, however, is not direct but by means of confirmation as the organic and indispensable achievement of the Christian initiation.

Confirmation and the Eucharist

When the early Church (and the Eastern Churches still, to a certain extent) concluded the Christian initiation by the communal celebration of the Eucharist, this was not for the same reason as, for example, a solemn Mass terminates a retreat or a convention. It was rather the visible expression of the great common experience and of a theological reality: the Eucharistic celebration being the proper end of the Christian initiation and henceforth the proper act of the Christian. Cyril of Alexandria expresses it this way: "If we come together for worship in the church or in other places, if we are alone or with two or three more, all those who have come together to sing the hymns are admitted to do so, because everybody can offer this sacrifice (of praise) together with those who are cleansed in baptism. But the one who is only a catechumen and who joins the perfect ones (the confirmed) to praise God will be sent away from the more elevated Mysteries and excluded from the sacrifice of Christ."

What is this organic binding between confirmation and the Eucharist? For the early Church, which expressed the heritage of the Lord and the faith of the Church in sacramental forms, it was very simple and clear. Whereas baptism gives us forgiveness of sins and reception in the People of God by a first *con-formatio* to Christ, in confirmation we receive the full participation in the messianic goods of that People and the capability of acting according to this conformation to Christ through the general priesthood of the faithful.

These fundamental features are repeatedly treated of by the Fathers, especially in their catechetical instructions. Christian initiation is not an abstraction, a theological scheme of concepts, but an active taking up into the concrete mystery of the Church itself, materialized in the communal celebration of the *Pascha Domini* as the proper and central act of the Church, because here the Lord comes back in order to constitute the People of God. As St. Ambrose teaches his newly baptized: they are now introduced into the second tent where only the high priest could enter once a year, they are now members of the priestly people and hence may draw near to the altar of God, where is the Body of Christ.

It strikes us how the organic binding between baptism (in water and the Spirit), the People of God, and the Eucharist was stressed from the first moments when the Church started reflecting upon her fundaments and declaring them. So the first Epistle of St. Peter, which can be seen as the first catechesis on the Christian initiation, turns about the main section of 2:4-9, explaining how this christening rite makes us into "a holy priesthood to offer spiritual sacrifices (*pneumatikás thusias*) . . . a chosen race, a royal priesthood . . . that you may proclaim the perfections of Him who has called you out of darkness into His marvelous light." This was the fulfillment of the prefiguration in the old chosen people, as was expressed in Exodus 19:4-6: "You will be for me a kingdom of priests and a holy nation." But as Justin interprets it in the second century: "We are made the true highpriestly tribe of God, through our christening rite."

Now, since "baptism" introduces us into the People of the Covenant (our baptism), it has to enable us to offer the sacrifice of this Covenant (confirmation), which is the Eucharist. So we understand why the initiation is not completed without the communal celebration of the Eucharist. Hence the Christian initiation, that is, baptism and especially confirmation as the final preparation, should be looked upon from this final fulfillment, the Eucharist, all-comprising token of the messianic goods for the new Covenant.

Is this not in contradiction with the way the apostolic Church understood confirmation, as being entirely directed to the Holy Spirit and not to the Eucharist? If we look closer, we see that both come together in the same root. The Holy Spirit was not looked upon as a private, personal gift, as we tend to see it now, for our own comfort, but as the active summary of all the messianic promises and goods, which are exclusively realized in the bosom of the priestly People of God. Now, the sacramental act through which we share in these messianic goods and which is at the same time the proper and constitutive act of the New Covenant, is precisely the celebration of the Eucharist, especially in its full shape of the Easter Vigil, because then the Lord of the Covenant comes Himself among His gathered people to celebrate His Passover from death to life, core of the whole economy of salvation.

Hence we understand why the pneumatical Church of the beginnings looked upon the *charismata* as tokens of the fullness of the messianic times, whereas the more institutionalised Church felt the Eucharist as the same token, but now sacramentalised in the sign of the Lord coming back among His people. So the Holy Spirit and the Eucharist coincide in the concrete celebration: the Holy Spirit being the *arrha* (guarantee) of the coming *aion*, and the Eucharist is already the anticipation of this coming *aion;* and only the one who possesses this *arrha* is able to participate in the Eucharistic celebration of God's people, for the only true worship is the place where the charismatical gifts are practiced.

Practical Applications

The relation between confirmation and the Eucharist can be contemplated from a double point of view:

the *actual administering* of confirmation in respect to first Communion, that is, seen as the first participation in the common celebration of the Eucharist;

the *habitual effect* of this administration in its relation to the Eucharist, that is, relation between the *sacramental character* of confirmation and *participation in the Eucharist* in the daily Christian life.

Confirmation and First Holy Communion

It is noteworthy that the whole Church of East and West has always respected the primitive practice of joining first Communion immediately to confirmation, as the third part of the one Christian initiation. This applied even for little children. And this practice was so far above discussion that the Church considered it an apostolic institution, inherited from the Lord Himself. So, for example, Theodulf of Orleans (ninth century) tells us that "the Church has received from the Lord Himself the custom of nourishing with

His Body all those who are reborn from water and the Spirit; for, as He said, only by force of this food can one remain in Christ and He in him and attain, like Elias, the top of the mountain which is Christ."

Bishop Jesse of Amiens, another Carolingian theologian (d. 836), appeals to Christ's words to justify the baptismal rite in the Easter Vigil: "Finally (that is, after baptism and confirmation) the baby is strengthened with the Blood of Christ. So he becomes a member of Him who died for him and has risen, as the Lord has said Himself: 'Who eats my flesh. . . .' Just as our body cannot live without soul, likewise only the one who is strengthened with the Body of Christ has the spirit of life. Consequently he who wants to live, let him draw near, let him believe that he lives from God, that he is incorporated in God in order to be vivified."

The Greek theologian Simeon of Saloniki (d. 1429) gives the decisive reason for this practice: "One objects that babies do not know what they receive (and hence reason prohibits us from admitting them to Holy Communion). What a silly objection! Why then do you baptize them and sign them with holy chrism?"—for, in principle, baptism is the seal on a conscious faith in the receiver. So we can understand why the Eastern Churches have preserved this practice up to now.

St. Thomas gave the theological foundation (although he lived at the beginning of the devotionalistic era):

> The Eucharist is the achievement of Christian life (III, q. 73, a. 13), and contains the eternal life to be passed on to us (III, q. 79, a. 2).
>
> Consequently all the sacraments are ordinated to it as their goal (III, q. 73, a. 3); this especially applies to "baptism" (as the Fathers did, St. Thomas names thus the twin sacrament of our baptism plus our confirmation), which ordinates us directly to participation in the Eucharist (III, q. 65, a. 3).
>
> Moreover, nobody has one grace before receiving the Eucharist or at least desiring it (III, q. 79, a. 1); so, if the baby has some grace (q. 73, a. 3), this proves he has been ordinated to the Eucharist in virtue of this membership in the Church; and since he believes through faith of the Church (and *hence* can be baptized), likewise he desires the Eucharist through the intention of the Church.
>
> The initiation rite works out in us a participation in the universal priesthood of the faithful, "deputes" us to the true worship in the bosom of the priestly People of God; and the proper and full act of this priesthood is the Eucharist, bond of the actively participating community (III, q. 63).

Modern theology would circumscribe this in the following way. Holy Communion is not above all a nice devout tea-party with the sweet little Jesus (fortunately He is not little), whom these pretty boys and girls receive in their little hearts, to whom they may tell all (what?) now, the little hands nicely before their eyes, and so on. The Eucharist is a celebration, an action, where the Church exercises her priesthood according to the capacity of her members and edifies herself as the Mystical Body of Christ (1 Cor 10:16-17), for the Eucharist should be administered so that the organic link between them is preserved; that is, so that:

1. no sacramental act will intervene between baptism and confirmation;

2. if possible, the first celebration of the Eucharist (which is more than an individualistic reception of the sweet little Jesus) should immediately and sacramentally follow the administration of confirmation;

3. this should be done at the proper moment, that is, the Easter Vigil.

In regard to the first conclusion: no sacramental act between baptism and confirmation. This supposes that confirmation has to be administered:

—either immediately after baptism, in one and the same ceremony, because they both belong together (see above) and this was the general practice in the centuries of "sacramental boom" and still is in the East, in Spain, and in other countries; even in the West, in the episcopal churches, up to the end of the Middle Ages;

—or as soon as possible after baptism, and so that the organic unity of this twin sacrament is not broken by another sacramental act; for the longer one delays confirmation, the more danger there is of destroying this unity and twisting the whole meaning of confirmation.

This is certainly the meaning of the *Codex Juris Canonici*, 788: confirmation may not be delayed later than the age of seven years; this is to be considered as a real delay (*differatur*) since both belong together, and it may not be protracted; and at any rate confirmation has to be administered before first Holy Communion, as is officially stated by the *Commissio Authentica* of the Canon Law, June 30, 1932, ratifying the Spanish custom and prescribing confirmation *before first Holy Communion* as the normal way "since confirmation completes and fulfills baptism."

So the main problem could be solved very simply, by the single expedient of carrying out the prescriptions of the Church. Moreover, one of the purposes of the Apostolic Constitution *Spiritus Sancti munera* of September 14, 1946, giving pastors permission to confirm little children of their parish *in articulo mortis*, was to restore the sacramental unity of baptism and confirmation. This is certainly conformed to the spirit of the Church and, what is more, the spirit of the liturgy; for that reason Pope Leo XIII strongly approved the design of Bishop Robert of Marseille in 1898, of administering confirmation in earliest childhood; the main argument is that the young Christian needs this "strength from heaven," in order to go through the physical and psychological maturation process in harmony and grace.

Finally, the custom of administering confirmation after first Communion dates from very recent years; that is, from after the acceleration of first Holy Communion by Pius X. Up to the French Revolution, in the countries where confirmation was administered, this was given to children between one and three years old; that is, as soon as possible after baptism when the bishop made his tour through the villages.

In regard to the second conclusion: first Communion right after confirmation; if possible, in one and the same celebration.

Sacraments are not things, but a personal meeting with the glorified *Kyrios* in one of the salvific moments of his earthly life. The initiation sacraments are not a transitory act of a mere meeting, rather they give as well the ontological structure and organic direction toward the fullest encounter with the glorious Lord upon earth, the Eucharist and its extension in Christian cult.

Now, in confirmation as the final achievement of the initiation process, the Holy Spirit gives us the direct structure toward the Eucharist as meeting with the Lord and with His people. And for that reason no other sacramental act may intervene between baptism and confirmation or between confirmation and the Eucharist (for example, first Communion before confirmation) and confirmation and first Holy Communion should take place in one continuous celebration, for the Eucharist is the constitutive sacrament of the Christian community, in which confirmation gives a priestly function; that is, above all, active participation in the Eucharist. For initiation implies that the community in question performs effectively this admission and this happens finally in order to and by means of the common celebration of the constitutive token of all Christian community, the Eucharist.

This raises a serious problem; if this connection between confirmation and Eucharist is so close, how can our general custom of giving first Communion before confirmation be justified? We could answer by another question: how could the pretty general custom of not administering confirmation at all, right before the rise of Protestantism and before the French Revolution, be justified?

Neither of these customs can be justified at all, because they are an abuse, and of very recent date and exist only in the Western Church. Theologians may try to explain how this practice is not completely against the sacramental economy although it distorts the whole initiation rite. The key to this explanation is this. Since baptism is the first wing of the initiation triptych, it is organically structured toward the other wing, confirmation, and the central panel of all is the Eucharist. This structure is so existential that baptism contains already a certain "confirmation of desire" (parallel with the expression "baptism of desire"). This means that every baptism already includes implicitly but objectively—that is, in the very sacramental structure itself—a desire for its fulfillment through confirmation and hence also for the Eucharist.

We can therefore understand why the late Carolingian Ordo . . . stressed so much that confirmation should be administered by the bishop if he is present; but it adds that the Eucharist should be given anyhow after baptism if the bishop is not present, because of the Eucharistic celebration and the Christian initiation, even if one of the elements of this initiation is lacking by reason of purely external obstacles. Hence the "general custom" cannot be invoked against the real structure of the Christian initiation (and it is not "general," since none of the Eastern Churches follow it).[8]

In regard to the third conclusion: confirmation and the first Communion in the Easter Vigil. This is the final conclusion following from the preceding two points. We would not maintain that the Easter Vigil is the only fitting moment for confirmation and/or for first Communion. But it is certainly the right and best moment, for many reasons.

First of all, the very fact that the primitive Church, as soon as she started institutionalizing the divine heritage of grace into an adapted sacramental system, took the Easter Vigil as being the only moment for the Christian initiation in its threefold stage of baptism, confirmation, and first Communion. This very fact must be an argument sufficiently strong to rule out the posterior theological considerations.

Indeed, what are the theological foundations of this practice? The Church not only *gives* us the Eucharist and the other sacraments, but she first received them from her Lord, precisely as the effective token of her oneness (*com-unio*). Hence all the members of this community have to cooperate in bringing about this token, as soon as they are reasonably able to (early Communion). But they have to perform their first act of this cooperation under its right sacramental and ecclesial conditions; that is, after an appropriate initiation and in its Paschal environment. For it is in this Paschal context that the purified Church reaches the all-comprising culminating point of her life in order to communicate it to her newborn children: the Paschal Eucharist celebration.

Hence the early Church concluded: the Easter Vigil is the moment par excellence for first Communion, because only in this Paschal context does this Communion get its right meaning and perspective:

1. It is the act of full participation in the community of the risen Lord, the members of which live in this holy night their decisive exodus from the Egypt of sin and death into the promised land of life, so that they are at least for one night what they should be throughout the whole year: a Paschal people (see the *Exsultet*).

2. It is sacramental union with the risen Lord, who takes His gathered people and especially His new members up into His victorious Passover from death to life; this happens in every Eucharist, indeed, but when a new Christian experiences it for the first time, this should happen in its fullest and most effective form, in the Easter night.

3. The more so since this happens after the long sacramental (thus effective) preparation of both the new candidates and the admitting community, during Lent; in the right sacramental context after baptism (or renewal of the baptismal vows) and confirmation; and further developed and deepened during Easter Week.

It is beyond our plan to develop this last point. But we would stress very much the utmost importance of this sacramental preparation (Lent) and development (Easter Week) of the Paschal Night celebration. We may never forget that the primitive meaning of the

Holy *Quadragesima* is to prepare the candidates and the community for the great event of the Easter night; that is, not only for baptism, but for the whole admission rite, which includes confirmation and the Eucharist as well; and that Easter Week is properly meant to develop the riches of the first Holy Communion that the newly confirmed had received during the Easter Vigil: the whole liturgy of this week is devoted to developing this Eucharistic dimension of Easter; it is the most authentic "Eucharistic octave" of the primitive Church.

If we believe in the sacramental realism of the liturgy, we must bring confirmation and first Holy Communion, as far as possible, back to their original context; we have to take the primitive Lenten liturgy as the framework for our preparation for these sacraments, and the liturgy of Easter Week as the basis for their working out in the practical life. We are fully aware of the difficulties this arrangement involves. But then at least we will be able to "devotionalize" first Holy Communion and give it its full sense for the whole further life since it has been given within the right sacramental context.

Confirmation and Eucharist

The *habitual* relation between confirmation and the Eucharist in virtue of the *sacramental character* is not so immediate as is its actual administration in the context of the whole Christian initiation. It goes through the medium of the general priesthood of the faithful. Confirmation is the proper sacrament of the priesthood of the faithful, and the act par excellence of this general priesthood is the Eucharist.

We presume that both of these statements are now so generally accepted by the theologians who *ex professo* have studied the question that they do not need to be proved any more. We give here only some outlines in regard to our subject, and would like to refer to our book, *La Confirmation, doctrine et pastorale* (Brugge, 1958), for the theological and practical development.

1. The people into whom the Christian initiation rite introduces the new candidates is a "priestly people," the *regale sacerdotium* of 1 Peter 2:5-9, which was prefigured in Exodus 19:4-6. For that reason the Apocalypse describes the Church as a worshipping community, dedicated above all to the worship of God (Ap. 1:6; 5:10; 22:6). This does not mean that the Church has an exclusively

liturgical function, and certainly not in a rubricistic and legalistic sense. But that all the other levels of the Church's life (social, hierarchical, eschatological, and so forth) originate from and converge in this cultural character of the People of God.

Although the demarcation between the proper attributions of the two sacraments is not very clear, we might say with the Fathers and the liturgies that a new candidate becomes a member of the People of God through baptism; he goes through the door into the house of God (Council of Trent); but through confirmation he receives his organic function in that living organism; he receives, so to say, a "job in that house of God," he becomes an adult with his own responsibility in the bosom of the People of God, as a permanent structure, which enables him to exercise validly the acts that belong to that function.

Since the People of God is first of all meant to be a worshipping community, created for the glory of God, the proper function the new Christian receives in this community will be a worshipping function. And since the Eucharist is the vital center and goal of all Christian worship, confirmation has to create a special and permanent relation and structure toward the celebration of the Eucharist. This has been the strong conviction of the Church from the beginning, as she expressed, for example, in the Eucharistic liturgy itself. So the choir of the people sings after the Consecration, in the Armenian Rite: "Spirit of God, who, coming down from heaven, effect *through our means* the Mystery of him who is glorified," and so on.

This sacramental realism perhaps sounds unusual to us, for a double reason. First, since confirmation has been torn loose from its organic setting in the whole of the Christian initiation rite, its cultual and Eucharistic connection has been lost, and the social aspect (*robur ad pugnam*) has been stressed; this is a very real and important effect of confirmation, but not the primary and original one.

2. Secondly, we have lost the realization of the general priesthood of the faithful: during the Counter Reformation the theologians tried by every means to devaluate this priesthood and to prove that it has no real content, although for the Fathers and the whole of Christian antiquity the first who share in the priesthood of Christ (the unique priesthood of the New Covenant) are the faithful. In order to weaken this sacramental realism of the *regale sacerdotium* against Protestantism, they had recourse to all kinds of homemade subter-

fuges; for example, the priesthood of holiness as being distinct from the cultual priesthood, and the latter still further dehydrated into a mere metaphor.

To support these subterfuges they have to twist the real meaning of St. Thomas,[9] to overlook the Fathers and the primitive Church, and to empty the biblical realism. The "common or general consensus of biblical scholars" is that the *pneumatikài thusiai* of 1 Peter 2:5 has very little to do with "spiritual offerings" in relation to sanctifying grace and merely moral acts; but means real cultual "offerings in the Holy Spirit," that is, to which we are enabled by a special (that is, sacramental) intervention of the Holy Spirit, and that is confirmation. Of course, all worship has to be the expression of interior holiness (*devotio* as St. Thomas calls it), so that we would empty the real sense of worship *and* of spiritual life by making a cleavage between spiritual life and liturgy. But this "surrender to God" as such is neither offering nor worship nor priesthood. Priesthood always supposes and requires worship as its proper act and object, that is, the social and "sacramental" expression of the *devotio* of the Church as bride of Christ.

Now, through confirmation these acts of worship share in the priesthood of Christ, in its effectiveness and mediatorship. Moreover, through confirmation the whole life of the Christian receives a cultual finalization, as being ordinated to worship (Rom 12:1-2), not through a nonexistent priesthood of holiness, but through this ontological (because sacramental) priestly "trend" of our whole life effected by confirmation. This explains why the Bible sees a double element in the priesthood: the Word in order to witness and the worship. Both are the proper attribution of confirmation, but always in order to edify the Church as a worshipping community, gathered for their all-comprising act, the Eucharistic celebration, as the Apocalypse describes the ideal Church. Indeed, the privileges of the Levitic tribe of the Old Testament have passed to the whole priestly people of the New Testament.

3. This cultual dimension of confirmation becomes even clearer when we contemplate the sacramental system from Christ out, Head of the People of God and leader of their worship. A certain rite is a sacrament because it applies to us a certain salvific moment of Christ's historical life as the New Adam. Through baptism Christ extends to us His own sonship of the heavenly Father and the Holy Spirit makes us Christiform. Through confirmation we share in His

being filled with the Holy Spirit to act effectively according to our Christiformity.

From the earliest Fathers and liturgies on, baptism has been brought into relation with Christ's incarnation (and with His death and resurrection, but on a different level); confirmation with the mystery of Pentecost, when the glorious Lord communicated to His Church His own anointing and fullness by the Holy Spirit (*Christos*—the anointed one). Through confirmation the holy adventure of Pentecost is communicated to the Church throughout the centuries. That is the meaning of the original rites of confirmation: imposition of hands (communication of the Spirit) and anointing (sharing in the Anointed One par excellence).

Now, Christ's fullness of the Holy Spirit is His priesthood, as the Fathers unanimously point out; that means, the power giving an effective sanctifying and redeeming value to His incarnate sonship. In the Spirit His historical salvific acts are translated into ritual acts, that is, into worship, with the same redeeming dimension and effective strength, but now brought about together with His members, that is, with all who participate liturgically in these acts.

Confirmation, then, makes us share in this priesthood of Christ, lifts our worship up into the level of Christ's action; that is, makes these cultual acts really "priestly." This applies especially to the central act of all Christian worship, the Eucharist. We know that the Prayer of the Church is a more primary worship, because it is the expression of our fundamental relation to God, and hence it is a more basic object of the general priesthood of the faithful. But the Eucharist is the center of all Christian worship because Christ Himself takes our worship into His own Passover from death to life, the climax of His whole salvific life and of the whole economy of salvation.

Through active participation, for which confirmation qualifies us, the Eucharist, as supreme act of our Head, becomes the supreme worship of His members, and the holy token of our oneness in Him. For that reason theologians take the Christian community (that is, with Christ and between each other) as the *res et sacramentum* of the Eucharist. That implies that confirmation qualifies us to act in such a way that we *realize* the sacramental token itself of this Christian unity; and this capability applies not only to the priest but (*servatis servandis*) to the whole congregation as well, because only through their active participation can the Eucharist be the token of this oneness in Christ. This is strongly expressed by the famous sentence of St. Augustine: "This is the sacrifice of the Christians: many being one body in Christ." And for the same reason the catechumens had to leave before the Eucharistic service began, for only the full members of the priestly People of God were able to perform it.

Seen from below, this also implies that the Eucharist is the expression of the whole Christian life, just as His Passover from death to life (His sacrifice) was the expression of the whole priestly existence of Christ, from the first moment of the Incarnation until His ascension into heaven.[10] Likewise through this priestly "coining" by confirmation our whole life is ordinated to worship, which reaches its climax in its central act, the Eucharistic celebration.[11]

Conclusion

It is beyond our purpose to treat here of all the practical implications of this teaching of the Church. We would only submit the following ones to the benevolent attention of our readers.

All those who are engaged in these problems are of the opinion that the Easter Vigil should be restored as *the* confirmation day par excellence, and for the first communicants at least in the episcopal churches: by no other means could the sublime greatness of the bishop be better shown than through this solemn admission of young Christians to the full participation in the Paschal riches of the new People of God and in the Eucharistic celebration.

As to the parishes, the same privilege should gradually be extended to the pastors (they only) and only for the Easter Vigil and for the first communicants. This, of course, does not depend on us. But we are not the only ones who are convinced that it will be very difficult to revaluate the Easter celebration in its full meaning and all its dimensions unless we bring confirmation and first Holy Communion back to their right sacramental context. We are convinced, as well, that this implies many practical difficulties. But, on the contrary, we must not think that this was not true also for the primitive Church.

Then we will be able to give the real and full meaning back to Lent and to Easter Week, center of the whole liturgical year. Lent will again be the preparation for a real common celebration in which the whole Christian community is engaged. And Easter Week will be the festival extension, celebrated by the whole family of God, of the Eucharistic Easter celebration. . . .

References

[1] C. Vaggagini, *Theological Dimensions of the Liturgy* (Collegeville, 1959), explains this extensively. We suppose this general principle here sufficiently known.

[2] We find a parallel description in Acts of the Apostles 19:1-6: "Now it was while Apollo was in Corinth that Paul, after passing through the upper districts, came to Ephesus and found certain disciples; and he said to them, 'Did you receive the Holy Spirit when you became believers?' But they said to him, 'We have not even heard that there is a Holy Spirit.' And he said, 'How then were you baptized?' They said, 'With John's baptism.' Then Paul said, 'John baptized the people with a baptism of repentance, telling them to believe in him who was to come after him, that is, in Jesus.' On hearing this they were baptized in the name of the Lord Jesus; and when Paul laid his hands on them, the Holy Spirit came upon them, and they began to speak in tongues and to prophesy."

[3] Edited by Gregory Dix, *The Treatise on the Apostolic Tradition by Hippolytus of Rome* (London: Society for Promoting Christian Knowledge, 1937).

[4] Martène, *De Antiquis Ecclesiae Ritibus*, IV, c. xxiv, Vol. III, 158 (Rouen, 1700). Other examples and texts will be given further on. For a more complete documentation see our study "Première Communion, célébration pascale," *Paroisse et Liturgie*, 42 (1960), 18-42.

[5] For the full explanation of the following we would refer to our book *La Confirmation, Doctrine et Pastorale* (Belgium: Brugge, 1958).

[6] We know, however, that the "sacramental grace" of each of the sacraments refers to a very different "moment" in the history of salvation: baptism makes us participate in the mystery of Christ's death and resurrection; confirmation in the pouring out of the Holy Spirit on Pentecost. But it is not our task to treat of this here.

[7] The same mistake has been made by some theologians who study the place and power of the bishop, starting with some "marginal cases" and belittling and deforming the bishop. See our study, "De l'Evêque" in *Quest. Lit. Paroiss.*, 37 (1956), 197ff.

[8] On June 5, 1959, The *Catholic Telegraph* published a picture of the Holy Father giving first Holy Communion to young men, after having required that they should first be confirmed. The paper's letterpress rightly adds that this act of the Holy Father "put into new focus the growing movement to confer the Sacrament of confirmation prior to first Communion."

[9] Perhaps the best example of misinterpreting St. Thomas is III, q. 63, a. 3 c and ad 1, invoked in favor of a so-called priesthood of holiness, although the real point of this text is to prove just the opposite; i.e., that the sacramental character gives an ontological *deputatio*, i.e., structure and ability for real worship.

[10] See the beautiful Chapter 10 of Hebrews, especially vv. 5 and 14.

[11] Further explanation in our study "Confirmation Today," *Worship*, 33 (May 1959), 343ff.

JOHN H. MILLER, C.S.C.

Until He Comes—
the Eucharist and the Resurrection

A problem concerning the use of signs is the fact that they can become anachronisms. When this happens it is difficult (or even impossible) to comprehend the meaning of a sign. In this article, the Eucharist is seen as the symbol of the resurrection. Historical examination and biblical considerations show why the sacrifice of the New Dispensation looks not only to Christ's death but also to His resurrection.

Father Miller is an associate editor for the *New Catholic Encyclopedia*. He is working at The Catholic University of America, Washington, D.C.

We are all quite familiar with the Pauline doctrine of baptism as our dying and rising together with Christ from weak, sinful, and mortal humanity to a transfiguring union with God. What so many of us do not sufficiently understand is that the New Testament presentation of the relationship of the Eucharist to Christ's redemptive work is just as forceful and realistic, if not more so. It is not without significance that the Lord chose the passover meal, the sacramental memorial of the Israelites' exodus from Egypt, as the sacramental memorial of His passage, or exodus, out of the flesh of sin to the body of the Spirit, the passing over of His humanity from its fallen condition to its transfigured life in God.[1]

This article first appeared in *Thy Kingdom Come*, in the Proceedings of the Twenty-Third North American Liturgical Week. It is reprinted here with permission of The Liturgical Conference.

Surely if St. Paul advises the Corinthians that "as often as ye eat this bread and drink the cup you proclaim the death of the Lord until He comes," the farthest thing from his mind is that Christians should walk around half dead. If water had such an extraordinary prophetic importance in the Old Testament as a symbol of life and was so pointedly fulfilled by our Lord in the New,[2] so much the more is the meal used in the Bible as a symbol productive of union with God, divine life in man. It is a source of much discomfort to see so many writers speak of the presence in the Eucharist of Christ's death alone. They seek to find ways and means of representing His death in the very ceremonial of the Mass and stop short with that.[3] I submit that this was not and is not the import of the Lord's institution.

I would suppose that this emphasis on symbolizing only Christ's death in the Mass rests squarely on an incomplete understanding of His redemptive work, as though the crucifixion of our Savior was salvific in itself and by itself alone—a misconception which, I trust, Père Durrwell's book has dissipated. Just as every coin has two sides, so redemption necessarily involves being ransomed from the power of sin and Satan and reconciled to the love of the Father. In this vein the Apostle Paul says so pointedly that Christ "was delivered up for our sins and rose again for our justification." [4] Hence, the Resurrection of Jesus Christ is essential to His saving deed; it is what gives meaning to His death; it is the specifically divine transforming action. If I am correct in seeing the central message of the New Testament as redemption meaning "human-nature-glorified-by-union-with-God-in-Christ," then this must be essentially the meaning of the Savior's chief sacrament, the Eucharist. And if this divinizing transformation of humanity is the effect of the Sacrament, then can we not expect to see the symbol of God giving His divine life as essential to the sacramental sign of the Eucharist, as the theological axiom "sacraments effect what they signify" would demand? The Eucharist, then, must symbolize the Resurrection also and primarily.[5]

What is the symbol which the Savior chose in order to insert us into His Resurrection? The answer in scripture is clear. The New Testament writers do not seek to categorize the Savior's sacrifice by reference to the Old Testament holocausts. Rather they very emphatically explain it as the fulfillment of a communion sacrifice: the Pasch. St. John relates the crucifixion of Jesus to the Passover in Chapter 19 (vv. 14, 31, 36). St. Paul declares that "Christ our Pasch is sacrificed." [6] In Matthew and Mark the Eucharist which itself refers to the cross is related to the paschal meal. Luke reports our Lord to have begun the meal by saying, "With great longing have I desired to eat this Passover with you before I suffer." [7] And though the account of the institution of the Eucharist is lacking in St. John, in Chapter 6 he locates in the proximity of the Pasch the multiplication of loaves—symbolic of the Eucharist—and Christ's promise to give Himself as food: "Now the Passover, the feast of the Jews, was near." [8]

In the Semitic religions the idea of union with God was certainly one of the elements constituting a sacrifice. Man tried to create a bond between himself and God by establishing with Him a community of blood or food, the same means which served to solidify social relationships among men themselves.

Though less significant perhaps than the sacrificial meals, the blood rituals were nonetheless emphatic in this respect. The slaughter of the animal was not part of the liturgical rite;[9] it was killed beforehand by someone other than the priest.[10] After some of its blood had been poured on the altar, the people were sprinkled with the rest of it. Since this blood had entered God's possession, by being sprinkled on the worshippers it consecrated them to Him; it set up a bond between them and God. The touch of blood united to God, put one into contact with Him. And the flow of blood between altar and people symbolized a flow of divine life between God and His People. Leviticus 17:10ff. gives us the key for interpreting this blood ritual: "Blood atones, insofar as it is life." The essential idea in all this, then, is not death or substitution, but life and union with God.[11] Blood symbolized life in the Old Testament, and life was God's property.

But among the Semites the sacrifice of communion seems to have been the earliest form of worship and, later on at least, the most widespread rite. Through the sacrificial meal man entered into the intimacy of God. Having covered God's table with gifts, the offerers sat down with Him partaking of the victim which, through rites of offering, had become God's property and was given back to men as sanctified and bearing God's life. And though among the Hebrews the holocaust and sin-offering, in which the meal was either foregone altogether or reserved for the priest alone, somewhat overshadowed the communion sacrifice, apart from these later exceptions sacrifice normally included a meal. The offering of first fruits, the first born of the flock, of tithes all ended with a meal. In fact, says J. Coppens, "Sacrifice in their vocabulary was almost synonymous with eating and drinking before Yahweh. All sacrifices . . . other than holocausts seem to have included a meal." [12] The idea basic to all this was that a victim consecrated to God drew all who fed upon it into the orbit of divine life and holiness. Israel was a nation united within itself and wedded to Yahweh because it sat at table with its God. Most particularly the eating of the paschal lamb constituted a sacrificial meal and, for that reason, created a union between God and men.[13]

The paschal meal was essentially a memorial meal which effectively brought that original saving Passover into the very midst of the Jewish family. As they ate this meal, the Jews could relive mystically, sacramentally, the events of the deliverance and Exodus from Egypt; they became contemporaries of their forefathers and were saved with them. At the same time they were brought closer to the messianic fulfillment of that prophetic deliverance.

The paschal meal was invariably preceded by the *Haggadah*, a discourse relating the meal and its various elements to the saving event of the exodus. After the preliminary *Kiddush*, or declaration of the holiness of the occasion, the washing of hands, the eating of the parsley appetizer, and the breaking of the middle matzah, the narrative, or *Haggadah*, begins with the youngest child asking the meaning of this celebration. The father of the family then relates the story of the first Passover. Only after God's great deeds in favor of His people are recounted does the Jewish family re-enact the Passover meal. The meal concludes with the recital of those same saving acts of God in prayer form—a thanking of God by re-thinking or recalling His mercies. We have, then, three components to this meal: the *Haggadah*, or telling about God's wonderful work; the *berakah*, or blessing, thanksgiving, the grace at the meal; and the actual redoing of the saving event, or the eating of the meal.

And here is our Christian Mass in its most essential parts: Mass of the Catechumens, the narrative of God's words and deeds; Mass of the faithful, man's grateful response of thanksgiving which sacramentally re-enacts those saving deeds, thus making him a part of them, making those same saving deeds vitally his own. Continuing the distinguishing characteristic of Judaic worship, the Church makes God's word and deed the stuff of worship, stuff for sacra-

mental recital before God in thanksgiving. The congregation is first
confronted anew with God's mighty saving actions and then makes
them the material of its worship, its response, as it engages in the
sacrificial meal.

At the Last Supper the Lord fulfilled the Passover meal by sub-
stituting Himself for the paschal lamb and commanding His disciples to do the same thing as His memorial—not just as a remembrance of Him, but as a sacramental reliving of His "once for all"
deliverance of mankind. The New Testament writers saw clearly
that the Eucharist was the Lord's way of allowing them to communicate in Himself as victim, in His sacrifice which transformed
and divinized His humanity. Just as all those who partook of the
communion sacrifices of old were drawn into the same sanctification
as the victim, so in this Eucharistic sacrificial meal the believer
takes possession of the resurrected body of the Savior, receives
divine life from the victim of Calvary transformed by God in the
resurrection. In fact, Christ's passage from death to life now becomes the believer's as he becomes the resurrected body of Christ.
Yes, the Eucharist creates the Church, for through the Eucharist
each and every member of it re-experiences Christ's death and resurrection, dies and rises with Christ, becomes the transfigured Christ
by eating of His transfigured Body. In the Eucharist the Christian
surrenders himself to Christ and thus dies with Christ in order to
be clothed with Christ, permeated with the divine life and power
of His resurrected Body which he now eats. Once he has died to his
life of sin and opened himself to God's saving influence, that same
specifically divine transfiguring action which raised Christ's dead
Body from the tomb now grips him and lifts him to a more intimate
share in the divine life.

Paul was not speaking metaphorically when he said, "Because the
bread is one, we, though many, are one body, all of us who partake
of the one bread." [14] Yes, "we, though many, are one body in
Christ." [15] "It is no longer I that live, but Christ lives in me." [16] In
very truth, "as often as ye eat this bread and drink the cup you
proclaim the death of the Lord until He comes," [17] not because you
are dead, but because you are filled with the divine life of Jesus
Christ, you have become His resurrected Body, and thus are dead
to the things of the world which are opposed to God. Paul himself
insists that "the death He died, He died once for all to sin; the life
He lives, He lives unto God." [18] He explains further: "You also

when you were dead by reason of your offences and sins wherein you once walked according to the fashion of this world . . . were by nature children of wrath. But God . . . by reason of His very great love, even when we were dead by reason of our sins, brought us to life together with Christ, and raised us up together and seated us together in heaven in Christ Jesus." [19]

Note, too, that at the end of the Passover meal Luke introduces the institution of the Eucharist with these words of our Savior: "I say to you, I will not drink from henceforth of the fruit of the vine, until that day when I shall drink it with you, new, in the kingdom of my Father." [20] The favorite symbol in rabbinic literature to describe the messianic kingdom was that of a banquet. "That day" is the day of Christ's glorification; the kingdom begins with His entry into glory. Though our Lord's words bear an eschatological perspective, the banquet was not to be relegated to some distant future. Christ gave an unexpected deepening to the rabbinic image: the messianic meal was a paschal meal, symbol of national community, source of its intimacy with God.

Thus the very words which herald the great messianic banquet also set by its side the Eucharist in such wise that the Eucharist appears as the earthly sacramental anticipation of the feast to be celebrated in the Kingdom of heaven; and the heavenly banquet as a prolongation of the Eucharistic supper. Christ, in fulfilling the Pasch, inaugurated His kingdom in which His disciples could already share by eating of His paschal body and blood and in this way communicate in the redemption and receive in Christ God's glorifying action. And how well did St. Paul perceive the connection! "We all, with faces unveiled, reflecting as in a mirror the glory of the Lord, are being transformed into His very image from glory to glory, as through the Spirit of the Lord." [21]

As we feast upon the flesh and blood of the resurrected victim in the Christian Passover we are ourselves being resurrected bit by bit until we are ready for fullest participation in the banquet of the heavenly mansion of our Father. And so, St. Paul looks forward to the end with realistic eyes: "If you have risen with Christ, seek the things that are above, where Christ is seated at the right hand of God. Mind the things that are above, not the things that are of earth [meaning an earth opposed to God]. For you have died and your life is hidden with Christ in God. When Christ, your life, shall appear, then you too will appear with Him in glory." [22]

References

[1] The theme of this paper has been treated more fully in the author's book, *Signs of Transformation in Christ* (Englewood Cliffs, New Jersey: Prentice-Hall, Inc., 1963).

[2] John 3:5; 7:37-39; 19:34; Romans 6:3ff. See F. X. Durrwell's commentary on John 7:37-39 in *The Resurrection* (New York: Sheed & Ward, 1960), pp. 81-91.

[3] Cf. *Yearbook of Liturgical Studies*, 2 (1961), 231-32.

[4] Romans 4:25.

[5] Durrwell, *op. cit.*, pp. 324-28.

[6] 1 Corinthians 5:7.

[7] 22:15.

[8] V. 4.

[9] C. Stuhlmueller, C. P., "Teaching the Sacraments from Scripture," *Perspectives*, 5 (Sept.-Oct. 1960), 23.

[10] Leviticus 1:1-13; 3:2, 8; Ezechial 44:10-11.

[11] C. Stuhlmueller, *op. cit.*, 23.

[12] "Eucharistie," *Dictionnaire de la Bible, Suppl.* col. 1157.

[13] Durrwell, *op. cit.*, p. 74.

[14] 1 Corinthians 10:17.

[15] Romans 12:5.

[16] Galatians 2:20.

[17] Corinthians 11:26.

[18] Romans 6:10.

[19] Ephesians 2:1-6.

[20] 22:18. Matthew (26:29) and Mark (14:25) place these words after the institution. It is Luke who gives them their natural position. Cf. Durrwell, p. 156, note 7; P. Benoit, "Le récit de la cène dans Luc xxii, 15-20" *Revue Biblique*, 48 (1939), 357-93.

[21] Corinthians 3:18.

[22] Colossians 3:1-4.

WILLIAM W. BAUM

Sin, Repentance, and Forgiveness

A central problem in the history of theology is the meaning of
concupiscence. It is universally recognized as an effect of man's
original failure to live up to the condition in which God created
man. Concupiscence is an enduring effect which persists even
after man has been essentially restored by God's gifts to a state
of harmony with his creator. The presence of concupiscence suggests man's continual need for a healing process, and the sacraments of penance and extreme unction supply this need.

Monsignor William Baum is Vice Chancellor of the diocese of
Kansas City, Missouri.

On the holiest of all nights, in the course of the Easter Vigil,
the Church sings exultantly:

> "This is the very night which delivers all who believe in Christ
> from worldly vice and from darkness of sin which restores them to
> grace and makes them co-sharers with the saints."
> "This is the night in which Christ burst the bonds of death and
> came forth as Conqueror from the grave. For unless we had been
> redeemed, it would avail us nothing to be born."

Every Easter the Church rejoices in the Pasch of the Lord and
every Easter the Church beholds the rebirth of her children who
die in Christ and rise with Christ from the waters of baptism. The
Easter Liturgy is filled with this sense of the newness of all things,
this sense of deliverance from sin and guilt. The primal curse laid
upon Adam our father, and upon all of us, his children, has been
lifted. The state of sin, the alienation of man from God, has been

This article was read at the Twenty-Second North American Liturgical
Week and it was first printed in its Proceedings, *Bible Life and Worship*.
It is reprinted here with permission of The Liturgical Conference.

ended. The sinner, baptized in Christ, has been reconciled with his God; indeed he has become a son of God.

Scarcely is the Paschal solemnity completed, however, when the Christian is reminded that he still remains a sinner, that he still remains subject to sickness and to death, that he still suffers that disorder in his being called concupiscence, and that he is still capable of rebellion against his Creator. The mystery of iniquity still confronts him, and as he well knows, many a Christian has lost his baptismal grace and returned to sin, to the condition of alienation from God.

The infant Church, filled with the realization of the Paschal mystery, was profoundly dismayed by the recurrence of sin on the part of baptized Christians. In that precious document of the sub-Apostolic age, known as the *Shepherd of Hermas*, we find this mentality vividly portrayed in these words of the Shepherd:

> Commandment 4. 3. "From some teachers I have heard, sir, said I, that there is no other penance except the one when we went down into the water and received remission of our former sins. You have heard well, said he to me, for such is the case. Surely it were only right that he who has received remission of his sins should sin no more, but should persevere in purity."

He who has received remission of his sins should indeed sin no more. Is there no hope for such a one? The Shepherd continues:

> "But since you demand exactness in all your questioning, I will make this point clear to you as well, without, however, giving the wrong impression to those who are about to believe, or to those who have just come to believe in the Lord. For those who have just come to believe or who are about to believe, do not undergo penance for sins, but (through baptism) have remission of their former sins. It is then for those who were called before these days that the Lord has established penance. For the Lord who knows the heart and has knowledge of all things in advance, knew the weakness of men and the manifold wiles of the devil, and how he would do the servants of God some evil, and work some knavish trick upon them. Therefore did the Lord, who is rich in mercy, have mercy on the work of His hands and establish even this penance. But I tell you, said he, after that great and holy calling [of baptism], if anyone is tempted by the devil and sins, he has but one penance. For if anyone should sin and do penance frequently, to such a man his penance will be of no avail; for with difficulty will he live.

The Lord is merciful to spare. He offers a second chance at salvation, but this second chance according to the Shepherd is offered but once. There is displayed here a rigorous view towards the fallen Christian which well exemplifies one current of thought found in the early Church; and this rigorous tendency grows stronger during the century which follows the sub-Apostolic age.

The Church has long since clarified her position. She teaches that all sins can be forgiven and invites all men to do penance and seek this remission. There still remains, however, a tension within the Church created by this coexistence within her members of Divine Life and sin. There is also a tension resulting from the differing, and sometimes conflicting, meanings which we attach to terms like original sin, concupiscence, guilt. It is far from our purpose . . . to define these terms or to analyze them or to present a synthesis of Christian thought on these points.

We live at a moment of doctrinal and theological development, and there is no theologian today who maintains that a satisfactory synthesis has been achieved.

It will suffice . . . for us to touch upon certain themes and concepts and to suggest certain lines of thought. In any such attempt we shall find in the Sacred Scriptures, as well as in the Sacred Liturgy, an inexhaustible source.

Old Testament

When God led the children of Israel out of Egypt, He did more than rescue them from bondage in the house of death. He rescued them in order that they might become His people, an elect nation raised up to witness to Him before the world and to be the bearer of the great promise. The Covenant of Sinai was the great event in the sacred history of the people of Israel. On Mount Sinai Moses received the law, and Moses descended from Sinai to give this law to his people and to announce to them the Covenant whereby they became God's People. This Covenant of Sinai was inaugurated with sacrifice—a sacrifice which was intended both to purify from sin and to seal the covenant. The blood of the animals slain in sacrifice was poured both on the altar and sprinkled upon the people. While this rite took place, Moses spoke to the people: "This is the Blood of the Covenant which the Lord hath made with you concerning all these words" (Ex 24:8).

Even after the Exodus and the Covenant of Sinai, the people of Israel kept alive the memory of these saving events and renewed them by means of their cultus, the cycle of feasts and prescribed sacrifices.

Although this people had been led out of Egypt and had become the people of God, sin still remained and there were appointed sacrifices to be made as "sin offerings." Aaron the priest, and the high priests, his successors, were commanded to come annually before the Ark of the Covenant to make expiation for the sins of the people (cf. Lv, 16). Through this day of atonement the people of Israel sought forgiveness of their sins. The high priest not only offered sacrifice but also confessed, that is, acknowledged both his own sins and the sins of his people.

For Israel, sin was rebellion against God, the rejection of God's law, and, in a sense, the repudiation of the Covenant between Yahweh and Israel.

The individual Israelite was saved through his belonging to the people of God; and the sin of the individual Israelite was not only rebellion against God but also because it was so opposed to the Covenant, an injury to the whole people.

It would be a distortion, however, to present the spirit of repentance as found in the Old Testament as merely ritual in character. It is true that for the Israelite, friendship with God was bound up with membership in the community, with belonging to the chosen people of God. It is also true that the Israelite depended upon the cultus to maintain this relationship with God. But it is also true that the prophets of Israel raised their voices repeatedly, insistently, angrily to remind the people that mere ritual without true personal sorrow was not only inadequate but even offensive in the sight of God. Thus the prophet Amos:

> I hate and reject your festivities:
> I have no pleasure in your solemn assemblies.
> If you offer me your holocausts and your oblations,
> I will take no pleasure in them,
>   and your sacrifices of fat calves—
> I will not even look at them.
> Take away from me the noise of your canticles,
>   that I may not hear the sound of your harps.
> But let judgment flow like water,
>   and justice like an unfailing torrent.

> (Am 5:21-27)

The God of the prophet is the God of holiness and of justice requiring both fear and sorrow on the part of His sinful people—a

God who threatens chastisement if the people remain hard of heart. But this same God of holiness and justice, is shown by the prophet Osea to be also a lover who is grieved by the sin of His people— even as a loving husband is grieved by the infidelity of a wayward wife; and as a forgiving husband offers pardon and protection to a repentant wife, Yahweh assures the repentant people.

> I will espouse you to myself for ever:
> I will espouse you to myself in justice and judgment,
>   in mercy and in tenderness;
> I will espouse you to myself in faithfulness.

> (Os 2:19-20)

Since sin entailed both personal rebellion against God and also infidelity to the Covenant which bound the people to God, sin was punished by the people, that is, by the community. The sinner was not only left to the judgement of God but even, on certain occasions, cast out from association with the people. What might be called "excommunication," cutting off from the common life and common worship of the people, was a punishment frequently imposed among the Jews of antiquity.

In the intertestamental period, the time between the composition of the last books which are part of the canon of the Old Testament and the birth of Christ, we find a development of this spirit among those people sometimes called "Essenes." These people lived in a kind of monastic life in the desert and felt themselves to be a people separated not only from the Gentile world but even, in a sense, from the rest of Israel. These people of the desert, the men of Qumran, about whom we have learned much in recent years from the discovery and study of the so-called "Dead Sea Scrolls," believed themselves to be a very special community, enjoying a unique relationship with God—people of a new Covenant. More rigorously than their forefathers, these men, hungering for justices and holiness, excluded the sinner from their midst until the sinner was purified:

> Whosoever among the men of the Community—of the Covenant of the Community—turns away insolently from any commandment, he shall not participate in the purification of the holy men nor shall he have any knowledge of any of their deliberations until his deeds are purified from all iniquity and until he walks in perfection of way. He shall (then) be admitted to the Council according to the judgment of the Great Ones, and afterwards he shall be enrolled

in his assigned position. This same rule shall be enforced on all those who join the Community ("Discovery in the Judean Desert," Vermes, pp. 148-49).

The New Testament

> Therefore as through one man sin entered into the world and through sin death, and thus death has passed unto all men because all have sinned, yet death reigned from Adam until Moses even over those who did not sin after the likeness of the transgression of Adam, who is a figure of him who was to come. Now the law intervened that the offense might abound. But where the offense has abounded, grace has abounded yet more; so that as sin has reigned unto death, so also grace may reign by justice unto life everlasting through Jesus Christ our Lord (Rom 5:12-21).

This is St. Paul's doctrine on the universality of sin, the solidarity of the human race in the state of sin. But, at the same time, if there is solidarity in sin, there is also solidarity in grace, the grace of Jesus Christ. Jesus Christ is the new Adam who has poured forth His blood, who has given up His life because He has taken upon himself the sins of the world. Paul is bold enough and blunt enough to declare:

> We exhort you, for Christ's sake, be reconciled to God. For our sakes He made Him to be sin who knew nothing of sin, so that in Him we might become the justice of God (2 Cor 5:20-21).

By reason of original sin we are all involved in the mystery of iniquity, in the mystery of death. We come into existence devoid of holiness, alienated from God, oppressed by the guilt of the sin of Adam and disfigured by its stain.

In the Epistle to the Romans, St. Paul tells us of God's plan to rescue us from this condition.

> Do you not know that all we who have been baptized into Christ Jesus have been baptized into His death? For we were buried with Him by means of Baptism into death, in order that, just as Christ has arisen from the dead through the glory of the Father, so we also may walk in newness of life.

The Christian, then, reborn in Christ, the second Adam, is delivered from the sin of Adam; he is dead to sin but alive to God in Jesus Christ.

The baptized Christian, even though he now is a member of the Body of Christ, still remains subject to sin. When the baptized

Christian sins, he rebels in a way impossible for an infidel. By sin, the Christian repudiates the New Covenant which has been inaugurated by the Blood of Christ—wounds the very Body of which he is himself a member; and the whole Body suffers the consequences of his rebellion. How does the Body react against such a threat? St. Paul decreed, in writing to the Corinthians with terrifying severity, excommunication for the sinner.

> It is actually reported that there is immorality among you and such immorality as is not found even among the Gentiles, that a man should have his father's wife. And you are puffed up, and have not rather mourned so that he who has done this deed might be put away from your midst. I indeed, absent in body but present in spirit, have already, as though present passed judgment in the name of our Lord Jesus Christ on the one who has so acted—you and my spirit gathered together with the power of our Lord Jesus— to deliver such a one over to Satan for the destruction of the flesh, that his spirit may be saved in the day of our Lord Jesus Christ (1 Cor 5:1-5).

Is there nothing more to be said? The baptized member has been cut off from the Body. Can he rise again to a newness of life? Can he be reconciled with the community of the faithful? The Gospel of Christ has not left us uninstructed on this point. After His resurrection Our Lord appeared to His Apostles:

> When it was late that same day the first of the week, though the doors where the disciples gathered had been closed for fear of the Jews, Jesus came and stood in the midst and said to them, "Peace be to you." And when He had said this, He showed them His hands and His side. The disciples therefore rejoiced at the sight of the Lord. He therefore said to them again, "Peace be to you. As the Father has sent me, I also send you." When He had said this, He breathed upon them, and said to them, "Receive the Holy Spirit; whose sins you shall forgive, they are forgiven them; and whose sins you shall retain, they are retained."

It is in this way that the Savior instructed His Church concerning the sacrament of penance, the sacrament of reconciliation. The Church teaches that the Christian who sins is offered the "second plank of salvation" to save him from eternal death. With true interior sorrow for sin the sinner approaches the tribunal where the priests sit in judgement; he confesses his sins; the priest pronounces a solution, his sins are remitted; the repentant Christian is restored to friendship with his God.

Is there more to be said? How can any man, as the priest claims to do, forgive sins? Does it not suffice for the sinner, praying as the psalmist of old to prostrate himself before his God and beg forgiveness? Why this intervention on the part of the priest? It should be recalled that the Pharisees, when the Saviour cured the man sick with palsy and declared the man's sins to be forgiven, raised this same question, "Who can forgive sins, but God only" (Mt 5:18-24).

To attempt an answer to this question one must see the mystery of Christ as the mystery of the God-man, Christ Jesus, in union with His members. In other words, one must have a vision of the "Whole Christ." Just as sin on the part of a baptized Christian is not an action which is performed in splendid isolation—just as the state of sin, which is the consequence of the act of sin, is not a condition which endangers only the sinner himself but also the Church, so too the forgiveness of the sinner is not imparted as to an isolated individual. Forgiveness is granted to one who has been incorporated into the Body of Christ, and no one can find forgiveness and restoration to eternal life apart from this Body of Christ.

This aspect of penance is vividly portrayed in the penitential liturgy of earlier centuries. In the penitential practices and rites of the Church we see very clearly that the sinner was "excommunicated," cut off from the Eucharistic life of the Church, excluded from the sacrifice, denied the flesh of the Lord as his food. Before the sinner could return to his place in the Eucharistic assembly he had first to be reconciled with the Church. Sozomen describes the penitential liturgy of Rome in the fifth century in these words:

> There [at Rome] the place of those who are in penance is conspicuous: they stand with downcast eyes and with the countenance of mourners. But when the divine liturgy is concluded, without taking part in those things which are lawful to the initiated, they throw themselves prostrate on the ground with wailing and lamentation. Facing them with tears in his eyes, the bishop hurries towards them and likewise falls to the ground. And the whole congregation of the church with loud crying is filled with tears. After this the bishop rises first and raises those who are prostrate; and after he has prayed in a fitting manner for those who are repentant of their sins, he dismisses them. Then each one by himself willingly spends as much time as the bishop has appointed in exercises of hardship, either in fasting, or in not bathing, or in abstinence from meats, or in other ways which have been prescribed. On the appointed day, having discharged his penalty after the manner of a debt, he is absolved from his sin, and takes part in the assembly with the people.

The bishops of the Romans have guarded this procedure from times long past up to our own day.

It was the bishop who received his confession, assigned him his penance and finally, by the imposition of hands, offered him peace and restored him to communion with the Church. The severity of the early Church in imposing harsh penances has long since disappeared. The practice of public penance is today all but unknown. The postponement of absolution until after the performance of works of penance is out of the ordinary. The rite of penance is today so simple and the circumstances so private that the *social* character of forgiveness is not readily apparent.

The idea of frequent confession not only of mortal but also of venial sins has become an important part in the life of Christians. The simplicity of rite and the privacy of the confessional undoubtedly encourage the sinner. Frequency of confession also gives every Catholic an opportunity to receive some individual spiritual direction. In other words, if something has been lost of the ancient awareness of penance as the "Sacrament of reconciliation with the Church" much has been gained.

It is more than possible that the liturgical renewal of our age will lead to a re-emphasis on the "communal" aspects of penance and will, moreover, lead to a synthesis of the "public" and "private" elements of this sacrament.

It is also well to remember that the administration of the sacrament of penance is an act of "jurisdiction" and belongs properly to the bishop. Presbyters, priests of the "second rank" must receive "faculties" (jurisdiction) from the bishop in order to absolve, to reconcile, to restore the sinner to Eucharistic communion. On this point it may be illustrative to recall an admonition of the third century uttered by St. Cyprian, the bishop of Carthage:

I hear that some of the presbyters are neither mindful of the Gospel nor do they consider what the martyrs have written to me, nor do they reserve to the bishop the honor of his priesthood and chair, but they have already begun to communicate with the lapsed and to offer in their behalf and to give them the Eucharist, when it was proper that they should have attained all this through approved procedure.

On this notion of jurisdiction as well as that of reconciliation St. Thomas Aquinas with his usual lucidity remarks:

Through the sacraments a man is not only reconciled to God, but must also be reconciled to the Church: but he cannot be reconciled to the Church unless the sanctification of the Church reaches him . . . and in Penance the sanctification of the Church can only reach him through the Church's minister, and hence although one who confessed to a layman in a moment of danger may have won forgiveness of God . . . nevertheless he has not been reconciled to the Church, so as to be admitted to the sacraments of the Church, unless he is first absolved by a priest, just as he who has been baptized by Baptism of desire is not admitted to the Eucharist.

Extreme Unction as the Sacrament of the Sick

. . . [Now I would like to discuss] extreme unction as the sacrament of the sick. One must confess a certain hesitancy in approaching this subject. . . . [I do not intend] to plunge into the controversy concerning the nature and effects of this sacrament. Preachers and theologians are divided in their approach, and even noted experts on the Liturgy differ one from another. Some present extreme unction as the "anointing for glory"; others see this sacrament as one which "looks to the bodily, psychological, and moral condition of a man when his organism begins to fail." [1] Both sides can call upon impressive authorities for support.

This controversy however, does not obscure certain fundamentals. Despite baptism and absolution the Christian remains weak and inclined to sin, subject to sickness, suffering and death—all of which are manifestations of our sinful condition—signs of our "apartness" from God. Until the Son of Man in all His glory comes again, these consequences of sin will not entirely disappear.

Anointing of the sick, whatever else is to be said of it, *sacramentalizes* this process of dying. The sick man (or the dying man) is by means of anointing, configured to Christ in a unique way. The external rite, the *sacramentum tantum*, produces a "symbolic reality," the *res et sacramentum*, which endures through the course of the sickness and continues to cause the grace, the *res sacramenti*, as long as the sickness lasts.

The soul is indeed a substance distinct from the body, but soul and body go together to make up this being called man, and man is one. When we assert that anointing is primarily for the benefit of the soul and secondarily for the benefit of the body do we not perhaps make too clean and sharp a distinction? It is true that the anointed person is not always restored to full health, but the sacrament does have its effect on both soul and body and becomes "a help granted to the whole person to enable him to live intensely his supernatural life notwithstanding the special encumbrance of sin . . . a comfort bestowed upon the body so as not to impede the life of the spirit, that is, a help that partially restores order among the various faculties with respect to the total finality of the person." [2]

Conclusion

The Christian, although reborn in Christ remains subject to concupiscence, sickness and death, suffers the buffeting of Satan, and even retains the capacity of personal sin—of rebellion against his God. Every sin, even venial, is a kind of withdrawal from God.

It is in Christ that man encounters God. No one comes to the Father except through the Son. Sin on the part of a baptized person becomes also a rebellion against Christ and consequently a withdrawal from His Body. Sin on the part of a Christian is an attack on the whole Body of Christ which is the Church and incurs a special penalty: The sinner is cut off from the Sacrament-Sacrifice of the Eucharist—excluded from the assembly in which the Sign of the New Covenant is renewed.

In the Sacrament of Forgiveness the sinner once more encounters the risen Christ; he is restored to communion with the Body; he is readmitted to the assembly of the faithful and through the Son is reconciled with the Father.

The Lord took upon Himself our condition of weakness, which is a sign and a consequence of sin. He became obedient even to the death of the Cross, and death is the greatest of the signs and consequences of sin. But in suffering and dying the Christ becomes Victor over death and Victor over that which is signified by death—sin. The Father accepted the Sacrifice of His Son, the Son rose from death, ascended to the Father and sent the Holy Spirit to vivify His Church.

Mysteriously, the human condition, which includes the state of concupiscence, suffering, and death, is consecrated by the Church. By means of her sacraments of forgiveness and healing we are more perfectly configured to, more perfectly united with the Christ, Who for us was made to be sin.

For those who are engaged in the liturgical apostolate these are themes and concerns of great moment: the Mystery of iniquity, solidarity in sin, rebirth in Christ and reconciliation with the Mystical Christ, consecration of suffering and dying. Perhaps it would not be inappropriate to apply to ourselves these words of the Gelasian Sacramentary used by the Roman Pontiff in reconciling sinners to the Church:

O God who has fashioned and has most graciously refashioned the human race, who by the blood of thine only Son has redeemed man when cast down from eternal blessedness by the devil's envy, quicken now him who Thou in no way desires to be dead to Thee, and Thou who does not abandon what is crooked, take back what has been straightened. May the tearful sighs of this Thy servant move Thy fatherly kindness, we beseech Thee, O Lord. Do Thou heal his wounds. Do Thou stretch forth Thy saving hand to him while prostrate, lest Thy Church be deprived of some portion of its body, lest Thy flock suffer loss, lest the enemy rejoice over the harm done to Thy family, lest a second death grip him who was reborn by the saving bath of Baptism. To Thee then, O Lord, as suppliants we pour forth our prayers, to Thee our heartfelt tears. Do Thou spare the one who confesses, that by Thy mercy he may not incur the punishments which now threaten him and the sentence of the judgment to come. Through Christ our Lord. Amen.

References

[1] B. Leeming, *Principles of Sacramental Theology*, p. 371.
[2] Alszeghy, *Theology Digest* (Spring 1961), p. 109.

MAUR BURBACH, O.S.B.

The Bible, Marriage, and Worship

The most commonly cited Pauline text which deals with the sacrament of matrimony is "This is a great mystery—I mean with reference to Christ and to the Church" (Eph 5:32). The significance of this text for sacramental theology is not immediately apparent, and the context of the statement raises difficulties concerning its exact meaning. Nevertheless, this text highlights the most important feature of matrimony, the dimension of mystery. It is this distinctive feature of marriage which is treated in the following article.

Father Burbach is the Rector of Immaculate Conception Seminary in Conception, Missouri.

. . . In a context more comprehensive than marriage, Father Pierre Teilhard de Chardin in his book, *The Divine Milieu*, observes that according to the most sacred articles of his creed, the Christian believes that life here below is but a prelude to a life, the joy and intensity of which are quite incommensurable with the present conditions in our universe. This disproportion by itself would be enough to rob us of our taste for the world and interest in it. Yet to it is added a positive doctrine of condemnation and contempt for a fallen world. "Perfection consists in detachment: the world about us is vanity and ashes." The believer is constantly reading or hearing these austere words. How can he reconcile them with that other counsel, usually coming from the same master and in any case written in his heart by nature, that he must be an example unto the

This article was originally a paper printed in *Bible Life and Worship*, Proceedings of The Twenty-Second Annual North American Liturgical Week. It is reprinted here with permission of The Liturgical Conference.

Gentiles in devotion to duty, in energy, and even in leadership in all the spheres opened up by man's activity. Every spiritual director knows that there are many for whom the difficulty takes the form and importance of a constant and paralyzing perplexity. Such Christians, set upon interior unity, become the victims of a veritable spiritual dualism. On the one hand a very sure instinct, mingled with their love of being and their taste for life, draws them toward the joy of creation and knowledge. On the other hand a higher will to love God above all else makes them afraid of the least division or deflection in their allegiances. In the most spiritual layers of their being they experience a tension between the opposing ebb and flow caused by the attraction of the two rival stars, God and the world. Which of the two is to make itself more nobly adored?

The dichotomy and tension here outlined is a universal problem for Christians today, but it affects more keenly, perhaps, than any other group, those Christian married couples who are at all sincere both about their religion and their marriage. The apparently irreconcilable polarity between God and nature, complicated by the duality of human nature itself into body and spirit, makes such violent demands on the loyalties of most married couples that marriages can almost be classified in one way according to the triumph of God over nature or nature over God; and in another way according to the triumph of spirit over body or body over spirit. Titus and Bertha, to give them their "canonized" names, are torn day by day between such alternatives as buying a new car or having another baby; between moving to a parochial school or staying where they are; between remodeling the basement or contributing to the fund drive for a new church; between dinner out and dancing or a week-day Mass next morning; between a movie or a C F M meeting; between *Gunsmoke* or confession; between washing the diapers or June devotions.

Frequently these conflicts and tensions are gradually resolved in favor of religious fanaticism on the one hand or secularism on the other. Or, then, they are resolved by compromise, by a double life. Clinging to the principle that love of God must be undivided, some married couples renounce, if not in fact at least in theory, as much of God's creation as possible, including each other. Others, driven by instinct and intuition to accept the worth of life and its fullness, will turn their backs on religion which seems intent on robbing them of wholeness. Finally, and here we deal with the majority, a neat compromise, a double standard, is adopted: part of life and time and action is given to God, part to the world; a share is assigned to the soul and a share to the body, so that the polarity of these tensions, far from being resolved, is only heightened by an unwilling resignation to imperfection, frustration, and insincerity. None of these three tempting avenues of escape from the basic tensions that surround marriage offers release, and the agony consequent on any one of them is immensely increased if one partner chooses to seek relief along one path while the other selects a different one. Whether we become distorted, disgusted, or divided, the result is equally bad.

Fortunately another road is open to us. . . . Nothing is more certain, theologically, than that the whole of human life can be sanctified. Wedded life in all its mean and precious details, in its ecstasies and in its miseries, in its glory and in its lowliness, in its spiritual grandeur and in its physical roots, is open to sanctification. Faith is that road. And faith tells us that marriage is a revelation; that it is a mystery; that it is worship.

Marriage is a revelation, a divinely established and divinely revealed plan for life. It is not some evolutionary accident, some freakish twist of nature. That the division of the sexes and their union was established and blessed by God may be learned from the first pages of Holy Writ.

. . . [Even a] cursory acquaintance with Sacred Scripture, erudition aside, will reveal basic ideas and themes like the following: that marriage in its very origin is in intimate continuity with God's creative work; that the plan of divine providence is to be achieved through the marriage bond; that the union of man and woman is so blessed in its origin that even the Fall could not destroy its goodness; that salvation history unfolds in a family context; that the very economy of redemption has its roots in a family; that the love of Yahweh for Israel is fittingly expressed in the strongest conjugal terms; that the division of man into male and female and their union in marriage can give us an insight into the divine; that the relation between Christ and His Church is that of bridegroom and bride; that, in fact, the whole psychological and literary framework of theology is shot through with marital, conjugal, and familial concepts and terminology.

However different the two creation accounts in Genesis may be, they agree in this, that conjugal and domestic life form the apogee

of their story. Whether we contemplate the unfolding panorama of
the seven days or the poetic beauty of the garden of Eden, the
crown and climax is the same—man, man not in the abstract sense
of rational animal, but man in the concrete sense of male and female,
man and woman together, in partnership, the image of God, becoming two in one flesh. The union itself and its fruitfulness, both are
bléssed and blessed. "And God created man to his own image; to the
image of God he created him, male and female he created them, saying: 'Increase and multiply, and fill the earth and subdue it. . . .'"
"And God saw all things that he had made, and they were very
good." "And the Lord God said: It is not good for man to be alone:
let us make him a help like unto himself." "And Adam said: 'This
now is bone of my bones, and flesh of my flesh.'"

God's plan of salvation is from start to finish a "family plan."
From promise to fulfilment, from the "seed of the woman" to the
Holy Family, the context is ever the same. "God's people" are a
family. "The house of Israel" is a family. Jesus is of the "House
of David." Those genealogical lists, which we are inclined to skip
in the Scriptures and listen to impatiently in the liturgy are still of
the essence of God's plan of salvation. God's holy people are a
family, one in flesh and blood, the flesh and blood of Adam now
superseded by the flesh and blood of the new Adam, Christ.

But in the narrower sense, too, of family, in the sense of conjugal
love and fidelity, abstracting from the fruitfulness of marriage, it
is a revelation. Whole books of the Bible have conjugal union as
their basic theme. Apart from the Canticle of Canticles, in the literal
sense a love song, in a spiritual sense the hymn of loving union between God and His people, between Christ and His Church,
between the saints and their Savior, the book of Osee is an example
of how marital love and fidelity represent union between God and
man.

In fact, if one were to go through the Scriptures striking out all
family terms—husband, wife, bridegroom, bride, father, mother,
brother, sister—and then reread them, he would find that the heart
had been taken out of revelation. If only we look at marriage as
God does, as He Himself has told us to look at it, that basic tension
which arises from the notion that God tolerates it could never be.

Marriage is a mystery. St. Paul calls it that. "That is a great
mystery—I mean in reference to Christ and to the Church." The
text is quoted often enough, especially in sermons. Most frequently,

however, its interpretation is confined to a pious exhortation to married couples to pattern their love on the love of Christ for His Church. The key word, rather, is mystery. And mystery here is used in the full Pauline sense, that is, to express the totality of God's creative and redemptive plan, which is hidden from all eternity in the heart of the Trinity. This mystery is given expression in the creation of man and woman. When it encounters sin God arranges for the destruction of sin by the incarnation of the second Person whose death sets up in His blood a new covenant wherein men are identified in His Body and so, united to Him in the love of the Spirit, return to the bosom of the Father. St. Paul's observation is inspired by the words of Genesis: "and they shall become two in one flesh." He does not hesitate to apply this ancient text to the reality of the Mystical Body in which Christians are made to be flesh of flesh and bone of bone of the Body of the Lord. Marriage is more than a symbol of this mystery. It is part of it. It is rather this very mystery made present, made concrete. Husband and wife are two in one flesh, two in the one flesh of the Lord. Already so identified by baptism and the Eucharist their identity in the Lord is deepened and intensified by marriage. Such identification far outstrips the wildest pagan fantasies bent on personalizing and divinizing conjugal love. For the depth of the Christian mystery is that the husband's love for his wife is in fact, while not less a love of her, truly love of his own flesh and, even more, love of the Body of the Lord, so that human love and divine encounter one another and fuse into a single unity.

Can we really speak this way of married love, and speak literally? Yes. And this is the one tremendous area of fundamental difference between Christian and pagan love. Christian love does not have to stop, cannot stop, with the beloved but finite partner. The Christian knows that Christ made the other partner in the marriage member of His own Body at baptism. He knows that God lives in the other. He can say in literal and full truth, "It is the Lord I love and am united to." As the great theologian, Scheeben, expressed it, "the married couple are wedded to Christ in their marriage to each other." God's love from on high meets mutual human love from below and the three loves become one through the instrumentality of the union of bodies of bride and bridegroom caught up ineffably in the oneness of the flesh and blood of the Lord. Husband and wife, and children too, fruit of the union, and by baptism and the

Eucharist incorporated in the mystery, are thus in very fact and not in mere image, the Mystical Body in miniature.

At the outset I referred to the perplexity and even paralysis which afflicts so many married couples because of the tension between love of life and love of God. For the married couple who deeply apprehend and believe the mystery of marriage, that "they are wedded to Christ in their marriage to each other," this tension is nonexistent. Christ, in giving them their sacrament, planned that no tension should arise.

But I would like to emphasize here the word "believe." Marriage is a mystery of faith. And, as we experience with every aspect of Christian life, there are times when faith is not, as it were, perceived. For many married couples, years of humble endeavor and cooperation with God are required before this greatest reality of their marriage, their union with God in each other, is recognized.

Marriage is a sacrament of the New Covenant. The Church so teaches and we gratefully give assent, little realizing, perhaps that in so doing we confess that it is worship, that it is sacred liturgy. Like the other sacraments, marriage is worship of God, divine cult.

Nor should we limit marriage to those brief moments, however essential, before the altar, when a man and woman, as ministers of the sacrament, pledge themselves, their love and fidelity, to one another. Somehow, the courtship which precedes and the life-long bond which follows, form an integral part of the total structure of the sacrament. Marriage is a continuing sacrament, abiding, extended, and renewed through the vicissitudes of joy and sorrow, poverty and riches, sickness and health that enter the life span of the married couple. When we say that marriage is a sacrament we are saying that it is a form of worship, a kind of liturgy, which glorifies God. But we are saying more. We are saying that as sacrament it gives grace. And by grace I mean more than the power to endure, the patience to persevere, the strength to forgive. I mean more even than the blessings of joy that come with happy union. Grace is more than God's help enabling the married couple to be loving and faithful, patient and brave, selfless and helpful. Grace means more than divine assistance to accept the duties of the married state. It means divine life, salvation, sanctification, union with God growing stronger day by day. It means God Himself, communion in the infinite fullness of His unspeakable glory. All this is indeed hidden under veils of faith and hope. But all this exists and is intensified for the married couple by their sacrament.

Marriage is a sacrament, and so, like every other sacrament, it is an echo of the Eucharist, whence it arises because the Eucharist makes the partners two in one flesh, and toward which it is directed because, like the Eucharist, its goal is the upbuilding of the Body of Christ.

Marriage is even a kind of Eucharist. For the Eucharist is Christ's death by which He purchases for Himself a spotless bride. In marriage each partner reproduces the death of the Lord by the entire surrender of self, by dying to self, first by the total giving of self to win the spouse and then by the daily living of this devotion, the daily laying down of his life for the spouse. When a person in the fullness of his freedom and in Christian faith, embarks upon the bold and holy venture of a unique choice of love and fidelity for life, he enters somehow into the mystery of God's choice of man as an object of His love unto death, and in a way re-enacts the Eucharistic mystery of redemption. To risk self, heart, life, destiny, dignity of person, to surrender one's entire existence in faith and love to the unknown and inscrutable mystery of another human person is truly to lay down one's life for one's spouse.

Such total and mutual self-donation, all-embracing and all-containing until death consummates it, is not merely an imitation of Christ's redemption, it is rather a participation in it. Every Christian marriage fills up what is wanting in the sufferings of Christ, and leads infallibly to the ecstasy of the eternal marriage feast of heaven.

To reflect deeply on these Eucharistic aspects of marriage, on marriage as worship, love, sacrifice, and union, and deeply to live them is the sure way to terminate the tragic division of life into the things of God and all else that troubles so many Christians. Love of God must indeed be undivided and in Christ's plan it cannot be divided between spirit and flesh, between God and creation, because He is all in all, and every Christian marriage is in Him.

A sacrament is by definition a means of sanctification and of fullness, not a source of imperfection and frustration. Yet that is what we find today in so many marriages. Marriage today is characterized by tensions, surrounded by inanities and stupidities, portrayed in ridicule, and spoken of largely with vulgarity. For the sake of those who are married, and all those who will marry, this great sacrament needs imperatively to be understood and lived in the light of the mystery of God and His Church, not as an escape from the real world, but as the only way, for them, of truly entering upon reality.

Only faith in its fullness can resolve the tensions between God and nature, between body and spirit. The age of the laity calls unceasingly for a definition of its way to sanctity, its path to God. There is no need for the fanaticism, despair, or compromise. God heard that call of our century when He gave the laity their sacrament. But each marriage must dedicate itself unceasingly to a fuller response to His reply. Married people today must fulfill what God offers by sharing more fully in His divine life, and more perfectly offering Him that worship of praise and thanksgiving which is uniquely theirs.